The Changing Consumer:

Markets and Meanings

**Edited by Steven Miles,
Alison Anderson and
Kevin Meethan**

London and New York

658.
834
MIL

First published 2002
by Routledge
11 New Fetter Lane, London EC4P 4EE

Simultaneously published in the USA and Canada
by Routledge
29 West 35th Street, New York, NY 10001

Routledge is an imprint of the Taylor & Francis Group

Typeset in Goudy by Taylor & Francis Books
Printed and bound in Malta by Gutenberg Press Ltd

British Library Cataloguing in Publication Data
A catalogue record for this book is available from the British Library

Library of Congress Cataloging in Publication Data
The changing consumer: markets and meanings/edited by Steven Miles,
Alison Anderson and Kevin Meethan
p. cm–Studies in Consumption and Markets
Includes bibliographic references and index
1. Consumption (economics) 2. Consumers. I. Miles, Steven. II.
Anderson, Alison. III. Meethan, Kevin. IV. Studies in consumption and
markets series
HC79.C6 C493 2002
658.8'3–dc21
2001048178

ISBN 0–415–27042–1 (hbk)
ISBN 0–415–27043–X (pbk)

Contents

Contributors

Alison Anderson is a Senior Lecturer in the Department of Sociology, University of Plymouth, UK. She is author of *Media, Culture and the Environment* (UCL 1997) and has written widely on the media representation of environmental issues. Her research interests are in the fields of mass media, the sociology of risk and the environment, and social movements, science and technology.

Russell W. Belk is the N. Eldon Tanner Professor at the David Eccles School of Business, University of Utah, USA. He is the author of *Collecting in a Consumer Society* (Routledge 1995, 2001) and various other books, articles, and videos focusing on consumption, materialism, gift-giving, and the development of consumer culture in less affluent societies, including China, Romania and Zimbabwe.

Ben Crewe is a researcher in the Department of Sociology, University of Essex, UK. He has recently submitted his Ph.D. thesis, 'Representing Men: Cultural Production and Producers in the UK Men's Magazine Market'. He is particularly interested in masculinity, media institutions and the prison service.

Paul du Gay is the Sub-Dean (Research) at the Faculty of Social Sciences, The Open University, UK. He is the author of *Consumption and Identity at Work* (Sage 1996) and *In Praise of Bureaucracy* (Sage 2000) and has published widely on questions of cultural identity and cultural production.

Adrian Franklin is a Reader in Sociology at the School of Sociology and Social Work, University of Tasmania, Australia. He is the author of *Animals and Modern Cultures* (Sage 1999) and *Nature and Social Theory* (Sage 2001). He is currently writing new books on tourism and retro culture and working on a major national study of human–animal relations in Australia.

Elaine Lally is the Assistant Director of the Institute for Cultural Research at the University of Western Sydney, Australia. She is author of *At Home with Computers* (Berg, forthcoming). Her research interest is in culture and

information technology, and in particular how new technologies are transforming everyday life.

Liz McFall is a Lecturer in Sociology at the Open University, UK. She has
published a number of articles exploring the cultural economy of advertising
practice from a historical perspective. Her current research interests are in
the sociology of economic life.

Kevin Meethan is a Senior Lecturer in the Department of Sociology, University
of Plymouth, UK. He is author of *Tourism in Global Society: Place, Culture,
Consumption* (Palgrave, 2001). His research interests are tourism, globalisation, consumption and cultural change.

Steven Miles is Principal Lecturer in the Department of Sociology, University
of Plymouth, UK. He is author of *Consumerism as a Way of Life* (Sage 1998),
Youth Lifestyles in a Changing World (Open University Press 2000) and *Social
Theory in the 'Real' World* (Sage 2001). His research interest is in youth and
consumption, and he is currently co-writing a book on consuming cities,
with Malcolm Miles.

Simone Pettigrew is a Senior Lecturer in the Faculty of Business and Public
Management, Edith Cowan University, Australia. She is editor of *The Journal of
Research for Consumers*. Her primary research interests are consumer educa-
tion and qualitative consumer research.

Steve Spittle is a Senior Lecturer in Media and Communication at the
University of Wolverhampton, UK. He was formerly a Teaching Fellow at
the University of Central England in Birmingham. His research interests
centre around New Media, Television and Consumer Culture.

Alan Warde is a Professor of Sociology at the University of Manchester, UK,
and Co-Director of the ESRC Centre for Research on Innovation and
Competition. His recent books include *Consumption, Food and Taste* (Sage
1997) and, with Lydia Martens, *Eating Out: Social Differentiation, Consumption
and Pleasure* (Cambridge University Press 2000). A volume co-edited with
Jukka Gronow, *Ordinary Consumption*, will be published by Routledge in the
autumn of 2001.

Janice Winship is a Lecturer in Media Studies at the University of Sussex, UK.
She has written widely on women's magazines. Her current research interest
is in advertising, consumption and shopping, and she is currently working
with a colleague on the cultural significance of the retailer Marks and
Spencer.

1 Introduction

The meaning of consumption; the meaning of change?

Steven Miles, Kevin Meethan and Alison Anderson

The consumer ethic is ubiquitous. Everything we do, see, hear, and even feel appears to be connected in some way to our experience as consumers. The increasingly high academic and media profile of debates over consumption, consumer culture, consumer behaviour and consumer rights reflects a world undergoing rapid change. In *The Changing Consumer* we hope to chart the nature of that change and to discuss why it is that consumption is so important to the state of the world in which we live, and what role, if any, consumption plays in actively underpinning social, economic and political transformation. The papers in this collection originate from a conference entitled *Consuming Markets; Consuming Meanings*, which was hosted by the Research Group on Consumption and Representation at the University of Plymouth. The conference attracted a diverse number of consumer researchers from fifteen countries and a wide variety of disciplinary backgrounds. But this book isn't a conference collection in the conventional sense. Indeed, the editors consciously commissioned authors whose work seemed to get at the crux of what it means to be a consumer at the beginning of the twenty-first century. Some of the chapters presented here have a historical dimension, but, more importantly, the book as a whole is concerned with why consumption is important and why it is important now. *The Changing Consumer* represents an effort to take one step back in order to consider what constitutes the so-called consumer society, and why, if at all, that consumer society appears to be more well entrenched at this point in time than it ever has been before. The consumer society may well have changed. This book is concerned with how and why that change, apparently driven by the market, seems to have had such a fundamental impact on the meanings through which human beings relate to a world of consumption which is, at one and the same time, both constraining and enabling, individualising and conforming.

In 1995 Daniel Miller made the polemical statement that consumption, rather than production, was '... the vanguard of history' (Miller 1995: 1). Behind Miller's assertion is the recognition that the relationship between the social and the economic has undergone significant changes at a global level just as much as at national and more localised levels. There are of course a number of reasons: economic, political, ideological and theoretical for instance, which have contributed to many disciplines, shifting the focus of their attention from issues of production to those of consumption (see, for example, Miller 1994, 1995, Corrigan 1997, Miles 1998, Edwards 2000). Foremost among these we can identify the near-universal adoption of neoliberal market policies, the growth of multinationals, the global spread of media and information technologies and the globalisation of production, in particular the displacement of Fordism by post-Fordism. Changes to the organisation of manufacturing have also led to the decline of class- and work-based solidarity, and their replacement with more fragmented and diverse forms of social identity which appear to champion diversity and individualisation (Giddens 1991, Beck 1992, Bocock 1993). With the demise of the regulated state, and with freedom of choice dominating the rhetoric of the political economy, the apparent global triumph of free-market economic policies leads to a common assumption that, in the early twenty-first century, the modern developed economies are characterised as consumer societies. Although it could be argued that, after all, this is not a wholly new phenomenon (Benson 1994), this shift is also indicative of changes in a number of theoretical approaches. One of the most significant was the cultural turn in social theory and the discovery, or invention, of post-modernism.

Leaving aside the problems of defining this term, and the way in which it now appears to be subsumed under the rubric of globalisation, the important point is the way in which the apparent certainties or 'meta-narratives' of modernity have been progressively challenged if not dismantled, to the extent that the social world is characterised by difference and fragmentation. The predictability of the life course has, from this point of view, been dissolved, to the extent that consumers are at one and the same time both liberated and yet subject to a world of increasing uncertainty. Arguably, consumerism plays a key role in this process, when the functional aspects of commodities are replaced by aesthetic concerns (Lyon 1999: 72), where image and style take precedence over content. Whatever the merits of such approaches, there is no denying that what we see are a number of interlinked processes which taken together result in an apparent disaggregation or 'de-differentiation' of mass society and indeed mass markets (Featherstone 1991). Whatever label we wish to put to it, there can be little doubt that contemporary consumerism is driven by diversity and choice, by an emphasis on difference, and the conscious and deliberate promotion of material goods as status indicators for particular market segments. Marketing orthodoxy therefore links a range of commodities and their associated cultural and symbolic capital to more or less coherent lifestyle images (Slater 1997: 191).

In theoretical terms we can also see that conceptualisations of commodity forms have broadened to include the importance of sign or symbolic value, a recognition that the significance of commodities cannot be reduced to economic criteria such as exchange value alone, but need to be seen in the social contexts from which they derive symbolic value. This concern is in part a reaction against the notion, largely derived from Marxist theory, which argues that the significance of commodities lies in their capacity to conceal or falsify social relations (Callinicos 1999: 88). The logical consequence of this approach leads to viewing the desire for goods as some sort of fetish. However, if we adopt an approach which recognises that the uses to which goods are put are more than an apparent satisfying of basic or utilitarian needs (Bocock 1993, Warde 1996), then a rather different set of concerns emerge in relation to the communicative aspects of consumption.

The first point to note is that the producers of commodities have little or no control, despite the rhetoric of marketing and advertising, over their deployment and use. Therefore we should not fall into the naïve fallacy of assuming that the 'intentions' of the producers are simply absorbed whole and unmediated by the unsuspecting and passive 'consumer' in whatever social or cultural milieu they are located (Howes 1996, Meethan 2001). As Miller (1995: 41) notes, although consumption may be globalised, it can also act as a way for local groups to both create and maintain a sense of difference (see also Clifford 1997, Friedman 1994, Gurnah 1997).

To view consumption as communication also implies that we consume in order to tell others who and what we are (Corrigan 1997) or to put it another way, that social differentiation is constantly maintained through practices which more or less consciously utilise the symbolic nature of material goods (Bourdieu 1984). For example, the possession of goods, or the wearing of items of clothing which signify a particular status or allegiance, also implies the existence of a group for whom a particular commodity has a particular meaning. Now, in certain situations, there is little doubt that possessions and goods, even the most apparently banal, can be used as 'markers' of identity (Bourdieu 1984, Belk 1995, Hitchcock and Teague 2000). Yet it must also be acknowledged that the same material object may well have many different and contradictory 'messages' other than that intended, if indeed any was consciously intended in the first place (Campbell 1995: 114–16). In addition, as Kopytoff (1986) argues, the biographies of commodities themselves can be seen as a series of transformations, as objects enter into and even leave spheres of exchange, accumulating or shedding different meanings and values in the process. In short, a communicative model of consumption is not something that can simply be accepted as given without careful qualification, for although it may appear to be liberating, it can also be viewed as conspiratorial or manipulative (Edwards 2000: 10), the former in terms of the apparent power wielded by producers, and the latter in terms of utilisation of consumption patterns.

To adopt what may be termed a celebratory approach to see the advent of consumerism as a form of liberation, inasmuch as it seemingly provides the opportunity to create a new 'self', is to risk falling into the trap of assuming that consumption is all about unfettered individualism and 'identity'. Although consumption is a means by which self identities *may* be defined and maintained (see, for example, Friedman 1994: 103), it is not the only one. Factors such as gender, ethnicity, kinship and age, for example, may in fact be more salient ways of expressing identity, or of mediating patterns and forms of consumption (Edgell and Hetherington 1996, Warde 1996). In fact, consumption may simply be a vehicle through which more significant aspects of identity are expressed.

We also need to remember that access to forms of consumption is far from evenly spread within and across societies, and to many, the apparently liberating aspects of consumption, and the opportunities that it appears to offer are not something to be celebrated, but rather to be resisted. We can, for example, point to the forms of direct action that took place during the Seattle and the May Day protests in London; to populist criticism (Klein 2000); to the value inversions of performance art (Landy 2000); as well as to the more academic concerns of Ritzer's (2000) dystopian vision of a rationalised McWorld. The apparent radicalism of such approaches needs to be treated with some caution too. For example, as Parker makes clear, Ritzer's approach is concerned with maintaining a rather élitist view of culture (1998: 8), a reiteration of a rather old theme, that modernity flattens out diversity and difference, and that affluence is equated with a loss of authenticity (Miller 1994: 205). Despite these caveats, there is a serious issue to be addressed here, which is the tension between control and choice, between approaches which see consumer society as a global conspiracy to be resisted and those which see it as the epitome of freedom, to be celebrated. As this brief overview has argued, there are a number of reasons why consumption is high on the academic agenda, and why it also figures significantly in more popular forms of discourse, in particular the perhaps belated recognition that the practices associated with consumption are not simply some form of misguided or fetishistic behaviour, but, whether a cause for celebration or not, are an inseparable part of social and individual life in the early twenty-first century.

Given the fact that aspects of consumption appear to be so high up on the academic agenda, it is of particular importance that the ways in which we study aspects of consumption are as sophisticated and as flexible as the phenomenon we seek to study. An underlying concern of this book is that this has not always been the case and that to the extent that the development of consumer studies as a discipline or sub-discipline in its own right, has been hamstrung by the constraints of academic boundaries. In other words, there has been and there continues to be an inevitable tendency to view aspects of consumption through specific disciplinary lenses (Miller 1995). For instance, marketers are often concerned with facilitating consumption or at least maximising the chances that consumers will consume. Sociologists meanwhile take a more critical line. Often they are interested in why and how consumers consume, but they seek to understand what consumption means in terms of the ideological nature of social change and the way in which individuals relate to society. Although it is difficult to generalise about the specifics of what any discipline seeks to understand about consumption, what is certain is that these alternative perspectives are complementary; they have to be. The consuming experience is so ingrained in contemporary lifestyles that the ability to consume or indeed the inability to consume can be said to affect almost every aspect of what we do and how we do it. Single disciplines simply do not have the tools to come to terms with levels of such complexity. Moreover, each discipline is bound up in its own particular predispositions, which channel such research in a specific – some would say blinkered – direction.

The Changing Consumer cannot in itself transform the study of consumption into a cross-disciplinary science. But what it can do is take a first step towards breaking down the barriers that prevent us understanding consumption and consumers as well as we might. To this end, the authors presented here represent a variety of disciplinary backgrounds, including Sociology, Cultural Studies, Media Studies, Marketing and Intercommunal Studies. Many of the disciplines represented in the chapters here are also informed by complementary disciplines. For instance, a common thread is the suggestion that approaches to consumption are all too often ahistorical. By advocating a multidisciplinary approach to consumption, the intention is therefore to promote a more rounded approach to consumer studies. We therefore agree with Miller's contention that:

> The key to progressive consumer studies is disaggregation ... the individual consumer is disaggregated as they are found, not to find some clear coherent cultural imperatives, but often partially connected, partially formulated, and quite contradictory sources of value and desire.
>
> (Miller 1995: 53)

In a similar vein, Gabriel and Lang describe the contemporary consumer as unmanageable. What they mean by this is that the nature of consumption is becoming more and more spasmodic and *ad hoc.* It is very difficult to understand consumers if consumers are inconsistent, unpredictable and contradictory, '... today, there is no single entity, the consumer' (Gabriel and Lang 1995: 191). The experiences that consumers have are so divided that consumers are indeed 'unmanageable' or 'uncontrollable'. The task for the consumer researcher is therefore an exigent one. Perhaps we can never truly understand the complex underpinnings of consumerism. However, an underlying theme of this book is that we can at least begin to understand what it means to consume if we focus on the everyday meanings with which consumers endow what they consume. Debates surrounding consumerism are all too often clouded by abstract theory and rhetoric. *The Changing Consumer* represents an effort to push aside the rhetoric, to cast doubt on approaches that see consumption as entirely controlling or entirely liberating, in order to construct a rounded, grounded and cross-disciplinary foundation to allow us to begin to understand what it actually *means* to consume.

Structure of the book

Chapter 2 sets the scene by providing a broad overview of the key issues at stake. It traces the emergence of contemporary patterns of consumption in the general context of the shift from Fordism to post-Fordism. Here Warde highlights the major issues that will continue to fascinate researchers of consumption for the foreseeable future. In turn, he begins to consider, and indeed answer, some of the central questions that currently interest consumer researchers: how can we usefully comprehend the vast complexity of the consumer? How, indeed, can we define 'consumption' – mundane or otherwise – in such a fragmented world? And whatever happened to the politics of consumption?

In Chapter 3, *Consuming Women: winning women?* Winship charts the changing profile of women as consumers. Noting that women, as opposed to men, have always been perceived as maintaining this role in some form or another, Winship argues that recently women have been perceived, notably by advertisers, as being increasingly sophisticated in their consumption habits. In particular, the suggestion is made that, in the context of consumption, femininity is increasingly associated with the freedom of the outdoors, as opposed to the enclosed, constrained spaces with which male consumers tend to be associated. Winship considers the extent to which the representation of women as consumers reflects a real change in how women experience consumption at the beginning of the twenty-first century.

The concern with gender as a central dimension of everyday expressions of consumption is carried through in Crewe's following chapter, on *Consuming men: producing loaded*. The apparent split between men as producers and women as consumers has been severely undermined in recent years as the market has woken up to the potential of men as consumers in their own right. This chapter charts the changing experience of men as consumers as a symptom of long-term social change. Focusing on the emergence of the men's magazine market as an illustration of this apparent transformation, Crewe argues that such a trend may have as much to do with the social, cultural and gender identities of cultural intermediaries as it does with the changing experiences of men as consumers. Are men really consuming in markedly different ways to those in the past?

The next chapter focuses upon the representation of consumption. For a long time, television has been arguably the most influential medium through which representations of consumption have been presented. In Chapter 5, *Producing TV: consuming TV* Spittle charts the changing nature of these representations, arguing that television no longer simply portrays consumption, but actively promotes it as a way of life. Using the popular British DIY transformation show, *Changing Rooms* as a case study, Spittle argues that consumption is a very paradoxical process in so far as, on the one hand it is seen as life-enhancing and expressive, while, on the other, consumers display ambivalent attitudes towards aspiration.

Chapter 6, *Consuming advertising: consuming cultural history*, focuses upon the role of the advertising industry in influencing patterns of consumption. McFall and du Gay argue that economic and commercial life, as expressed through advertising, has tended to be misunderstood by theorists such as Wernick, Lash and Urry, who tend to underestimate the cultural contexts in which meanings are endowed through advertising. After presenting a historical genealogy of 'persuasion' in advertising, the authors suggest alternative ways of conceptualising the consumer in this context. They conclude by suggesting that we need to exert caution in how forms of advertising are interpreted as indicative of the broad shift towards the increasing significance of cultural, as opposed to economic, aspects of life.

Chapter 7 examines the changing nature of design. The consumption of consumer goods is more than the straightforward purchase of a product. Indeed, the very act of purchasing a product can be said to traverse aspects of production and consumption. Design plays an important role in linking the two. In this chapter, Franklin charts the changing nature of design and its influence on consumption. He then goes on to present a case study which looks at the emergence of retro consumption culture and, in particular, the way in which consumers are drawn towards collecting specific kinds of designed objects. He concludes by suggesting that the collecting of such objects invokes nostalgia for a national modernism in which the élite arts and crafts movement of the early twentieth century was democratised by high-design and mass production.

In Chapter 8, *Consuming alcohol: consuming symbolic meaning*, Pettigrew considers the symbolic and emotional role of consumption and how it appears to both reflect and reinforce prevailing social orders. Drawing upon the consumption of alcohol as a case study, Pettigrew's argument is that pleasurable consumption has important implications for the construction of gender relations, but more generally, that the consumption of products plays a key role in the ways in which processes of self-construction are socially specified.

In Chapter 9, *Consuming home technology: consuming home computers*, Lally presents an insightful account of how the home computer has become an increasing focus for domestic consumption and leisure. By drawing upon interviews with home-computer owners, this chapter highlights the significance of technological forms of consumption, while raising the key question: where will technology take consumers next?

In the penultimate chapter, Miles argues that Consumer Studies has tended to be preoccupied with the more melodramatic aspects of consumption. He notes how researchers have increasingly recognised the importance of young people as a growing consumer market and as a barometer of societal change. Using examples from his own research, Miles suggests that the way in which we conceptualise the consumer needs to be readjusted, with the prioritisation of the much-abused notion of 'lifestyle'. Young people are faced with a series of dilemmas bound up with fast-paced social, cultural and structural change as a routine aspect of their lives, and the main way in which they deal with this is through the maintenance of consumer lifestyles.

In the final chapter of the book, Belk usefully highlights the key themes that underlie a re-conceptualisation of the changing consumer. Arguing that the diversity of approaches which characterise Consumer Studies represents an opportunity as opposed to an insurmountable hurdle, Belk summarises the main characteristics of the changing consumer as we enter the new millennium, while pointing out the challenges that these changes bring for consumer researchers, as well as for consumers themselves. The world in which we live is constantly changing, as are the meanings with which we, as consumers, endow that world. *The Changing Consumer* seeks to come to terms with that change, and the role that the market has in underpinning it. In short, our concern here is with how far our role as consumers shapes who and what we are at the beginning of the twenty-first century.

References

Beck, U. (1992) *Risk Society: Towards a New Modernity*, London: Sage.

Belk, R. (1995) *Collecting in a Consumer Society*, London: Routledge.

Benson, J. (1994) *The Rise of Consumer Society in Britain 1880–1980*, Harlow, Essex: Longman.

Bocock, R. (1993) *Consumption*, London: Routledge.

Bourdieu, P. (1984) *Distinction: a Social Critique of the Judgement of Taste*, Routledge & Kegan Paul: London.

Callinicos, A. (1999) *Social Theory: a Historical Introduction*, Cambridge: Polity Press.

Campbell, C. (1995) 'The sociology of consumption', in D. Miller (ed.) *Acknowledging Consumption: A Review of New Studies*, London: Routledge.

Clifford, J. (1997) *Routes: Travel and Translation in the Late Twentieth Century*, Cambridge, MA: Harvard University Press.

Corrigan, P. (1997) *The Sociology of Consumption*, London: Sage.

Edgell, S. and Hetherington, K. (1996) 'Introduction: consumption matters', in S. Edgell, K. Hetherington and A. Warde (eds) *Consumption Matters: the Production and Experience of Consumption*, Oxford: Blackwell.

Edwards, T. (2000) *Contradictions of Consumption: Concepts, Practices and Politics in Consumer Society*, Buckingham: Open University Press.

Featherstone, M. (1991) *Consumer Culture and Postmodernism*, London: Sage.

Friedman, J. (1994) *Cultural Identity and Global Process*, London: Sage.

Gabriel, Y. and Lang, T. (1995) *The Unmanageable Consumer: Contemporary Consumption and its Fragmentation*, London: Sage.

Giddens, A. (1991) *Modernity and Self Identity*, Cambridge: Polity Press.

Gurnah, A. (1997) 'Elvis in Zanzibar', in A. Scott (ed.) *The Limits of Globalization*, London: Routledge.

Hitchcock, M. and Teague, K. (eds) (2000) *Souvenirs: the Material Culture of Tourism*, Aldershot: Avebury.

Howes, D. (ed.) (1996) *Cross-Cultural Consumption: Global Markets, Local Realities*, London: Routledge.

Klein, N. (2000) *No Logo*, London: Flamingo.

Kopytoff, I. (1986) 'The cultural biography of things: commoditization as process', in A. Appadurai (ed.) *The Social Life of Things: Commodities in Cultural Perspective*, Cambridge: Cambridge University Press.

Landy, M. (2000) *Breakdown*, London: The Times/Artangel Commission.

Lyon, D. (1999) *Postmodernism*, Buckingham: Open University Press.

Meethan, K. (2001) *Tourism in Global Society: Place, Culture, Consumption*, Basingstoke: Palgrave.

Miles, S. (1998) *Consumerism as a Way of Life*, London: Sage.

Miller, D. (1994) *Modernity: an Ethnographic Approach: Dualism and Mass Consumption in Trinidad*, Oxford, Berg.

——— (1995) (ed.) *Acknowledging Consumption: a Review of New Studies*, London: Routledge.

Parker, M. (1998) 'Nostalgia and mass culture: McDonaldization and cultural élitism', in M. Alfino, J. S. Caputo and R. Wynyard (eds) *McDonaldization Revisited: Critical Essays on Consumer Culture*, Westport: Praeger.

Ritzer, G. (2000) *The McDonaldization of Society*, Thousand Oaks, CA: Pine Forge Press.

Slater, D. (1997) *Consumer Culture and Modernity*, Cambridge: Polity Press.

Warde, A. (1996) 'Afterword: the future of the sociology of consumption', in S. Edgell, K. Hetherington and A. Warde (eds) *Consumption Matters: the Production and Experience of Consumption*, Oxford: Blackwell.

2 Setting the scene

Changing conceptions of consumption

Alan Warde

Introduction

When Featherstone (1990) reviewed developments in the sociology of consumer culture at the end of the 1980s, he identified three analytic perspectives. The first he called the 'production of consumption' approach, which focused on the dispro-portionate power of capitalist producers and the nature of the commodity. A view associated initially with the Frankfurt School, it has been more recently developed in the early work of Baudrillard (1998[1970]) and by Jameson (1984) who depicted post-modern culture as an effect of the logic of the commodity in late capitalism. The second perspective he referred to as the 'modes of consumption' approach. This concentrated on the role of consumption in social classification, because 'the symbolic associations of goods may be utilized and renegotiated to emphasize differences in lifestyles which demarcate social relationships' (Featherstone 1990: 8). The work of Pierre Bourdieu was singled out for particular attention because of his analysis of the way in which cultural capital generated a knowledge of and conflict over legitimate taste, around which social classification was accomplished. Featherstone suggested that the proliferation of commodities in consumer culture made this process of classification less straightforward because it became more difficult to read displays of goods as signs of social status. The third perspective, not yet fully formed, was more heterogeneous, being concerned with the 'dreams, images and pleasure' associated with consumer culture. Featherstone pulled out some aspects of post-modern culture for scrutiny. He suggested that attention be paid to: issues of excess and waste (after the fashion of Bataille); carnivalesque events; the 'dream worlds' of department stores and arcades (following Walter Benjamin); the creative potential of mass culture and the apparent collapse of the boundary between high and popular culture instigated by post-modernism; the aestheticisation of everyday life; and the collapse of the boundary between the artistic *avant garde* and the new *petite-bourgeoisie* represented in the plural lifestyles of the new cultural intermediaries.

Accepting Featherstone's portrayal as a reliable account of the situation in the sociology of consumption, or more specifically of consumer culture, a decade ago, we might ask: what has changed? My view is that the concern with understanding the cultural aspects of consumption, images, signs and symbols, which was central to Featherstone's portrayal of movements in the 1980s, has continued, but with increasing emphasis on notions of personal identity rather than collective practice. In the process we have seen:

- a serious decline in the prominence of the first perspective;
- a rearguard action to preserve treasured aspects of the second perspective, which has resulted in some promising development; and
- a proliferation of attention to selected elements of the third perspective.

The next section of this chapter makes a very few observations about the downward trajectory of approaches 1 and 2. The third section identifies ten reasons which scholars, most of whom work out of approach 3, have evinced for celebrating consumption, for asserting it to be a most welcome feature of advanced societies. The fourth section identifies briefly some of the theoretical, methodological and practical consequences – some unintended, others unrecognised – of adopting the celebratory assessment. In particular, I suggest that sociologists have increasingly come to adopt the premises of a common-sense view of the world of consumption which owes much to the penetration of commercial and promotional discourse into social science. The celebratory approach does not entail, but appears to have encouraged, a tendency to turn the benevolent aspects of consumption into a legitimisation of commercial culture and an apology for liberal capitalist markets. Some alternative perspectives and sociological projects, marginalised as a result, are reviewed.

Laying aside classical approaches

Indifference towards producer power

There has been a general decline in interest in the ways in which producers mould consumption. The reputation of Adorno and the Frankfurt School has waned markedly. It has become conventional wisdom that producers are unable to manipulate wants through advertising or simply to market those products that it best suits them to produce. There are many reasons for this, important among which are:

- a view of media audiences which denies that they passively absorb messages;
- an enhanced appreciation of the symbolic, as opposed to the use-value of goods;
- a withdrawal from the critique of the commodity, perhaps as part of the accommodation to the triumph of capitalism and the ideological rehabilitation of market mechanisms;
- a diagnosis of the emergence of a post-Fordist economy, where the capacity to produce niche products indicates a greater responsiveness to consumer desires; and

- a continued and apparent uncertainty of producers about what consumers want (witness their vast expenditure on market intelligence) associated with competition among capitalist organisations.

There are many ironies in this tendency. Advertising budgets continue to grow. Production is becoming increasingly concentrated and the potential power of the big corporations is augmented accordingly. Globalisation has resulted in the targeting of the same products at ever-larger audiences, with apparent success in many instances where global brands predominate. Manufacturers and designers now are not embarrassed to talk about 'creating needs', admitting precisely the main point of Marcuse's (1964) much-contested critique. Above all, commodification is accelerating, with the alternatives to commodity exchange – through state provision, communal reciprocity and household production – consequently in decline. Sociologists seem to be losing interest in the determining aspects of the system of commodity production and exchange just as it seems set to consolidate further its grip on consumption behaviour.

Distinction in transition

Consideration of the connections between hierarchical social inequalities – especially of class – and consumption behaviour, constituted sociology's main contribution to the field for many years. The most distinctive feature of the sociological arsenal was its understanding of conspicuous consumption: the possession and display of goods as a means of demonstrating superiority in a system of social status. This basic idea was developed, without much discipline, in many directions. Among the mechanisms that were added, and which actually result in a rather complex and contradictory series of variants, include Hirsch's notion of positional goods, emulation, the trickle-down effect, distinction and neotribalism (e.g. Hirsch 1978, Bourdieu 1984, Maffesoli 1988, Fine and Leopold 1993). The predominant view, I would suggest, is that such an approach is becoming less useful. Among the reasons advanced are:

- horizontal differentiation is, increasingly, more socially significant than vertical divisions;
- there is a less clear classification of consumption practices – a function of the democratisation of taste; wider access for most of the population to previously exclusive consumption activities; a proliferation of cultural items which makes it very difficult for most people to recognise and rank all of them; and a growth of cultural omnivorousness which collapses the separation between high and popular culture;
- class is becoming a less important social division;
- consumption behaviour is becoming increasingly individualised, so that lifestyles can no longer be associated with social groups;

- everyone, except those on the lowest of incomes, can participate in a similar way in consumer culture, each pursuing his or her own preferences in a self-conscious and self-regarding fashion.

If that is the principal tendency, there are nevertheless still constructive programmes of research into the modes of consumption. The influence of Bourdieu (1984) has been very considerable across Europe and America and there are still many sociologists attempting to apply the varied aspects of his corpus to different groups in different countries (Lamont 1992, Thornton 1995, Holt 1997). The injunction to consider consumption as a system of communication ensures that, because language has to be interpersonally meaningful among erstwhile strangers, the classificatory potential of consumption remains in focus. Also, the commercial imperatives of marketing ensure that there are many empirical investigations to identify associations between the characteristics of groups and individual tastes.

Expunging guilt, or ten benefits of consumption

Whereas the first two of Featherstone's perspectives typically exhibited considerable ambivalence about the virtue of deregulated or decontrolled consumption, the third perspective is characterised by its wholeheartedly positive appreciation of consumer culture. The moral uncertainties which surrounded consumption in modern Western, especially Protestant, societies for a couple of centuries are suspended, rejected or overcome in a celebration of the personal and social benefits of living in an advanced consumer society. I can identify at least ten different reasons, each canvassed and elaborated by several different sociologists, why we should suspend our predominantly critical attitude towards a commodified culture of consumption and embrace the human potentiality of mass and post-Fordist consumption.

Consumption fosters meaningful work

The criterion of satisfying work applies to many areas of non-necessity, with consumption delivering the known benefits of non-alienated work, as Moorhouse's (1991) study of hot-rod enthusiasts, Finnegan's (1989) research on amateur musicians in Milton Keynes and Stebbins' (1992) analysis of serious 'leisure' demonstrate.

Consumption promotes an aesthetic attitude

The everyday world may contain more aesthetically appealing items which many more people are in a better position to appreciate by orienting themselves to a style of living in which bare necessity, survival and functional requirements do not determine their accoutrements and surroundings. While there remains a symbolic (and pecuniary) distinction between mass-produced and designer

14   A. Warde

goods, the benefits of thoughtful and artistic design are increasingly present in the former. Mass-media technologies make available the finest music to the entire population, and people regularly exercise aesthetic judgement, with studies of audiences for advertisements and TV indicating a reflective and critical attitude to their production and content. Moreover, rapidly changing fashions, in items of all kinds, keep issues of taste constantly on the agenda. What is more, as Edwards (1997) implies, British men of the 1990s are able to look prettier and smell sweeter than those of the previous generation!

Consumption facilitates social rebellion

De Certeau (1984) demonstrated that consumption is one channel for expressing resistance in everyday life. Many others noted a feature of the use of fashion in the 1960s was the capacity for a younger generation to shock orthodox conservative opinion by flouting conventions of many kinds and to express visually their social disaffection through clothing and other collective cultural practices (Hebdige 1988). Many observers have noted that new patterns of consumption might provide what Cohen and Taylor (1992) called 'escape attempts' – ways of dissociating themselves from the constraints of a given everyday reality.

Consumption is enjoyable and pleasurable

In most accounts, hedonism is considered morally dubious, if no longer entirely reprehensible. Investigation of the origins of consumerism has rehabilitated pleasure and enjoyment (something more than mere satisfaction) as pertinent objectives of human conduct. The extent to which traditional pleasures are supplied by consumption, and the rather more ephemeral and qualified way in which modern hedonism is entangled with the imagination and transcendence of new wants, has been usefully charted in works like that of Campbell's *The Romantic Ethic* and *The Spirit of Modern Consumerism* (1987). To the extent that consumption reliably delivers pleasure (Hirschman 1982), and there is evidence that it often does (Warde and Martens 2000), then it should be applauded.

Consumption nurtures possessive individualism

Although politically contested, there are many who would argue that commodified consumption rewards people because private possession entails unconstrained use of goods, which enhances self-esteem and ontological security (see, for example, the argument about owner-occupied housing in Saunders 1990). The competitive individualism often said to be encouraged by conspicuous consumption, which offers opportunities for pursuit of status, distinction and display, may be welcomed because it positively encourages hard work and increases economic productivity. Certainly, robust demand for consumer goods is a major systemic requirement of capitalist economic growth, upon which levels of employment are so critically dependent. The emergence of a so-called 'work-and-spend' culture (Schor 1992, Cross 1993) has among its preconditions the privatised household consumption patterns associated with suburbanisation and the belief that access to the rewards of consumer culture is, and should be, by means of individual effort.

There is a certain disdain, particularly on the part of intellectuals, regarding the merits of accumulating property and possessions. Yet, in some forms at least, it may be a quite harmless, and indeed stimulating, source of personal satisfaction. For example, Belk, in *Collecting in a Consumer Society*, explored the explosion of the habit of collecting – that is making collections of almost anything – in the USA. His conclusion warrants examination:

> collecting is consumption writ large since it involves the perpetual pursuit of inessential luxury goods. It raised the question of whether the collector's quest for self completion and happiness in the marketplace is a realistic one. For some people collecting is a harmful addiction, while for others it is an heroic and selfless act of love that saves unappreciated cultural treasures for future generations. For the vast majority of collectors who are neither addicted nor saviors, collecting appears to be a relatively healthy activity that invigorates consumer life with passion and purpose while it provides the collector with self-enhancing benefits that may be unavailable in their careers and households. Rather than being manipulated pawns of marketers, collectors are proactive decommodifiers of goods who creatively wrest meaning from the marketplace.
>
> (Belk 1995: 157–8)

Hence, at least this form of possession is beneficial rather than pathological.

Consumption supports socially meaningful practices

Much purchasing of commodities is directed towards social and altruistic ends. Gift-exchange is increasingly a matter of swapping manufactured goods, but it is no less meaningful a basis of social bonds for that. Much consumption is implicitly or explicitly an expression of caring, as with the processes associated with the provision of family meals, so delicately described by Marjorie DeVault (1991). 'Enthusiasms', of which collecting is but one example, absorb much contemporary leisure time and, except where conducted in total isolation, are generally considered positive both for the individuals concerned and because they involve social participation which builds social capital and sustains relationships of civil society. Yet few could now operate without either the availability of commercially manufactured equipment or commercially organised events and meetings. Participating or attending a classic car rally, a professional football match, a flower show, or a sheep-dog trial are means of confirming group membership and belonging.

Consumption supplies intellectual stimulation

Television documentaries, films, newspaper crosswords, computer games, books, museums and theatrical productions provide intellectual stimulation. The psychological stimulation of novelty and new experience is well attested; new technological devices require understanding, travel broadens the mind, and exotic food items require culinary experimentation.

Consumption provides refreshing entertainment

The capacity for consumption to provide practical and mental diversion from activities with more serious consequences, those requiring concentration or commitment, is much underestimated. The idea that legitimate consumption and leisure should be purposeful is one of the burdens of a society where people are increasingly fearful of having insufficient time. Although the wasting of time is no longer so often viewed in the context of work left undone or financial loss, as in the perspective of Benjamin Franklin, it nevertheless generates considerable anxiety. Hence people tend to be apologetic about their exposure to light entertainment. Watching television is probably the classic instance. The most popular of leisure activities, engaging the average Briton for about twenty-five hours a week, watching TV is a source of relaxation, of passing time, of cessation of the vigorous and compulsive activity that is so much encouraged by models of the active self and of self-development. As Darier (1998) points out, one of the most environmentally friendly of all commitments would be for everyone to do less. For instance, being prepared 'merely' to be entertained at home by a technological device where the marginal cost of watching two or three times as many programmes is negligible, would be very beneficial. Consumption fostering laziness and inactivity should be welcomed.

Consumption sustains comfort

Mass consumption has raised the standards of comfort and cleanliness and reduced the amount of sheer toil required in the daily material reproduction of most people. While few would be so eulogistic about mass consumption as Lebergott (1993), who suggests that this pursuit has been largely successful, his rhetorical questions regarding who would be prepared to give up the improvements in the general standard of life witnessed by Americans since 1900 are worthy of serious consideration. Mass consumption has indeed made life comfortable for those who are its beneficiaries – a substantial majority in Western societies – and at a level that few would willingly let fall.

You can *always* get what you want

Demand is increasingly effective, which is partly a function of the further extension of commodity exchange into areas previously governed by other relations of provision, and partly the effect of consumer organisations which are increasingly influential in ensuring that producers are subjected to regulation with a view to providing satisfaction to consumers (Gabriel and Lang, 1995).

Some reservations

There are, then, many plausible arguments contained within the body of recent literature which celebrate modern consumption practice. Consumption can promote comfort, pleasure, self-esteem, escape and decontrol. Such a thorough appraisal of the diversity of ends to which goods and services can be applied invalidates any deterministic 'production of consumption' thesis, explains and legitimises the often intense popular concern with securing access to more commodities, perhaps excuses reduced scholarly concern with the role of consumption in invidious social comparison, and countermands the authority of a long tradition of puritan evaluation of consumption. To the extent that societies of high consumption increase opportunities for self-development, independence, control, gratification, tolerance and comfort, their contribution to the improvement of the human condition should not be denied. However, I would argue that the overall impression given is potentially misleading as a foundation for an understanding of contemporary consumption in at least three respects:

1   First, it has been complicit in the exaggeration of the role of individual choice in consumption behaviour.
2   Second, it loses sight of what might be called the dull compulsion to consume, the mundane, unreflective ordinariness of much consumption.
3   Third, it fosters a complacent suspension of critique regarding consumer culture in general.

Self-identity and individualism

I would contend that, increasingly during the 1990s, the lens through which contemporary consumption has been observed serves to emphasise its function in the creation of self-identity. This encourages a focus on consumption as a personal, individual and self-regarding matter (that is, it prioritises concern with the consumer as 'identity-seeker', in the terms of Gabriel and Lang's (1995) classification of nine social scientific 'models' of the consumer), rather than as a collective and socially-embedded set of practices. Arguably, the currently dominant model of consumption presupposes that people buy what they personally want and thereby satisfy their individual material, symbolic and emotional needs and aspirations. Such a view is constantly on the brink of reverting to a paradigm for understanding consumption which presumes the sovereignty of consumer choice and reduces explanation to the reasons why individuals make particular choices.

There is no logical entailment that leads from the identification of the positive functions of consumption to acceptance of the primacy of individual choice in the explanation of consumption patterns. However, acknowledgement of the diversity of ends served by consumption practice does seem to incline people to conclude that consumption provides a realm of radical personal freedom. I have insufficient space to elaborate this point, but one of the most stimulating of all books about consumption was the little volume, contributed to a series devoted to explicating key concepts in sociology, by Zygmunt Bauman which, with insightful irony, he entitled *Freedom*. This intriguing account of contemporary society maintains that greatest possible individual freedom is provided by the consumer market – despite the fact that the encompassing social system is entirely beyond the control of consumers. The first of these propositions has suffused recent analyses of consumption, while the second has been ignored. Consequently, sociologists have become much enamoured with accounts which start from an assumption of individual agency rather than social constraint, perhaps most popularly, in the claim of Giddens (1991), Beck (1992), Bauman (1988) and many others, that we no longer have any option but to choose who we are to be and that substantive choices are registered most powerfully through consumption behaviour.

The individual agent exercising self-control over personal destiny – a key figure in the discourse of late modernity – offers a seductive model. People like to think about themselves in this way, or at least the privileged and successful do. Yet how people think about themselves, while being one precondition of their behaviour, is not sufficient to explain what they do. It is necessary therefore to note some of the counterpoints to accounts of consumption as the outcome of the decisions of individuals. There is now an extensive, increasingly multifaceted, critique of the idea of individual choice. Warde and Martens (1998b), for example, in examining the concept of food 'choice' distinguished four different shades of meaning for the term choice:

1   to select;
2   to pick in preference;
3   to consider fit, or suitable;
4   to will or determine.

The rhetorical and ideological danger, ever present with respect to consumption, is to conflate the first two meanings with the fourth, which implies the existence of freedom for an individual to determine his or her own fate. They conclude that: 'The term choice inflates the importance of individual decisions and conflates qualitatively different aspects and levels of discretion', and that 'Availability of resources, systemic inequalities of power in decision-making, shared cultural and aesthetic judgement, and "situational entailment", all constrain the individual.'

In certain fields of sociological analysis, a strong emphasis on individual agency may be beneficial. However, in others, it may be prejudicial to understanding and, in the field of consumption, this is particularly the case at present. The danger is that we accept a model of the individual, who is very like our ideal versions of ourselves, and where the checks and balances, context and constraints are overlooked. Behaviour is collective and situational; and the appropriate methodological stance is collectivist or institutional. If the collective and institutional conditions of consumption are ignored, then the structure of unequal distribution of power in the various fields of consumption is also overlooked, and all actors are attributed with an equal capacity for control over their own situation.

The dull compulsion to consume

Second, the celebration of consumption tends to obscure the humdrum ordinariness of the behaviour of most consumers, where individuals are not being self-reflexive, nor taking conscious decisions in the face of consumption options. The increasing suffusion of models of the self-possessed, individual consumer choosing positively and freely in the light of personal wants in ever-expanding markets for commodified goods and services, tends to obscure and therefore underestimate the importance of other aspects of contemporary consumption. In an earlier paper, reflecting on the limitations imposed by taking conspicuous consumption as the classic focus for sociological concern, I argued that appropriate weight should be given to the mundane, routine, inconspicuous elements of consumption practice which, I believe, constitute a vast proportion of all consumption.

Consumption tends to be seen in decisionistic terms – as people making decisions about what they want. It has often been pointed out that if people were thoroughly reflexive and pondered on every act where there were alternative courses of action, daily life would become intolerable. In fact, there are many different points on a continuum between deeply reflected and considered selection among alternatives to unconscious replacement and repetition (Gronow and Warde 2001). It would seem that some purchases may be subject to reflection, but others occur completely without mental input. What we need to know is which are which; what proportion of purchases, and what types of purchase, follow a model of habit, as opposed to conscious reflection.

Much of what is consumed is largely impervious to mechanisms like status-enhancement or the pursuit of fashion (Shove and Warde 1998). This is true of the petrol for the car, the electricity for the lighting, the water for use in the new bathroom suite, precisely items which pose the major problems of waste and destruction of scarce resources. This recognition is particularly germane to understanding the processes of normalisation. How do things come to be defined as necessities, to be expected in all households and available to all people? This is a primary way in which demand is ratcheted upwards. Yet it is a kind of change or accumulation which goes unnoticed, is accreted rather than consciously acquired, and which is almost impossible to reverse.

Pantzar (1997) speculates on the tendency for newly invented items to be utilised first as playthings, then to become instrumental as technologies, and finally to become subject to aesthetic reflection as art (as with collections).

Many things have their greatest impact – because they are rapidly diffused to a mass public – in the middle phase. In the process they become unremarkable. As they become available to all, any associated 'magic' or social symbolic significance is drained from them. For example, the telephone is almost universal in British homes. It is acutely normal, its existence probably only remarkable in its absence. Processes like habituation, routinisation, normalisation and appropriation are key mechanisms in what might be examined as the bases of a compulsion to consume.

Diluted critique

Many of the positive values promoted by expanding commodity consumption are achieved at the expense of others. Autonomy may engender insecurity; self-development may lead to self-absorption; tolerance may encourage indifference; comfort may dull compassion. Moreover, there is a question whether these are the only effects of consumption, and indeed whether there are types of consumption which have none of these beneficial effects. My concern is the extent to which the sociological appraisal of consumer society loses its sense of balance regarding the nature of consumer behaviour and its consequences for social relations. Until recently, social scientists typically expressed considerable reservations about the effect of the rapid acceleration of commodified consumption. The problems generally held to characterise consumer society were neatly summed up by Schudson (1993), and included detrimental effects on character, waste, privatism and disregard for the people whose labour is embodied in commodities. Rather than these critiques having been refuted, they tend simply to have been laid to one side. One consequence of the cessation of critique is a marked convergence between the concerns of social science and the market research approaches to consumer behaviour, which reflects a tendency towards the commercialisation of mental life, and the subordination of intellectual reflection to the instrumental and practical purpose of selling goods and services (Warde and Martens 1998a).

That the contemporary literature on consumption desists from offering a general and total critique of consumerism and consumer culture is probably opportune, but the dearth of references to the politics of consumption is suspicious. While it is true that some new studies have highlighted the skirmishes of tactical opposition through consumption in everyday life and others have noted neotribal expressions of oppositional identity, there is scant analysis of the role of consumption in politics. There are some hypotheses regarding political conflicts and divisions over consumption. Bauman (1987) distinguished the seduced from the repressed, the latter, failed consumers, being increasingly exposed to state policing in order to preserve the sense of security of the former. Also, although now little mentioned, ·there was a debate about consumption cleavages, which identified political divisions between those primarily consuming through markets and those dependent on the state. But in most respects, except for the frequent, and very important, observation that the very different levels of financial resources between social groups may easily become a basis for mobilisation, there is surprisingly little discussion or structural analysis of potential political divisions over consumption.

One place to look for the basis of renewed critique is the contemporary world of political activism – to see who is campaigning about what. It is one of the great merits and a very distinctive feature of Gabriel and Lang's (1995) review of the field that they pay considerable attention to the practical politics of consumption. *Inter alia*, they describe at length various forms of political action deriving from, or centring upon, consumption behaviour. The issues and actors that they identify as the substantive content of consumption politics can be summarised as follows:

- value for money (Consumers' Association)
- poor-quality products (Consumers' Association)
- dangerous products (the Co-operative Movement historically, single-issue campaigns)
- overpricing and unreasonable profit-making (Co-operative Societies, Local Economic Trading Schemes, ethical investment trusts, utilities regulators)
- contestation of private property (politically motivated theft)
- expression of cultural hostility and symbolic rejection of norms of respectability (rebellious use of goods and services, especially by youth groups)
- sustainable and social exchange (Local Economic Trading Schemes, pop festivals)
- fair conditions of labour (Fair Trade schemes)

A number of things strike me about this list. First, it would be difficult to derive an explicit definition of the boundaries of consumption politics on the basis of its particular content, it being only a common-sense rendition of political practices which have engaged individuals in relation to consumption. In my view, a more disciplined and precise definition of consumption would make for a better set of criteria for identifying consumer politics. Second, it suggests that consumption politics is currently mostly concerned with issues of economic exchange, matters of price and quality. The importance of these should not be underestimated; the grounds on which the power of large organisations and corporations might be confronted by a consumer 'voice' rather than a mere 'exit' are central political issues (Hirschman 1970). However, the other types of mobilisation suggest the wide potential scope for a renewed critique of commodity culture. Each constitutes a major potential form of practical critique of the contemporary system of consumption. Denying the legitimacy of private property, rejecting dominant norms of respectability, circumventing the formal economy, and requiring that consumers consider the plight of the producers of items that they purchase – these amount to expressions of radical opposition to contemporary social arrangements. However, mobilisation around these issues commands comparatively limited support and has marginal impact at present.

Third, the list totally excludes issues of welfare, issues of what used to be called collective consumption. In many respects, the post-war welfare state was the most trenchant critique of commodified consumer behaviour, introducing practical policies to protect citizens, as workers and as consumers, from the ravages of markets. The effect of thinking about consumption primarily in terms of the purchase of commodities entrenches a narrow notion of the consumer and obscures struggles around alternative modes of provision. Charities seeking to combat homelessness and tenants' associations seem to me as much organisations of consumption politics as the Consumers' Association and the Co-operative Movement. Fourth, there is very little consideration of the political issues of control emerging from the context of use of goods and services. If consumption is conceived not just as purchasing, but as the appropriation and application of a vastly increased volume of commodities, then issues like pollution caused by the use of automobiles and aircraft, for example, should be included as political problems of consumer culture.

In principle, consumption politics might in addition address social exclusion with causes other than a shortage of money to purchase a socially acceptable minimum standard of living. It also suggests a range of issues which require democratic determination regarding control of other people's consumption. In these terms, the right to roam is a consumption issue just as much as town planning, traffic congestion and the impact of car use on pedestrians. Regulation of the amount of waste that any individual might be allowed to produce could be another agenda item. Because in this regard the effects of every individual's exercise of control in the sphere of consumption are intimately and intricately bound up with those of many others, a political field of conflict and negotiation opens up.

The suppressed politics of consumption hints at a basis for a more general social scientific critique of the consumer society, which would identify more connections among the social institutions implicated in sustaining contemporary consumption patterns. The insights to be obtained from imagining a broader politics of consumption might be the means to reinvigorate a tradition of critical evaluation of the returns to commodified consumption.

Summary

In sum, what seem to me to be the more important trends in the field in recent times include:

- A decline of interest in the mechanics of capitalist production and its impact on consumption behaviour;
- An increasing concern with the role of consumption in the construction of personal identity, with a correspondingly reduced appreciation of its role in the inegalitarian and invidious aspects of social classification;
- A welcome recognition of the positive contributions of consumption to human well-being;

- A declining concern with non-commodified modes of consumption, with an attendant danger of taking-for-granted, as inexorable and therefore unchallengeable, the disadvantageous aspects of the social relations of commodity exchange;
- An unhelpful presumption that individuals have the power each equally to determine a personally sculpted identity with an associated social standing;
- A continued and unjustifiable level of attention being given to conspicuous consumption at the expense of its more mundane aspects;
- A hesitancy in evaluating critically the general social effects of the recent expansion of consumerism.

References

Baudrillard, J. (1998) *The Consumer Society: Myths and Structures*, London: Sage.

Bauman, Z. (1987) *Legislators and Interpreters: on Modernity, Postmodernity and Intellectuals*, Cambridge, Polity Press.

—— (1988) *Freedom*, Milton Keynes: Open University Press.

Beck, U. (1992) *Risk Society: Toward a New Modernity*, London: Sage.

Belk, R. W. (1995) *Collecting in a Consumer Society*, London: Routledge.

Bourdieu, P. (1984) *Distinction: a Social Critique of the Judgement of Taste*, London: Routledge & Kegan Paul.

Campbell, C. (1987) *The Romantic Ethic and the Spirit of Modern Consumerism*, Oxford: Blackwell.

Cohen, S. and Taylor, L. (1992) *Escape Attempts: the Theory and Practice of Resistance to Everyday Life*, 2nd edn, London: Routledge.

Cross, G. (1993) *Time and Money: the Making of Consumer Culture*, London: Routledge.

Darier, E. (1998) 'Time to be lazy: work, the environment and modern subjectivities', *Time & Society* 7(2): 193–208.

De Certeau, M. (1984) *The Practice of Everyday Life*, Berkeley: University of California Press.

DeVault, M. (1991) *Feeding the Family: the Social Organization of Caring as Gendered Work*, Chicago: University of Chicago Press.

Edwards, T. (1997) *Men in the Mirror: Men's Fashion, Masculinity and the Consumer Society*, London: Cassell.

Featherstone, M. (1990) 'Perspectives on consumer culture', *Sociology* 24(1): 5–22.

Fine, B. and Leopold, E. (1993) *The World of Consumption*, London: Routledge.

Finnegan, R. (1989) *The Hidden Musicians: Music Making in an English Town*, Cambridge: Cambridge University Press.

Gabriel, Y. and Lang, T. (1995) *The Unmanageable Consumer: Contemporary Consumption and its Fragmentation*, London: Sage.

Giddens, A. (1991) *Modernity and Self-Identity*, Cambridge: Polity.

Gronow, J. and Warde, A. (eds) (2001) *Ordinary Consumption*, Reading: Harwood.

Hebdige, D. (1988) *Hiding in the Light: On Images and Things*, London: Comedia.

Hirsch, F. (1978) *Social Limits to Growth*, London: Routledge & Kegan Paul.

Hirschman, A. (1970) *Exit Voice and Loyalty: Responses to Decline in Firms, Organizations and States*, Cambridge MA: Harvard University Press.

—— (1982) *Shifting Involvements: Private Interest and Public Action*, Princeton, NJ: Princeton University Press.

Holt, D. (1997) 'Distinction in America?: recovering Bourdieu's theory of tastes from its critics', *Poetics* 25: 93–120.

Jameson, F. (1984) 'Postmodernism, or the cultural logic of late capitalism', *New Left Review* 146: 53–93.

Lamont, M. (1992) *Money, Morals and Manners: the Culture of the French and American Upper-Middle Class*, Chicago: Chicago University Press.

Lebergott, S. (1993) *Pursuing Happiness: American Consumers in the 20th Century*, Princeton NJ: Princeton University Press.

Maffesoli, M. (1988) 'Jeux de masques', *Design Issues* 4(1–2): 141–51.

Marcuse, H. (1964) *One Dimensional Man: the Ideology of Industrial Society*, London: Sphere Books.

Moorhouse, H. (1991) *Driving Ambitions: an Analysis of the American Hotrod Enthusiasm*, Manchester: Manchester University Press.

Pantzar, M. (1997) 'Do commodities reproduce themselves through human beings? Man vs. nature vs. technology: problems and new conceptualizations', paper given at the ESF TERM Programme Workshop, *Consumption, Everyday Life and Sustainability*, Centre for Environmental Change, Lancaster University.

Saunders, P. (1990) *A Nation of Home Owners*, London: Unwin Hyman.

Schor, J. (1992) *The Overworked American: the Unexpected Decline of Leisure*, New York: Basic Books.

Schudson, M. (1993) *Advertising, the Uneasy Persuasion: its Dubious Impact on American Society*, London: Routledge.

Shove, E. and Warde, A. (1998) 'Inconspicuous consumption: the sociology of consumption, lifestyles and the environment', in A. Gijswijt, F. Buttel, P. Dickens, R. Dunlap, A. Mol and G. Spaargaren (eds), *Sociological Theory and the Environment: Part 2: Cultural and Social Constructivism*, Proceedings of the Second Woudschoten Conference, SISWO, University of Amsterdam.

Stebbins, R. (1992) *Amateurs, Professionals and Serious Leisure*, Montreal and Kingston: McGill–Queens University Press.

Thornton, S. (1995) *Club Cultures: Music, Media and Subcultural Capital*, Cambridge: Polity Press.

Warde, A. and Martens, L. (1998a) 'Eating out and the commercialisation of mental life', *British Food Journal* 100(3): 147–53.

—— (1998b) 'Food choice: a sociological approach', in A. Murcott (ed.) *The Nation's Diet: the Social Science of Food Choice*, London: Longman.

—— (2000) *Eating Out: Social Differentiation, Consumption and Pleasure*, Cambridge: Cambridge University Press.

3 Consuming women

Winning women?

Janice Winship

Introduction

From mid February 1994, St Valentine's Day, when Wonderbra's advertising campaign hit the cities' billboards in Britain, 'the original push-up plunge' bra made headline copy. Voted 'Campaign of the year' in 1994 (*Campaign*, 6 January 1995: 21), a Jacky Fleming cartoon in *The Guardian* three years later critically mobilised Wonderbra within a post-feminist discourse:

> Janice, remind me, what's feminism?
>
> Um … girlie pop band
>
> fun fun fun …
>
> girlpower … wonderbra
>
> bloody hell, Jules, can't remember, BRAIN'S GONE.
> (*The Guardian*, 'Women' section, 27 March 1997: 5)

Wonderbra had blossomed into a popular cultural icon for the 1990s, seamlessly appropriated within *The Sun*'s sexualised tabloid journalism and hijacked by diverse promotions, including 'National Wonderbra Week', a breast cancer awareness campaign (*The Times*, 19 June 1998: 42).

Yet at first glance the image in this advertisement suggests little to differentiate it from a host of others that have graced the pages of women's magazines since the late 1960s. In one of an initial three variations, the newly discovered model Eva Herzigova sports a black Wonderbra, smiling as she gazes downwards at her ample cleavage. More careful scrutiny, however, throws up the real mark of difference – the ad's copy: against a white background in large black serif type: **'HELLO BOYS'**. Wonderbra is a product targeted at the female consumer but the ad's greeting explicitly acknowledges the male gaze and men's consumption of this image.

As a flip-side to Eva Herzigova's controlled self-confidence, the single thirtysomething heroine of Helen Fielding's best-selling novel and much-hyped film, *Bridget Jones's Diary*, experiences her body, emotions and life, as being constantly out of control.

Sunday 8 January

9st 2 (v. bloody g. but what is point?), alcohol units 2 (excellent), cigarettes 7, calories 3100 (poor).

2 p.m. Oh God, why am I so unattractive? Cannot believe I convinced myself I was keeping the entire weekend free to work when in fact I was on permanent date-with-Daniel standby. Hideous, waste two days glaring psychopathically at the phone, and eating things.

(Fielding 1996: 27)

For Bridget, the pleasures of guzzling chocolate, sparkling wine, mince pies, 'the last of the Christmas cake and some Stilton, while watching EastEnders', are traduced into shame and repulsion: 'I can actually feel the fat splurging out from my body' (p. 18). When her office email-flirtation falters she records: 'V. depressed. Going shopping' (p. 31). Exploring the frailties of femininity – its consuming passions and passion for consumption – the Diary does so in a comic mode whose humour depends on Bridget, and the readers, sharing a feminist self-awareness about the production of such femininity.

Lest it be thought Bridget's consumption excesses are out of step with her peers, focus group research has indeed indicated that in a '200% life!' their heaviest consumption is on 'alcohol, cigarettes, eating out, takeaways, clubs, gigs, cinema, theatre' on the one hand, and 'clothes, shoes, underwear' on the other (Fydler 1998: 16). Dubbed 'Winning Women' by the marketers, these 'high spending single females' (*Marketing* 1998a) also make inroads into hitherto largely male and premium sectors of the market. In 1997 around 40% of new cars were bought by women, with a prediction for 1998 that women aged 18–40 will be the dominant buyers – 'Women buyers mean business' (Roberts 1998).

In this chapter I intend to explore what Christine Gledhill refers to as 'the state of the contest' in gendered relations (Gledhill 1997: 383) through a discursive approach circulating around the figure of the 'consuming woman', in the several senses invoked above. First, women consumed by, or taken up with all things feminine; second, women consumed by men – their bodies and appearance subjected to a sexualised male gaze; third, women as a market segment conjured up by marketers; and fourth, women as active subjects who consume signs and commodities (Cronin 2000: 168). I switch between attention to the advertising industry's changing classification of women consumers, including their engendering of Winning Women and an examination of representational change in a number of controversial but successful print advertising campaigns loosely targeted at this group. Against some feminist analyses claiming that advertising blocks transformation of women's lives, I argue that the industry is increasingly in the business of mapping and representing change. As such, it renders tensions visible and is itself a player in the changing discourses of femininity.

After productionism, after consumptionism?

In the 1990s a strand of cultural studies research emerged that might be characterised as both post-productionist and post-consumptionist in its attempts to avoid the problems and fill in the gaps of productionist and consumptionist approaches, terms borrowed from Jim McGuigan (1992). I locate my study here in this context. Criticisms of the former approach point to its economic reductionism, an understanding of advertising and consumption as simply handmaidens of expanding capitalist markets, and its rendering of consumers as passive dupes of ideology. It does not see the need to engage with the experience of consumption or with the complex and differentiated ways in which audiences might understand and appropriate media texts into their own lifeworld. Within feminist approaches, so-called '1970s feminism' (Brunsdon 1997: 84) also partly fits this frame, operating within a patriarchal reductionism. It is anti-consumption because consumption is seen to reproduce a problematic femininity; it regards advertisements as circulating stereotypes and dominant ideologies of femininity; and assumes that women passively accept and take these on board. Advertising is thus antithetical to feminist demands and a block to change. In reaction to productionist approaches, McGuigan suggests consumptionism developed to become '*the* mainstream position for Anglophone studies of popular culture' (McGuigan 1992: 5). It emerged from a disengagement with an Althusserian Marxism and the adoption of Gramscian ideas around hegemony, so opening up a space to engage with a 'culture-from below' and with consumption. But as issues of pleasure and/as resistance were foregrounded by scholars, cultural relations and a symbolic economy became unhinged from production and the economic, which led to a 'drift into an uncritical populism' (McGuigan 1992: 70). Citing John Fiske as the exemplary figure, the complaint is that consumer power is overestimated and the approach slips perilously close to the views of consumer sovereignty lauded within a neoliberal political economy. As Martyn Lee more vividly describes: 'Popular culture is transformed into a marvellous subversive space', its 'forms and artefact … a cause for celebration' (Lee 1993: 53). Modes of enquiry deriving from the suspect humanities, such as textualist and post-modernist trends, are also fodder for the attack, apparently steering cultural studies away 'from its … material roots' (Ferguson and Golding 1997: xviii). The charges are therefore that cultural studies has failed 'to deal empirically with the deep structural changes in national and global political, economic and media systems through its eschewing of economic, social or policy analysis' (1997: xiii).

Many dispute this evaluation. Graeme Turner, for instance, argues that this is 'a version of current cultural studies theory and practice that most would find unrecognizable' (Turner 1998: 434) – the issues exercising Ferguson and Golding having long been debated. Certainly significant feminist contributions are badly served by this onslaught. Emerging in the space opened up by post-Fordist/post-modernist development, with its moral elevation of consumption and an intensification of sign culture, and by women's gains in economic and social fields, an upbeat '1980s post-feminism' challenged the dogmas and puritanism of '1970s feminism', both within and without the academy. As Lyn Thomas comments about the collection *The Female Gaze* (Gamman and Marshment 1988) its pages 'are haunted by the spectre of "the drab, dungareed dyke"' (Thomas 1997: 188). A focus on consumption brought an important aspect of women's experience out of the shadows and offered a means to refute the victim status of femininity. Instead, the latter was invoked as more performative, playful and pleasurable (Gamman and Marshment 1988), a resource to be nurtured and mobilised, not simply to reproduce patriarchal oppression:

> In westernized capitalist societies [consumption] is an inevitable experience that is part of being female. Indeed, it is a sphere where femininity is performed, where versions of femininity are legitimated and negotiated, or contested and rejected.
>
> (Andrews and Talbot 2000: 1)

The title of a study by Corinne Squire, Empowering Women? The Oprah Winfrey Show (1997), typifies the intent of the wave of work so damned by Ferguson and Golding, and clearly shows the use of post-structuralist approaches to challenge any singularity of female identity and to emphasise the 'complex connections between subjectivity, gender, and other social relationships' (p. 110). Yet feminist criticism too has been worried about the post-feminist and post-structural turn, with Michèle Barrett and Anne Phillips urging that feminist cultural analysis should not neglect a wider engagement with economic, political and social spheres (Modleski 1991, Barrett and Phillips 1992: 23).

If some cultural studies scholars have urged a return to basics insisting on the continuing value of Marxism to 'consider and analyse the processes of determination among and between different levels of production' (Smith 2000: 78), other research has addressed production, but in ways leaning more on Foucault than Marx. This research takes cognizance of the merits of productionism and consumptionism striving to hold on to both 'ends' of the 'circuit of culture' (du Gay 1997a: 3). If it holds that the former does not adequately problematise or fill out the economic, it regards the latter as limited because of the inattention to how the consumer and cultural industries 'make up' their consumers (Hacking, cited in du Gay 1996: 54), in other words, regarding some as more valuable than others, and thus designing products and marketing accordingly. These studies suggest that consumers' experiences are, at least in part, articulated in relation to these practices even as they are also fed back into 'production'. While studies differ in their emphasis, the common theme is a *culturalising* of production, the economic and the commercial (Jackson *et al.*

2000). In Paul du Gay's (1996) pioneering work on the transformation of work identities in the retail sector, the author examines the discourses of management, arguing that their advocacy of an entrepreneurial self blurs the boundaries between work and consumer subjectivities. Frank Mort (1996) and Sean Nixon (1996) have both researched 'new masculinities' in the 1980s by attention to knowledges and practices in the commercial domain as well as by a more ethnographic encounter with male consumers (see also du Gay 1997b, Nixon 1997a, 1997b and Crew in this volume). In turn, Angela McRobbie builds on Nixon's idea that the 'cultural knowledge wielded by the creative professionals actively *produces new economies*' (McRobbie 1998: 5, my emphasis) in her investigation into the livelihoods of cultural producers within the fashion industry.

These studies also insist on a 'historical specificity in consumption studies' (Mort 1997: 30), as in Erica Carter's study of the housewife–consumer in post-1945 West Germany. Deploying an explicitly Foucauldian vocabulary, Carter demonstrates how 'the expansion of scientific market knowledges' in the period 'enmeshed the female consumer in proliferating networks of what Foucault would have called "knowledge–power"' (Carter 1997: 8). Pertinent to this chapter, she goes on to advise that 'an adequate feminist response to that development cannot be simply to reiterate the old politico-economic maxim that expanding consumerism involves an extension of economic power over women' (Carter 1997: 8). Thinking about advertising in these terms is to shift how we think about its relation to change. William Leiss *et al.* have usefully suggested that the advertising industry possesses some specific features:

> It appears to be an independent business institution, but it can be more accurately described as the point of intersection for the major institutional forces. The industry absorbs into itself information about the world of products, the world of media, the world of consumers, and the world of audiences. Perhaps no other institution in modern society reflects and holds within itself such complex relations.
>
> (Leiss *et al.* 1990: 191)

As such it is 'the intermediary through which so many currents of social change come together' (p. 191) and 'through which social change is mediated – and wherein such change can be witnessed' (p. 191). However, Carter's more Foucauldian approach implies that the discourses of advertising and their 'knowledge–power' relations are themselves a productive site of change. Bearing these ideas in mind, in the next section I will set out some understandings of advertising's more recent developments, before engaging with one aspect of 'knowledge–power' relations, the industry's 'production' of audiences and consumers.

Managing the 'unmanageable' consumer?

Accounts of advertising and consumption point to a shift from mass to more segmented markets, from an advertising that is informative about the product –

making a rational appeal to consumers – to one that operates on an associative plane, keying in to consumers' emotions, values and beliefs and assuming that they are creatures of impulse and irrational choice (in the worst-case scenario depicting advertising as the 'hidden persuader', Packard 1981). If there is a splintering of solid market blocs and a fragmentation of the mass media, so marketing's demographic classification of its consumers is also surpassed. Consumers are more finely categorised by a host of so-called psychographic and other classification systems attempting to acknowledge difference and the diversity of 'lifestyles' (Brierley 1995, Chaney 1996, Nixon 1997b, Berger 2000). Such an account is partly true; it is also too simple. Segmentation, the assumption of the emotional consumer, and attempts to characterise consumers on lifestyle criteria have existed throughout the history of marketing (Marchand 1985, Bowlby 2000). Likewise, when it suits, contemporary advertising still targets a mass market and offers the informative ad, while demographic data, 'ABC1 women aged 35–44', continue to provide the bedrock currency for the media and marketing industries.

Still, some kind of qualitative shift in emphasis has taken place, characterised by an intensification in the processes by which consumers are mapped. This can be thought about as an aspect of the much deeper and far-reaching socio-economic and political change in the 1980s, encapsulated by the term 'post-Fordism', 'flexible' or 'reflexive accumulation' (Harvey 1989, Lee 1993, Lash and Urry 1994, respectively). Evaluations, however, differ. Armand Mattelart for one is deeply worried about processes which aim 'to penetrate the secret of the black box of the "consumer"', attempting 'to predict behaviour and maybe manage to control it' (Mattelart 1991: 170). Others are more sanguine, regarding such research as receiving a mixed response even inside the advertising industry, the general view being that 'creatives' are the most sceptical (Nava 1997). Moreover, as Michael Schudson points out, what the trade literature pretentiously claims to know about consumers is one thing and how they in fact practice their craft is quite another (Schudson 1993: 60).

The industry's reliance on a panoply of different forms of knowledge about the consumer has an economic foundation: quite simply, clients wish to know whether the millions that they are spending on advertising is being well spent. While Wonderbra and other campaigns might suggest otherwise, Sean Brierley advises that 'advertisers believe that their money has been wasted if the advertising is received by people who are not in their brand's market' (Brierley 1995: 28). For advertisers, the tension involved in matching markets to audiences is a perpetual one that they strive to minimise (Leiss et al. 1997: 126). Against this background, Mica Nava highlights the promotional value of consumer research as agencies establish credibility and pursue clients (Nava 1997: 40). Offering a stronger interpretation, Lury and Warde (1997) invoke the advertising industry as the small and dependent partner in an asymmetrical power relation with their often much-larger clients. In response to their weak position, the advertising industries assuage,

the anxieties of producers by promoting themselves as experts in guiding, controlling, influencing and predicting what consumers will be prepared to buy; that is, they are in the business of what Ien Ang calls 'desperately seeking the audience'.

(Lury and Warde 1997: 92)

Mapping and interpreting change, marking it out on the body, making it both visible and intelligible, are then key to the expertise that advertising can sell to clients. As a handmaiden of global capitalism, advertising is one tool in sustaining the unrelenting economic logic of accumulation achieved by a tireless construction of new markets and the 'refreshing' of old ones. The industry is ever mindful of even the smallest social and cultural shifts which, when translated into the ad context, might facilitate the selling of a new brand, or an old brand 'keeping up with' and getting closer to a particular consumer group. Or, to coin the phrase used by Yiannis Gabriel and Tim Lang, advertising is in the business of managing and regulating the 'unmanageable consumer' (Gabriel and Lang 1995).

Winning women?

The development of specific advertising aimed at the niche markets of 'Winning Women' offers an opportunity to examine many of the issues outlined above, in particular the ways in which advertisers attempt to create discrete segments of consumers in a bid to open up new markets and highlight the need for fresh approaches to advertising. This can be clearly seen in the case of a 1998 marketing conference entitled 'Winning Women'. As the publicity states:

> For marketers, understanding the course of ... change is essential. It is not good enough to rely on old stereotypes, or even last year's imagery ... young single women are the most challenging for marketers to keep up with.
>
> ('Winning Women', publicity leaflet 1998)

Evidence of mapping change and the strains of 'keeping up' can be seen in an earlier attempt at mapping the consumer, discussed in the trade magazine *Campaign* (Nixon 1997b: 225). Christine Restall, planning director from the advertising agency McCann-Erickson, excitedly introduces 'A breakthrough in the study of women', which 'throws new light on the complex make-up of women' (Restall 1985: 25). It revealed 'eight psychological and lifestyle clusters', evinced through the names attributed to them and anthropomorphised animal sketches. 'Avant Guardian' is represented as a slimline, trouser-wearing cat who rides a bicycle, her shopping visible in the front basket. Believing that 'There has not been a decline in morals', she is 'Young, up-scale, working – single or married with children' (p. 28). In stark contrast 'The Down-Trodden' is represented as a somewhat overweight floppy-eared rabbit hiding behind a baggy raincoat, weighed down by supermarket carrier bags and with a couple of young bunnies around her feet. 'Shy, negative, timid, indecisive, put upon', she is 'Married with children, no longer young, part time job' (p. 27).

It is easy to dismiss these representations as offering only further demeaning stereotypes (Nixon 1997b). But there are several pertinent points to observe. Implicit in the account is a hierarchy of types, from those most elaborated on and valued, to those seemingly skated over and less valued; respectively represented as 'slim/youthful' and 'dumpy/middle-aged'. Within the valued, all broadly ABC1 groupings, it is the 'leadership' segments, not the 'followers' – who nevertheless 'represent big business and have large and distinct brand franchises' (p. 28) – who are of most interest. The former, although constituting smaller segments, embody cultural change, and they mark out new markets. But visualising that embodiment is problematic. Restall (1985) interestingly refers not to stereotypes but 'clusters', emphasising that the 'gentle and witty drawings of animals' were used 'to avoid preconceptions' (p. 27). 'Clusters' and these animal drawings perhaps also point to how consumer mappings attempt to delineate and arrest cultures that are in flux, with any 'real-life' woman not, in fact, fitting any of the ways in which she is being imagined.

A feminist awareness also lies behind the animal coding, as Restall goes on to indicate: 'it is particularly difficult to comment on women (even for a female commentator) without falling into a morass of prejudices and latent sexism' (p. 27). The study, at the end of the European Decade of the Woman and following an earlier one on men, was partly intended to explore the nature of the differences between the sexes: whether 'there is anything real in the idea of the feminist'; whether if there is, there are 'sufficient of them to make a real marketing target' (p. 27). Restall expresses surprise that the data indicated strong parallels between women and men but whether this is being put forward to weaken a feminist case is not clear. However, the clusters can be seen through a feminist lens. If 'Avant Guardian' dovetails to a degree with the values of '1970s feminism', a post-feminist sensibility is to be seen in-the-making, embedded in the ambitious but outgoing, young-working-mum lifestyle of 'The Lively Lady'. Whereas 'The New Unromantic', 'typically young, working, single' appears to be a beneficiary of women's gains in the 1970s and 1980s, 'The Hopeful Seeker' only aspires to a more independent life.

Thirteen years on, the 'Winning Women' conference offered another mapping of change, focusing on an expanded segment of women consumers, ABC1 25–34 year-old, high-spending, single women. Part of a more general growth of the middle classes, they are the outcome of an expansion of higher education, an increased birth rate in the late 1960s, and the later age of first pregnancies. Without dependants and in reasonably paid jobs, they are significant consumers whose bald profile the London conference aimed to embellish culturally.

This process of classification attempted to arrest and assess a fluidity of developments whose popular cultural nodal points, referred to by various commentators, included the 1994 Wonderbra campaign and *Bridget Jones*. At one level, the conference served as a celebration and a status enhancer for certain advertisers (Nava 1997) but, as with the earlier 'Woman Study', its cultural elaborations, purporting to assist marketing in 'Winning Women' to their brands were framed by a feminist gloss:

Feminism has come a long way. Bras aren't burnt any more, they're flouted [*sic*.]. Lipstick isn't shunned, it's all part of being a girl. Men aren't hated, they're – well, just men.

Overhyped though they may be, the Spice Girls represent modern, independent womanhood: confident, up-front, choosy, sexy, uninhibited and free-spending. Girl Power is where feminism's rapid evolution has taken younger women in early 1998.

('Winning Women' publicity material 1998)

With the conference chaired and largely attended by women, but the papers largely delivered by men, the mark of feminism and a shift in gender relations was highlighted when one male speaker apologised: 'I am acutely aware that as a man, I am not the best person to be giving this speech' [on Women and Drinking] (Brown 1998). The representations of 'Winning Women' also emphasised the changed experiences of a new generation. So while 'Winning Women' share characteristics with the ABC1s identified in the 1985 study, the political edge of 'Avant Guardian' is less evident, and unlike the 'Lively Lady's' commitment to career and success theirs is a 'conditional commitment' – jobs and careers are, after all, insecure. Having less to prove, and in the 'stress society' needing to escape, they enjoy a good time outside of work, exhibiting 'a sense of humour' and 'an ability to laugh at life' and themselves (Fydler 1998: 8). With men their equals – 'colleagues – lovers, soulmates, boyfriends, confidantes' (p. 5) – they reject fixed roles and scorn stereotyped representations, at the same time experiencing a tension between 'the comfort of the old' – the traditional – and 'the excitement of the new' – the modern. 'Winning women feel caught in the crossfire.'

Another more general point that can be drawn from the conference is the way in which the several, often discontinuous, stages of the marketing gaze were made visible and unified into a seamless whole (Nava 1997: 42). Quantitative and qualitative data were collected; interpretations made to represent and imagine 'Winning Women'; appropriate advertising and media strategies broadly sketched; a series of campaigns, promoting particular brands, through particular constellations of media were offered up as successful in targeting this group.

Each stage of work/representation is in fact performed by vying groups of professionals. An advertisement is a 'temporary truce' in a conflict that is inherent and unresolvable (Jowles1996: 77). Since reputation depends on overt demonstration of their ability to 'manage the consumer' (Lury and Warde 1997), no wonder that, rather like a soap opera, the industry needs its moments of unity and celebration to suggest a co-operation fruitfully culminating in successful marketing. The problems of mapping the consumer and the risks involved in the cultural translation into advertising are glossed over. There are no failures here.

The significance of the conference is that it effectively put into circulation a number of discursive understandings of change and cultural forms of knowledge about a segment of women consumers. These are further elaborated in ad campaigns broadly targeted at 'Winning Women' (*Marketing* 1998a,

1998b, Davis 1998). Here I examine more closely what Gledhill refers to as the 'state of the contest' in gendered relations (Davis 1997: 383), or what we might also refer to as changed 'knowledge–power' relations, by focusing on linguistic tone and address and on the exchange of gazes. As Stuart Hall comments, 'you can tell a great deal about how the picture works as a discourse ... by following the orchestration of *looking*' (Hall 1997: 59).

Different looks

A range of campaigns from the mid 1990s joked with, made fun and/or perpetrated a symbolic violence against men. From Wonderbra's 'Hello boys' to Lee Bootcut jeans' 'Put the boot in', the ads provoked media and public interest. In 1997, the latter ad, featuring a woman's leg, her stiletto-heeled boot resting on the buttocks of a prostrate and naked man, received the second-highest number of complaints to the Advertising Standards Authority (ASA) – a total of eighty nine. Those who criticised the ad saw it as anti-men, 'condoning violence' and 'offensive' (ASA 1998), or in the case of Wonderbra and other bra ads they were 'sexist and offensive' (ASA 1998), such as Gossard's 'If I want something rough on my chest I'll find a man' (ASA 1998). However, these campaigns can also be seen through a different lens.

In the Lee ad, the patriarchal representational regime of the stiletto heel as fetish is undoubtedly there as a strong trace, but it is also turned around. The prostrate man cannot see the fetish. If there is an uncomfortableness, given the proximity of stiletto to anus, about the injunction 'Put the boot in', in their defence the advertisers claimed that the phrase 'expressed control' and reflected 'the prevailing "Girl Power" mood in Britain'. Any hint of violence or offence is dissipated by the woman's toe 'resting gently on the man' and his nudity being 'delicately presented' (ASA 1998). 'Delicately' presumably referring to an absence of genitals and the offering of his 'feminised' passive body to the female gaze. John Berger's classic statement: 'Men act, women appear' (1972: 47) is here reversed.

This *double* regime of signification, and the ad's incitement of the tension between the two, is common to most of these campaigns, seeming to fulfil the advice of keying into 'Winning Women's' need for both the 'comfort of the old' and the 'excitement of the new', and with the brand then embodying that tension. So too, while the orchestration of looking in the ads varies, there is a tendency for a double or 'cross eyed looking'. Berger's additional statement that 'Men look at women, women watch themselves being looked at' (1972: 47), is both in evidence and overlaid with other gazes. This shift is clearer when we compare the 'Winning Women' ads to earlier ones.

If 'Dress to kill' was the catch line used by the retailer Wallis in 1997, it also featured in an ad from the leather glove manufacturer Pittard in 1968. Both campaigns boldly play with the literal as well as symbolic meaning of the phrase, Pittard's by having a woman wield a gun (which she holds in her red-gloved hands behind his back), Wallis by its 'accident' dramas. Both rely on a complex of gazes. In the Pittard's ad, the man's vulnerable back is the object of the (female) spectator's gaze, so that the exchange of looks between woman represented and spectator excludes him. The spectator, sharing knowledge of the red gloves' power becomes complicit in the 'killing', in fact ideally placed to 'shoot'. With Pittard woman almost winking at the reader, this is a joke shared between women who know that men *don't* know: this man has not seen through the feminine ruse of 'dress to kill'. The absent but necessary presence is him gazing at her. Notwithstanding his vulnerability, patriarchal relations are affirmed: she is after all still 'getting her man'.

Wallis woman, however, has no such interest. Here a symbolic violence is mobilised to *comment* on the masculinity that the Pittard ad keeps in place. In all of the four versions, 'Crash', 'Barber', 'Metro' and 'Pulp Fiction', Wallis woman is shown oblivious to all around her. In 'Crash', for example, she is self-absorbed as she leans over the promenade rails gazing out to sea. Meanwhile, men look at her, riveted, and with (potentially) devastating consequences: the car has crashed, the barber may slit the client's throat and the guard is about to be decapitated as a metro train passes beneath a tunnel.

Significantly the men are trapped: the driver is momentarily immobilised in his crashed car, the barber is only able to gaze at the woman/the world through his shop plate-window. A woman's looks – as in Laura Mulvey's (1975) classic psychoanalytic account of the pleasures of film – stop the narrative, but in this moment of erotic contemplation masculinity is also undone. Male pleasure in looking is further interrupted by the (female) spectator's gaze, both privileged and key to the ad's humour. We laugh at men's predicament and relish the exercise of power our organising gaze grants us. Such a conjunction of looks is described by Christine Battersby, writing about feminist photography:

> it is only by adopting visual shocks that one woman can enable another to see with a doubleness of vision – irony, parody, anger, satire, humour, mimicry – which is a necessary part of gazing within a culture that adopts the male viewing position as the norm … female gazers have to be more cross-eyed … they have to disturb the directness of the male gaze, by looking in (more than) two directions at once.
>
> (Battersby 1994: 93–4)

Arguably these ads encourage a 'cross-eyed' gaze that does not eliminate the 'patriarchal gaze' but comments on and checks it.

A comparison of a Gigi lingerie ad, in the public eye in 1980, with Wonderbra's 1994 campaign also illustrates a reordering of gazes. In the Gigi ad, a woman, alone at night and dressed in outdoor clothes, stands side-on looking askance at the camera. In a smaller inset is a narcissistic image of (the same?) woman pulling open her blouse to reveal a 'tantalising deep plunging bra … with lace trimming'. The caption reads 'Underneath *they're* all Lovable' (emphasis added). But who is speaking? Whose is the absent gaze? Who/what is 'they'? In her 1987 article 'Underneath we're angry', Rosalind Coward provided one set of answers. Originally published at a time when memories of the Yorkshire Ripper's sexual murders still resonated, and written from the perspective of '1970s feminism', Coward observes: 'She's being propositioned by someone in the place of the camera and she's saying no. She may say no and be offputting but persevere, force her. Underneath they all want it. An invitation to rape.' The absent gaze in this ad is that of a man, who speaks of, not to her; she is also the generic woman linguistically elided with the product 'Lovable'. Women are thus without voice but spoken about – 'they're Lovable'. In contrast, the elision is absent from the Wonderbra ad and woman is the active subject directly addressing men: 'HELLO BOYS'. Here the tag line breaks into the traditionally unspoken assumptions about women as the object of a male gaze and, as with 'Dress to kill', checks that gaze to generate a laughter that 'Underneath they're Lovable' never could.

These orchestrations of looking, together with their captions, discursively reconfigure women's subjectivity. This strategy also changes the relationship between brand and consumer, a change summated in the tag-line 'fcuk advertising'. 'Fcuk™ advertising' was used by the fashion label French Connection UK in their long-running campaign beginning in 1996. At the bottom of the ad in very small letters is clarification of the tag line: 'fcuk is a trademark of French Connection UK'. Meeting with hostility from moralists, the ASA also expressed concern about the campaign bringing 'advertising into disrepute' (ASA 1998: unpaginated). But rather perhaps the phrase signifies an 'up yours' to more traditional advertising. No sign of the product, a large expanse of white space, small typography and a woman's face cropped beneath the eyes, confirms that view. As her face slips out of the frame, her look is steady rather than seductive: is she refusing to be object for the male gaze? 'Fcuk advertising' invokes the 'new sexual discourse' of women's magazines (McRobbie 1996: 187). It also implies a new savvy form of advertising.

The cynical view of the 'fcuk advertising' tendency is that like Benetton's controversial campaigns it aims to shock in order to harvest free publicity. While the latter is valued by advertisers, making small budgets go further, to focus on it alone is to miss the point.

One of the issues to emerge from the new discourse of 'Winning Women' was an awareness of the importance of not patronising an audience, of the brand not being the authoritative parent but rather 'sibling, supporter, challenger, or simply a mad friend!' (Edwards, 1998). The relationship between brand and consumer should be a two-way process, with the brand listening as well as sending messages. As Adam Lury, founding partner of the 'hot shop' creative agency HHCL, highlighted in the agency's 1986 manifesto, 'Marketing at a Point of Change':

> Customers are no longer prepared to be the 'child', ever credulous, submissive to authority … They want to be involved in the process and increasingly they want recognition that *it is their agenda that is being followed* … they *are equal partners in a deal whose terms are constantly changing*.
>
> (quoted in Lury 1998: 79, emphasis added)

The tone and address of the 1990s campaigns I have been considering attempt just that. The shift from 'Underneath they're Lovable' to 'Hello Boys' or 'fcuk advertising' marks a more equitable relation between brand and female consumer. The advertising speaks to the target group in a tone of voice and with a cultural sensibility that they recognise. As Alison Fydler suggests of advertising targeted at 'Winning Women', it should be 'entertaining, making fun out of life' but also be 'relevant' (1998: 38). There is, however, another dimension to be mindful of. Most of the campaigns placed ads both in the intimate medium of women's magazines and in public space where they could also be consumed by, among others, men (Winship 2000). In that way, whether intended or not, the tension of the double signification, the reconfiguring of subjectivity and knowledge–power relations are more heightened. The dialogic quality of these ads, as in other arenas of popular culture, encourages public response and reflection (Rose 1998: 30). The micro-politics of advertising connects up with other networks – a process I have referred to elsewhere as 'the thicker life of (shock) advertising' (Winship 2000: 43).

Conclusion

In this chapter I have argued that advertising is in the difficult business of representing cultural change, a representation that takes place not just *in* the ads themselves but in other production practices including the industry's attempts at classifying consumers. The event 'Winning Women' was as much emblematic as anything else, 'winning women' had arrived. It demonstrated marketing's efforts to get culturally close to, keep up with, and manage the consumer, which in this case means contributing to the 'state of the contest' in gendered relations.

This is a different position to that suggested by '1970s feminism', which tended to see itself as loftily beyond advertising, regarded the latter as having a vested interest in the 'consuming woman' and therefore 'no stake in subverting conventional forms of femininity' (Winship 2000: 178). At the same time it believed that the industry's awareness that it 'cannot afford to be seen as in any way oppressive or, worse, old-fashioned' (p.178) has led to advertising managing 'to absorb feminism' (p. 179), implying its dilution. While sympathising with this structural view of power, in this chapter I have stressed a more Foucauldian analysis concerned with the discursive production of knowledge–power–subject relations across different sites.

Marketing's gaze, having become ever-refined in differentiating 'lifestyle' categories is continuing to enmesh the female consumer. Yet, its processes have assisted the development of increasingly specific frameworks for product distribution *and* political expression. The bio-cultural power referred to by Lury and Warde (1997) locates the body as not only the privileged site of 'normalisation' but also of 'the struggles between different formations of power/knowledge' (Hall 1997: 50). In the advertising that I examined, such regimes were clearly shown to be playing across the female body. While I accept the warning that these cultural processes do not in themselves transform the structures of society, they are part of the proliferating, though discontinuous, networks constituting 'woman' and through which women's own sense of their shared and differentiated identities are forged, and fought out.

References

Advertising Standards Authority (1998) *Top Ten Advertisements 1997*, London: ASA.

Andrews, M. and Talbot, M. M. (eds) (2000) *All the World and Her Husband: Women in Twentieth-Century Consumer Culture*, London: Cassell.

Barrett, M. and Phillips, A. (1992) 'Introduction', in M. Barrett and A. Phillips (eds) *Destabilising Theory: Contemporary Feminist Debates*, Cambridge: Polity.

Battersby, C. (1994) 'Gender and the Picturesque: Recording Ruins in the Landscape of Patriarchy', in J. Brettle, and S. Rice (eds) *Public Bodies–Private States: New Views on Photography, Representation and Gender*, Manchester: Manchester University Press.

Berger, A. A. (2000) *Ads, Fads and Consumer Culture: Advertising's Impact on American Character and Society*, Lanham, Maryland: Rowman and Littlefield.

Berger, J. (1972) *Ways of Seeing*, Harmondsworth: Penguin.

Bowlby, R. (2000) *Carried Away: the Invention of Modern Shopping*, London: Faber & Faber.

Brierley, S. (1995) *The Advertising Handbook*, London: Routledge.

Carter, E. (1997) *How German Is She? Postwar West German Reconstruction and the Consuming Woman*, Ann Arbor: University of Michigan Press.

Chaney, D. (1996) *Lifestyles*, London: Routledge.

Cronin, A. M. (2000) 'Advertising difference: women, Western Europe and "consumer-citizenship"', in M. Andrews and M. M. Talbot (eds) (2000) *All the World and Her Husband: Women in Twentieth-Century Consumer Culture*, London: Cassell.

Davis, F. (1998) 'Fashion case study: Wallis', in *Winning Women: Marketing to High Spending Single Females*, London: Haymarket.

du Gay, P. (1996) *Consumption and Identity at Work*, London: Sage.

—— (1997a) 'Introduction', in P. du Gay (ed.) *Doing Cultural Studies: the Story of the Sony Walkman*, London: Sage.

—— (1997b) 'Organizing Identity: Making Up People at Work', in P. du Gay (ed.) *Production of Culture/Cultures of Production*, London: Sage.

Ferguson, M. and Golding, P. (eds) (1997) *Cultural Studies in Question*, London: Sage.

Fielding, H. (1996) *Bridget Jones's Diary*, London: Picador.

Fydler, A. (1998) 'Winning Women', in *Winning Women: Marketing to High Spending Single Females*, London: Haymarket.

Gabriel, Y. and Lang, T. (1995) *The Unmanageable Consumer: Contemporary Consumption and its Fragmentations*, London: Sage.

Gamman, L. and Marshment, M. (eds) (1988) *The Female Gaze: Women as Viewers of Popular Culture*, London: Women's Press.

Gledhill, C. (1997) 'Genre and gender: the case of soap opera', in S. Hall (ed.) *Representation: Cultural Representations and Signifying Practices*, London: Sage.

Hall, S. (1997) 'The work of representation', in S. Hall (ed.) *Representation: Cultural Representations and Signifying Practices*, London: Sage.

Harvey, D. (1989) *The Condition of Postmodernity*, Oxford: Blackwell.

Heller, Z. (1998) 'Dumped', *London Review of Books*, 19 February: 24.

Jackson, P., Lowe, M., Miller, D. and Mort, F. (eds) (2000) *Commercial Cultures: Economies, Practices, Spaces*, Oxford: Berg.

Lash, S. and Urry, J. (1994) *Economies of Signs and Spaces*, London: Sage.

Lee, M. (1993) *Consumer Culture Reborn*, London: Routledge.

Leiss, W., Kline, S. and Jhally, S. (1997) *Social Communication in Advertising*, 2nd edn, London: Routledge.

Lury, C. (1998) *Brandwatching: Lifting the Lid on the Phenomenon of Branding*, Dublin: Blackhall.

Lury, C. and Warde, A. (1997) 'Investments in the Imaginary Consumer: Conjectures Regarding Power, Knowledge and Advertising', in M. Nava, A. Blake, I. MacRury and B. Richards (eds) *Buy this Book: Studies in Advertising*, London: Routledge.

McGuigan, J. (1992) *Cultural Populism*, London: Routledge.

—— (1992) *Cultural Populism*, London: Routledge.

McRobbie, A. (1996) 'More!: new sexualities in girls' and women's magazines', in J. Curran, D. Morley and V. Walkerdine (eds) *Cultural Studies and Communications*, London: Arnold.

—— (1998) *British Fashion Design: Rag Trade or Image Industry?*, London: Routledge.

Marchand, R. (1985) *Advertising the American Dream: Making Way for Modernity, 1920–1940*, Berkeley: University of California Press.

Marketing (1998a) *Winning Women: Marketing to High Spending Females*, London: Haymarket.

—— (1998b) *Winning Women: Marketing to High Spending Females* (delegate details), London: Haymarket.

Mattelart, A. (1991) *Advertising International: the Privatisation of Public Space*, London: Routledge (translated by Michael Chanan).

Modleski, T. (1991) *Feminism Without Women: Culture and Criticism in a 'Postfeminist' Age*, London: Routledge.

Mort, F. (1996) *Cultures of Consumption: Masculinities and Social Space in Late Twentieth-Century Britain*, London: Routledge.

—— (1997) 'Paths to Mass Consumption: Britain and the USA since 1945', in M. Nava, A. Blake, I. MacRury and B. Richards (eds) *Buy this Book: Studies in Advertising*, London: Routledge.

Mulvey, L. (1975) 'Visual Pleasure and Narrative Cinema', *Screen*, 16(3): 6–18.

Nava, M. (1997) 'Framing advertising: cultural analysis and the incrimination of visual texts', in M. Nava, A. Blake, I. MacRury and B. Richards (eds) *Buy this Book: Studies in Advertising*, London: Routledge.

Nixon, S. (1996) *Hard Looks: Masculinities, Spectatorship and Contemporary Consumption*, London: UCL Press.

—— (1997a) 'Exhibiting Masculinity', in S. Hall (ed.) *Representation: Cultural Representations and Signifying Practices*, London: Sage.

—— (1997b) 'Circulating culture', in P. du Gay (ed.) *Productions of Culture/Cultures of Production*, London: Sage.

Packard, V. (1981) *The Hidden Persuaders*, Harmondsworth: Penguin.

Restall, C. (1985) 'A Breakthrough in the Study of Women', *Campaign*, 22 November: 26–8. Reprinted in P. du Gay (ed.) (1997) *Productions of Culture/Cultures of Production*, London: Sage.

Roberts, H. (1998) 'Cars case study: Nissan', in *Marketing Winning Women: Marketing to High Spending Single Females*, London: Haymarket.

Rose, T. (1997) 'Never Trust a Big Butt and a Smile', in C. Brunsdon, J. D'Acci and
   L. Spigel (eds) *Feminist Television Criticism: a Reader*, Oxford: Clarendon Press.

Schudson, M. (1993) *Advertising, the Uneasy Persuasion: its Dubious Impact on American
   Society*, London: Routledge.

Smith, P. (2000) 'Looking backwards and forwards at cultural studies', in T. Bewes
   and J. Gilbert (eds) *Cultural Capitalism: Politics After New Labour*, London: Lawrence
   and Wishart.

Squire, C. (1997) 'Empowering women? The Oprah Winfrey Show', in C. Brunsdon,
   J. D'Acci and L. Spigel (eds) *Feminist Television Criticism: a Reader*, Oxford:
   Clarendon Press.

Thomas, L. (1997) 'In love with Inspector Morse', in C. Brunsdon, J. D'Acci and
   L. Spigel (eds) *Feminist Television Criticism: a Reader*, Oxford: Clarendon Press:
   184–204.

Turner, G. (1998) 'Review of Ferguson and Golding: Cultural Studies in Question', *International
   Journal of Cultural Studies*, 1(3): 433–6.

Wilkins, J. (1998) 'Girl watching', in *Marketing Winning Women: Marketing to High
   Spending Single Females*, London: Haymarket.

Winship, J. (2000) 'Women outdoors: advertising, controversy and disputing feminism in
   the 1990s', *International Journal of Cultural Studies*, 3(1): 27–55.

4 Consuming men

Producing *loaded*

Ben Crewe

Introduction

In August 1997, *The Independent* devoted its main editorial column, as well as a half-page news story, to events in the UK men's magazine market. The coverage marked a striking and significant moment in British media history. FHM had overtaken the women's magazine *Cosmopolitan* to become the UK's most popular monthly lifestyle title, selling over 500,000 copies per issue. At its peak the following year, FHM's sales reached over 775,000, more than ten times that of five years earlier, while overall monthly sales of men's lifestyle magazines, narrowly conceived, topped 2.3 million. FHM's achievement was especially remarkable because, while general-interest magazines for women had flourished throughout the twentieth century and *Cosmopolitan* had been on British newsstands for twenty-five years, the equivalent sector for men had only been resuscitated in the late 1980s after twenty years of being labelled the 'graveyard' of magazine publishing.

The market's maturation seemed highly symbolic of a changing relationship between male identity and consumer culture. Introducing her analysis of women's lifestyle magazines in the 1970s, Marjorie Ferguson suggested that the absence of an equivalent sector for men signified their relatively more certain gender identity: 'a more powerful and confident male sex already "knows" everything there is to know about the business of being masculine' (Ferguson 1983: 2). Twenty years earlier, women's magazines had been central in constructing the notion of the skilled and reflexive 'consuming housewife', a figure ideally suited to the burgeoning domestic commodity markets of the post-war era (Winship 1987). Following this logic, the revitalisation of the men's press seemed to indicate an unfixing of masculine identity from the bread-winner ethic and patriarchal status codes, and its progressive integration into the world of goods and leisure. It was the figure of the style-conscious 'new man' who seemed to embody these shifts, an identity some distance from conventional scripts of British masculinity. It is to the genesis and significance of the new man that I shall now turn, situating him in some historical context before returning to the events that have seen him superseded by a new icon of masculinity within the men's magazine market.

Consumer culture and new masculinities

Contrasting with the unitary conceptions of masculinity often presupposed in sex-role theories (Parsons and Bales 1953) and notions of patriarchy (for example, Brownmiller 1975), the publication in 1977 of Andrew Tolson's *The Limits of Masculinity* and Paul Willis' *Learning to Labour* was crucial in highlighting the diversity of masculinities existing within social settings and society at large. Notably, both identified class as the major axis of difference between men, relating distinctions between working-class and middle-class masculinities to different structural experiences of education and capitalist working practices. While the characteristics of working-class masculinity were those of collective solidarity, physical toughness and presence, bravado, confrontation, anti-authority sentiment and the avoidance of 'feelings', middle-class masculinity was seen to rest on moral dignity, emotional restraint, 'respectability' and individualised notions of self-discipline, ambition and competitiveness (Tolson 1977, Willis 1977).

Two years later, another landmark study, Dick Hebdige's (1979) *Subculture: the Meaning of Style*, implicitly recognised that men's relationship to the world of goods was not merely as producers, and that male identity was not secured through the institutions of production alone. *Subculture* outlined a range of urban youth subcultures in which *consumption* preferences were central in the construction and expression of a range of masculine identities within an increasingly fragmented and racially inflected class landscape. Those of the mod and the biker were anchored not simply in production conditions, the workplace or in the local community but in broader cultures of consumption: leisure, clothing, music and style (see also Willis 1978, Cohen 1980). That these were subcultures of the young was unsurprising. For an older generation of men tied to discourses of provision, extravagant forms of consumption, self-indulgence and leisure invoked the threatening figure of the homosexual (Ehrenreich 1983). Younger men, keen to differentiate themselves from parent cultures, and often with the disposable income with which to do so, represented the vanguard of a new masculinity in which collective identity was celebrated and assured through the public display of style.

Hebdige's interest in the media was limited to its role in commodifying and 'engulfing' these subcultures into dominant frameworks of meaning, a process seen to destroy their authenticity. Recent accounts of cultural industries have offered an alternative reading of the relationship between popular identity and commercial media. Here, the latter, and the representational sphere they constitute, are not seen as the 'enemies' of 'authentic' identity, or as the untrammelled purveyors of false ideologies of consumption onto gullible populations. Instead, they are regarded as sites 'where the market meets popular experience and lifestyles on the ground' (Mort 1988: 215), as bearers of an increasingly intimate and sensitised relationship between commercial producers and consumers (Mort 1988, 1989, du Gay 1993, Nixon 1996, 1997, du Gay et al.1997, McRobbie 1999). Through the advertising and promotion of an expanding range of goods targeted at men, the marketplace has become a privileged site for the elaboration and construction of a proliferation of new masculine identities. From this perspective, consumer culture is both reflective and productive of lived masculinities, a site where the identities of 'real men' are constantly scrutinised, reflected, dramatised, remade and, literally, re-presented back to them.

The assumptions underpinning this perspective merit further explanation. In general, the changing dynamic of cultural production is associated with the shift from a Fordist production system of large-scale standardised mass production for homogeneous mass markets to a post-Fordist culture of flexible specialisation, characterised by small-scale short-run differentiated production aimed at segmented consumer markets. One significant feature of new production systems is their ability, through flexible manufacturing techniques (or 'just-in-time' production), to respond rapidly to changes in consumer tastes and trends. Such procedures depend on a number of technologies, including electronic point of sale (EPOS) tills that provide retailers with instant data on consumer purchases to be fed back into stock-keeping and manufacturing orders, and the computer-aided production methods that enable the rapid design and modification of products in response to such information (du Gay 1993, Nixon 1996).

This tighter and more integrated system of production, distribution and retailing, what du Gay labels 'co-ordinated flexibility' (1993: 568), is also driven by the growing amount of market research undertaken within commercial culture. Intensive supply-side competition and the perception of increasingly unpredictable, fragmented and discerning consumer markets have made the monitoring of consumer preferences and lifestyles a crucial aspect of the battle for market advantage (Lury 1994, Nixon 1996). By this means, consumers – and the social and cultural shifts affecting their lives – are drawn into decisions made in the production sphere. To perceive them simply at the end-point of a production 'chain' does not adequately account for the ways that they are folded into production dynamics or for the apparently consumer-led nature of many commercial markets, from fashion, where 'street style' leads the way in establishing production trends, to my own area of concern, the magazine industry. Increased sensitivity to differentiated consumer blocs has also necessitated new strategies for engaging with customers. Goods and services are tailored to niche lifestyle fractions through aestheticised, image-led advertising, comprising emotional rather than informational or rational appeals to the 'individuality' of consumers. This is not to say that appealing to the individual 'you' is a radically new promotional approach; rather, that recent years have seen an expansion in the number of individualities on offer (Mort 1988, 1989, du Gay 1993).

It is through such terms that Mort (1988, 1996) and Nixon (1993, 1996) have understood the emergence of the 'new man', as exemplified in the pages of the men's lifestyle press of the late 1980s. For Mort, the intensity of attempts to open up consumer markets aimed at men, and the consequent interrogation of the young British man throughout commercial culture, generated a range of identities for men that both recognised and promoted the increasing integration of modern masculinity and consumer culture. The new man was the most notable amongst these offerings, while the establishment of the general-interest men's magazine became the chief concern for those manufacturers, retailers and cultural producers keen to bind men ever more closely into the cultures of consumption. As Nixon (1996) demonstrates, from the early 1980s, the clothing industry had begun to see male markets as more fertile than the relatively saturated women's sectors. Meanwhile, companies such as Next started to open up menswear middle-markets, differentiating male consumers into more specialised, segmented blocs, co-ordinated and represented through 'lifestyle' rather than class referents. However, promoting these new menswear and grooming products to appropriate consumer groupings was problematic. Whilst there existed a range of lifestyle magazines for women and girls, men's magazines were devoted to single-issue areas such as sport, cars and pornography. These provided neither sufficiently glossy paper nor suitably relevant editorial environments for advertisers' requirements, forcing them to spread their budgets across several publications to reach their desired consumers (Nixon 1993).

Motivated by this enthusiasm for general-interest men's titles amongst advertising and retail communities, magazine publishers were also encouraged by formal and informal assessments of shifts in male cultures. Lifestyle and psychographic research conducted within advertising circles indicated the existence of a new set of 'Avant Guardian' and 'innovating' men whose 'contemporary' and self-conscious attitudes towards masculinity and consumption made them potentially receptive to the editorial and advertising appeals of a glossy men's magazine (Nixon 1996: 101–2, 130–1). Like retailers such as Next and the Burton Group, advertisers recognised that economic class and mass identity could no longer account for the consumption patterns of a more individuated and expressive male public. Developments in magazine culture itself also informed calculations of the viability of a men's lifestyle title. Some practitioners regarded the success of American men's lifestyle magazines in isolating the 'male yuppie audience' as the key to establishing similar magazines in the UK (Nixon 1996). Other industry insiders were dubious that the 'more mature' American male, conscious of style, fashion and appearance and informed by the women's movement, could be discerned domestically (Nixon 1996: 128; Mort 1996). Mobilising standard stereotypes of the 'typical British man', such sceptics claimed that men's interests were well served by other media (in particular newspapers), that they had no need for the 'men's clubs' that lifestyle magazines would offer, and that British masculinity was uncomfortable with the explicitly gendered style that a men's title would need to invoke (Nixon 1996).

The failure of The Hit, launched by IPC in 1985 for the late-teenage male market, only fuelled such assertions. The product was given considerable backing by IPC and attracted strong support from advertising agencies, but consumers proved less sympathetic – reluctant to induct themselves into the magazine's self-consciously male community, with its implications of personal weakness and effeminacy (Mort 1996: 21). In the light of this failure, it was the style press, in particular The Face, that set the terms for the establishment of the men's magazine market. The Face offered a formula of style-led journalism through which to target affluent, trend-setting young men. Its success also established the leverage for publisher-editor Nick Logan to launch *Arena* in November 1986, the first successful, openly-male lifestyle magazine for almost twenty years (Mort 1996, Nixon 1993, 1996). The addition of GQ to the news-stands two years later signalled the market's first stage of consolidation. While there were important distinctions between *Arena*'s tone of 'avant-garde metro-politanism' and GQ's 'modern conservative metropolitanism' (Nixon 1996: 164), their common characteristics were also striking. Both magazines vener-ated consumer culture, drawing heavily on a vocabulary of 'style' in presenting informed and self-conscious consumption as a crucial means of expressing iden-tity (Mort 1996: 77). Dress, grooming and discerning consumption were thus portrayed as the primary identifiers of masculinity, and personal liberation equated with an immersion in the offerings of commercial society.

Examining recent ideologies of manhood in the US, Ehrenreich (1983, 1989) positioned the new man as part of a long line of masculine identities, promoted in both scientific and popular discourses, that have disavowed the dominant breadwinner ethic of the post-war years in favour of a more irrespon-sible, self-indulgent and emotionally labile masculinity. These include *Playboy*'s 'bachelor consumer', countercultural identities such as the beatnik and the hippie, and new psychology's 'healthy male'. A different set of masculine prece-dents might be distinguished in the UK. Nick Logan's claim that *The Face*'s editorial content was inspired by a recollection of his own lifestyle as a fashion-conscious 18-year-old mod is particularly suggestive of the importance of the subcultural scripts I mentioned earlier. Nonetheless, in both countries, the trail leads to forms of masculine subjectivity ever more suitable for a consumption-oriented society: the legitimation of 'a consumerist personality for *men*' (Ehrenreich 1983: 171).

Interpreting this shift is by no means straightforward. Edwards (1997) has argued that the expansion of markets for men in the 1980s reflected a number of connected developments. These included the growth of service sector indus-tries such as the City, advertising and marketing that provided employment and income for young single men, while equating success at work with personal appearance. Ideologies of individualistic materialism and co-ordinated consumption were encouraged more widely within political culture and lifestyle advertising respectively, while the increasing number of men living alone or in childless relationships was also seen to be significant in fostering a male consumer culture. Although these appear to be social, cultural, demographic and ideological as much as economic developments, Edwards asserts that the redefinition of masculinity in terms of possessions rather than provision was an 'adaptation to a primarily economic precedent' rather than 'purely social change' or an *outcome* of shifts in sexual politics (1997: 50). Accordingly then, Edwards highlights the economically (as well as geographically, racially and generationally) stratified exclusions that a consumption-oriented masculinity promotes: 'Consumer society may well open up opportunities for some, yet it slams doors in the faces of others' (1997: 130). Conventional masculine hierar-chies based upon production roles may be undermined, only for class to reappear as an axis of inequality in the clothing, cars and consumer goods that different men can afford.

Other discussions of the new man highlighted the proliferation of representations that portrayed men as more narcissistic, emotional, self-conscious, domesticated and 'feminine' than the conventional figure of patriarchal authority, action, responsibility and machismo, and the breadwinning family man (Goffman 1979, Wernick 1987). Shifts in sexual politics deriving from second wave feminism, the men's movement and a thriving gay culture were often suggested to have informed such representations (Chapman and Rutherford 1988). Equally, the representations were themselves accorded the potential to undermine traditional conceptions of masculinity. In this respect, much attention focused on the visibility of the male body in new man imagery (Chapman 1988, Mort 1988, Pumphrey 1989, Nixon 1993, Simpson 1994). In established codes of looking, masculinity was associated with activity and looking, and femininity with passivity and being looked at. When men were presented as objects of visual attention, the kind of passive and inviting poses that could threaten the masculine status of their carriers and offer narcissistic and homo-erotic identifications for spectators were avoided and suppressed (Dyer 1983, Neale 1983). The new man, as featured in adverts for jeans and toiletries, appeared to rupture such conventions, inviting men to take pleasure in themselves and other men as sexual objects.

The most optimistic readings of such changes suggested that men and women were now able 'to appear with equal plausibility, at either end of the objectified–objectifying sexual scale' (Wernick 1987: 293). Less hyperbolically, Mort (1988) regarded the constant visual reassembly of masculinity in popular culture as significant in revealing masculinity as something mutable and socially constructed, encouraging men to experiment with self-identity through style. By soliciting men to consume images of themselves, the marketplace opened up the possibility of a self-conscious questioning of masculine identity and the potential for the formation of more progressive masculine selfhoods (see also Rutherford 1988). Nixon suggests that this explicitly gendered address was neither new nor necessarily progressive. What was nonetheless important and distinctive about new man imagery was that it represented a 'loosening of the binary opposition between gay and straight-identified men and extended the space available within the representational regimes of popular consumption for an ambivalent masculine identity' (Nixon 1996: 202). Forms of looking traditionally the sole preserve of homosexuality were made available to the heterosexual viewer. It was the inter-textual presence of such representations across a range of commercial industries, in menswear, design, retail, advertising and magazine publishing, and their continuity with structures of perception in earlier periods of consumer culture, that rendered them potentially disruptive.

Other analyses, sometimes more suppositional than informed, were more sceptical about the transformational potential of men's consumption. Some claimed that new man imagery still ultimately disavowed the vulnerability and homo-eroticism that could make it transgressive. The exhibition of male genitalia was promised but never delivered, and the phallic symbolism that protected against male nudity (bottles of champagne, saxophones, etc.) expressed conventional masculine notions of control, action and power (Chapman 1988, Simpson 1994). Others proposed that the hegemony of white, young, muscular heterosexual masculinities in mainstream visual culture remained relatively unaffected by new man imagery (Edwards 1997), and that the 'menswear revolution' was likewise limited to a sartorial élite (Spencer 1992). At the same time, the increasing visual objectification of men may merely mean that gender equality has been '"won" along precisely the lines upon which it had already been lost' (McRobbie 1994: 186; see also Ehrenreich 1989). Press reports of rising rates of male body surgery and anorexia attest to the negative consequences of men's gradual integration into cultures of consumption.

As Mort and Nixon acknowledged, the effects of the new man's representational regime on lived masculinities could not be easily deciphered from its imagery alone, particularly given the temporal specificity of its prominence (Mort 1988, Nixon 1996). Indeed, questions about the destabilising potential of the new man began to appear obsolete by the mid-1990s, as developments in the men's magazine market announced the emergence of a rather different masculine culture. It is appropriate now to examine the conditions of these shifts.

Cultural production and the men's magazine market of the 1990s

When *loaded* was launched in April 1994, there was no fanfare reception in the publishing trade press and no protracted debate over the likely success of this new kind of men's magazine. Details of IPC's forthcoming product, a 'cross between *Viz*, *The Face* and *i-D*', covering music, affordable fashion, sport, sex and comedy, had been announced in *Media Week* and *Press Gazette* three months earlier (28 January 1994: 1, 31 January 1994), but there was little subsequent discussion of its significance and barely any comment when it arrived on the news-stands. A short report in *The Guardian* represented Fleet Street's only interest in IPC's endeavour (G2, 11 April 1994). This virtual silence contrasted both with the publicity that accompanied *FHM*'s triumph three years later and the animated tone of the trade press when *Arena*, *GQ* and *Esquire* were thrust into the market a few years earlier. As these titles gradually built circulations of 100,000 copies per issue, industry insiders concluded that the market had reached a state of stable maturity. Despite an underlying feeling that the available publications were 'over-aspirational' and had limited appeal, trade reviews of the sector rarely raised the idea of a title aimed at the mass male public. When they did, it was only with a resigned sense of its impossibility.

Rod Sopp, advertising manager at Wagadon, whose titles had defied similar scepticism only a few years earlier, dismissed the notion of market expansion: 'there's not a market to launch into. ... I don't think we'll see a situation where we have lots of men's magazines selling between 60,000 and 80,000' (*Campaign*, 3 April 1992: 10). David Dent, a media strategist at the advertising agency

HHCL, reiterated his pessimism: 'the mass generic male is not catered for and he probably wouldn't be interested ... I could never see a mass men's magazine with a sale of 300,000 to 400,000' (*Ibid.*). Only two months before *loaded* entered the market, *Esquire* publisher John Wisbey restated the industry's received wisdom: 'men's magazines are never going to be anything more than niche brands' (*Marketing*, 10 February 1994).

Within only nine months of its launch, *loaded* had reached the circulation benchmark of 100,000 copies per issue, 60,000 above its original aim and a sales volume that had taken market leader GQ five years to attain. Readership figures released in June 1995 revealed that 73% of the magazine's readers were from social classes ABC1, a profile putting *loaded* on a par with *Yachting World*, *Empire* and *Esquire* in terms of its value for advertisers looking to target affluent men (National Readership Survey 1995; *Media Week*, 9 June 1995, 16 June 1995). By August 1995, *loaded* was the biggest-selling product in the sector and had rewritten the conventions of men's magazine publishing, laying the path for a host of competitors (*Maxim*, *Front* and *Bizarre*), new sub-sectors based around health and fitness (*Men's Health*, *XL*, *Men's Fitness*, *ZM* and *GQ Active*) and men's consumer products (*Stuff*, *T3*, *Boys' Toys*), and for *FHM*'s coming ascendancy. *loaded*'s success, and the expansion of the sector into a mass market, astonished the publishing community and most of those practitioners involved in its growth. The scale of *loaded*'s impact was all the more disturbing for the industry given its self-image as highly sensitive in translating shifts in the socio-cultural fabric into market opportunities. Trade analysts raised a number of pertinent questions: why was industry common sense so mistaken about the likely success of mainstream men's magazines? How were *loaded* and *FHM* allowed to enter the market like Trojan horses? And how was IPC persuaded to launch such a title?

Such issues were germane beyond consumer publishing. As I have suggested, academics have also emphasised the agility of post-Fordist consumer culture in general, and consumer publishing more specifically, in discriminating and rein-scribing transformations in lived experience (Winship 1983, Mort 1988, Nixon 1996). While market research and purchasing data are the means by which such sensitivity is putatively guaranteed, it is 'cultural intermediaries' who are charged with using such tools to mediate between consumers and producers in advertising, retailing and other consumer industries. Their role is to assess and interpret consumers, represent their values and preferences to cultural producers, and re-represent consumers back to themselves by appropriately associating goods and services with their lifestyles. It is the growing influence of such workers that has precipitated proposals from a variety of sources for further examination of their values, lifestyles, professional practices and intellectual and cultural formations (for example, Mort 1989, 1996, Featherstone 1991, Nixon 1996, 1997, Ferguson and Golding 1997, Nava 1997, McRobbie 1999). My analysis, based primarily on interviews with editorial and publishing staff in the men's press, seeks to add empirical flesh to what have mainly remained conceptual formulations and calls to arms, and to understand developments in the men's magazine market through an account of the conditions and knowledges that informed its production.

The launch of loaded

According to its editor-in-chief, Alan Lewis, there were three key factors that guaranteed the launch of loaded. One was the 'bullish mood' of the company. Sentient to the advertising revenues that it could attract from fashion, fragrance and wristwatch advertisers, IPC had been looking to enter the men's market since the start of the decade. As early as 1991 it had converted some basic ideas into dummies (prototypes) and had researched the existing market fairly thoroughly, but for some time was aware that its ideas lacked editorial clarity and focus. IPC also recognised that its staff had insufficient expertise, contacts and personal interest to produce a magazine like the sector's current offerings, founded on fashion, grooming and related forms of upmarket consumption. Since its research showed that there was general dissatisfaction with these titles amongst consumers, it made all the more sense for IPC to try to open up a new area of the market. The second significant factor then was that, in taking a leap into uncharted commercial territory, IPC had little to lose financially in its endeavour. loaded's development team was therefore given considerable scope with which to operate, something it needed when there remained little indication that there existed a market for its editorial ideas, only a sense of what not to be doing: the kind of 'very aspirational, very glossy, very posh, quite unrealistic' products that Lewis decried. Indeed, loaded was eventually launched despite rather than because of indications from research exercises. It was the third factor, the gut feeling held by key editorial and publishing staff that loaded would work even when formal evidence suggested otherwise, that proved decisive.

Focus group sessions organised towards the end of 1993 were inconclusive. Opinions within individual groups tended to polarise, and overall outcomes were negative as often as positive. In the light of such indications, the future of the project was by no means clear. If the company board had been in more cautious mood and had followed the research results closely, or if the market had been more competitive at the time, loaded would probably have been scrapped. The editorial team remained buoyed by its own faith in the project. Rationalising the research results, they concluded that focus-group participants had been 'the wrong people' and that the extremity of certain reactions to the magazine indicated that it was 'onto something'. Lewis explained:

> Because the men's magazines that were around were pretty upmarket and aspirational for the intended loaded reader, they [the research participants] weren't reading men's magazines at all. Therefore, in some of the research groups they simply didn't get it at all, because it wasn't a vocabulary, it wasn't a language ... they simply weren't in the habit, they hadn't even thought of buying a magazine ... [But] when you hit the right audience

there was a very strong connection there. And we thought 'we know this audience is out there'. In effect, the launch team pulled rank on what potential readers declared: 'I know the pure ethics of marketing are that you have to satisfy people's needs', proclaimed publishing director Robert Tame, 'but people didn't know that they wanted *loaded*'.

The instincts, motivations and informal cultural capital of the editorial team were also dominant in defining the magazine's tone and content. Lewis and co-founders James Brown and Tim Southwell had worked together on IPC's weekly music title the *New Musical Express*, where their brief had been to bring humour and irreverence to a title perceived to have become po-faced and pretentious. The project was evidently formative: Brown's editorial proposal for *loaded* was based explicitly on what he had liked about this transformation of the *NME* and the idea of bringing the tone of the music press to the men's lifestyle market. It was also representative of their personal preferences: *loaded* was designed by the editorial team in deliberate contrast to the existing market. Lewis recalled finding nothing of interest in the men's style titles, despite knowing that, as a 'London media type', he was within the target market. Southwell and Brown shared this sense of alienation from the current publications, as Brown outlined: 'Not one told me about my life. They never covered football or music or night-clubs, all of which were exploding across Britain. They were missing British culture' (*Financial Times* 4 September 1999).

More precisely, they were ignoring the cultures that defined his and Southwell's lives. Representing these cultures, and giving a voice to the men who inhabited them, was a key motivation for *loaded*'s co-founders: 'we took it to the level of the street and the nightclub and the pub, where guys were used to being ignored' (*Midweek*, Radio 4, 23 September 1998). *loaded* was pitched as a magazine for 'normal blokes', the term being used to suggest a clear distinction from the perceived consumers of *GQ*, *Arena* and *Esquire*. Summoning his first journalistic endeavours as a fanzine writer, Brown announced his ambition to create a national fanzine for an audience beyond the capital with its 'loft-spaces and tailor-made clothes'. Southwell's view of the style-press editors signalled his own preoccupation with the élitism that he saw as characteristic of their titles.

> It seemed pretty obvious that if you'd met the editor of any of these mags down the pub – or more likely the gentleman's club – he wouldn't have time for you, unless you knew someone with a chateau he could stay in during Paris Fashion Week. The best I could offer was a week in my uncle's caravan in Tenby.
>
> (Southwell 1998: 128)

What went into the magazine more specifically came down to whatever directly excited, interested and inspired the editorial team, rather than any more mediated or strategic sense of what readers might want. Editorial staff were assumed to embody their consumers, and therefore to be the best barometers for editorial composition. Brown's inspiration was 'to create a magazine that was for me and my friends, and an extension of my personality' (*The Independent* 8 June 1998). The various influences to which the magazine owed its character – most notably, *NME*, *Viz*, *The Sun* and a number of football fanzines – represented a coherent reflection of his own cultural preferences, training and identifications.

Research practices did little to mediate Brown's editorial technique. Through several remodellings, the title remained rooted in sport and comedy, and retained what Lewis described as a 'sparky sense of humour, a sense of the absurd and obviously a determination to have a lot of attitude'. Whereas the men's style titles preached discerning consumption and self-stylisation, Brown declared 'grooming is for horses' (*Media Week*, 28 April 1995). Affordable fashion was allowed into the title only at the behest of IPC advertising executives. Where Brown's preferences were elsewhere overruled, it was Lewis' instincts rather than research results that were responsible. Trial readers claimed to have little appetite for pictures of scantily clad women. Lewis simply vetoed their assertions: 'the men that we spoke to were either deluding themselves or were not being totally honest'.

With the focus groups in this way disregarded, it was gut faith alone that underpinned the magazine's progression. As Southwell recalled, uncertainty was therefore a prime characteristic of the launch:

> We basically came to the conclusion that it was either going to be an almighty success, immediately, or it was going to be a complete flop. Because all it was was a little fanzine, scrapbook of our ideas and doodlings at the time; just what we wanted to write about and what we wanted to put in, and it was no more than that. And we thought, if people pick up on it at all there's probably gonna be loads of them. But they might just think it's really crap.

Other launches

While the context of *loaded*'s genesis was unusual, a number of features of its development were recurrent in other launches within the sector. Most notably, research data played a subordinate role in market assessments and the development of products. Publishing companies saw little value in undertaking wide-ranging or longitudinal studies to track men's lifestyles, values and attitudes. When research was conducted, such as basic demographic analysis of potential markets, appraisals of existing publications, and focus-group testing of prototypes, it was treated with considerable suspicion by most industry practitioners, often serving little more than to frame editorial developments. Although research could offer negative indications that might lead to concepts being rejected, it was considered incapable of generating ideas for new titles or replacing creative 'vision'. Potential and actual readers were regarded by most practitioners as poor sources of information about their own interests: unable to predict their own purchasing motivations or to see beyond the products they already knew. Most importantly, editors maintained that, in volatile and unpredictable commercial markets, research data were always outdated before they could be mobilised usefully.

Research was often used only to support decisions that had already, effectively, been made. This was particularly the case once editorial figures were involved in market launches. Indeed, the use and influence of research was delimited by occupational function. While evaluating the basic potential of a market area was a job undertaken by publishing practitioners (those concerned primarily with the magazine's commercial position), actualising the idea was an editorial decision. For these latter personnel, research data represented a threat to their expertise, as one editor indicated: 'If you need a bunch of people sitting in a room telling you what you should be doing, then you're in the wrong job'. Once a readership was established, data about its social composition and consumption habits were used by people working in publishing and advertising roles in order to sell advertising space. Editors were often unaware of such data and had little concern with advertising considerations. Their daily understandings of readers were guided by more intuitive strategies. Like Brown, many 'instinctive' editors assumed themselves to embody their audiences, and projected their personal preferences, interests and preoccupations onto the pages of their publications with little further reflection. 'Professional' editors relied on a more mediated sense of their readerships, building a picture of the 'typical reader' to be used as a filter for editorial ideas. Although more often guided by readership and focus-group data, as well as emails, letters and established formulae about 'what worked', these editors nonetheless maintained that an intuitive 'feel' for the market and the magazine's consumer was what marked their expertise.

Conclusion

The paradigm shift that occurred in the men's lifestyle press in the 1990s is enlightened considerably by the patterns that I have outlined. Launches do not occur through some kind of abstract logic or 'rational calculus' (Jackson et al. 2000: 1), whereby gaps in the market are faultlessly translated into appropriate products. Rather, as Nixon (1996) has highlighted, 'economic' practices have 'cultural' conditions of existence, only coming into effect through understandings of commercial possibilities and representations of target markets that are discursively rendered. I have argued that both in the fleshing out of abstract commercial briefs, and in the ongoing formulation of editorial policy, it is the intuitive cultural knowledge of editorial personnel, their 'gut feel', 'hunch' and 'vision' rather than formal knowledge, that is decisive in articulating consumers with producers.

Indeed, while consumers are presented as the primary consideration of launch teams, actual readers or consumers themselves play little part in development processes, instead being invoked and mobilised in often different ways by various competing practitioners. For editors, being seen to understand the ever-elusive reader preserves autonomy and authority within and beyond the magazine company. This is not to say that real readers do not matter, or that editors are simply sovereign in representing them. The veto of consumer demand and advertising imperatives set real limits on the fortunes and focus of a title, as well as on the range of magazines in circulation in a market, while also circumscribing editorial freedom in significant ways. Nonetheless, in their monarchical position in the production of magazine identities, and through their representations of consumers on behalf of themselves, editors appear productive of as well as responsive to markets in important ways. The ways that men's markets are formed has to relate in some way to lived cultures and experiences, but precisely how the 'male consumer' is characterised or 'shaped up' is somewhat open to intervention. The normative power and cultural authority of editors are particularly effective given that lifestyle magazines are such aspirational and informational media, and when their very existence may imply that the traditional moorings of male identity have been cut loose. Exploring the cultural resources, assumptions and identifications of editors is, for this reason, all the more crucial. As masculinity and men's consumption patterns continue to shift, popular cultural configurations such as *loaded*, and popular authorities such as Brown, are crucial in channelling the ways that they do so.

As the pivotal figure in the market's articulation, Brown's assertion that 'men are more product and brand-conscious than they used to be – powdering their noses and talking about clothes – we're becoming just like women' was particularly striking (*Daily Telegraph* 20 October 1997). For rather than delineate a more feminised male identity, his magazine seemed to resurrect traditional heterosexual scripts, albeit dislodging them from production foundations. The consumers of the early men's style titles were addressed by narratives of individualised consumption that explicitly associated modern masculinity with clothing, accessories and consumer items. The consumers of *loaded* were hailed by a more nostalgic appeal rooted in forms of everyday, collective consumption such as football, music and drinking. These bindings still drew readers into a product in which forms of consumption and masculinity were conjoined, but on rather different terms from the existing/previous market.

Nonetheless, Brown's outline of his ideal consumer suggested a masculine identity in which both production and consumption were significant: 'blokes' who had turned 'their passions and private lives into jobs', setting up clubs and record labels, 'in fashion, or film or sports, or whatever'. The image of the ordinary self-made man – counterposed with the 'hoover salesmen' that Southwell cast pejoratively as the *FHM* audience – fitted Brown's own self-perception. What it highlighted also was the increasing number of men for whom knowledge from the sphere of consumption and everyday life has become integral to productive life. Men's magazine consumers are not primarily from the shrinking cohort of men in abstract labour functions, but those engaged in forms of service work where everyday social skills and 'personality' are key. The cultural capital distributed in the men's press through mappings of urban culture and digestible columns of facts is as much about the dispersal of 'character' as entertainment or information alone. Arguably then, men's lifestyle magazines imply not so much the breakdown of a masculinity rooted in production and patriarchy, but what du Gay (1993) suggests is a dissolution or blurring of identity boundaries between the sphere of production and consumption whose interconnection I have discussed in this chapter.

Acknowledgement

The research on which this chapter is based was funded by a three-year grant from the Economic and Social Research Council.

References

Brownmiller, S. (1975) *Against Our Will: Men, Women and Rape*, New York: Simon and Schuster.

Chapman, R. (1988) 'The Great Pretender: variations on the new man theme', in R. Chapman and J. Rutherford (eds) *Male Order: Unwrapping Masculinity*, London: Lawrence and Wishart.

Chapman, R. and Rutherford, J. (eds) (1988) *Male Order: Unwrapping Masculinity*, London: Lawrence and Wishart.

Cohen, P. (1980) 'Subcultural conflict and working-class community', in S. Hall, D. Hobson, A. Lowe and P. Willis (eds) *Culture, Media, Language*, London: Hutchinson.

du Gay, P. (1993) 'Numbers and souls: retailing and the de-differentiation of economy and culture', in *British Journal of Sociology* 44(4), 563–87.

du Gay, P. *et al.* (ed.) (1997) *Production of Culture/Cultures of Production*, London: Sage.

Dyer, R. (1983) 'Don't look now', *Screen* 24(6): 61–73.

Edwards, T. (1997) *Men in the Mirror: Men's Fashion, Masculinity and Consumer Society*, London: Cassell.

Ehrenreich, B. (1983) *The Hearts of Men: American Dreams and the Flight from Commitment*, New York: Doubleday.

—— (1989) 'A feminist's view of the new man', in M. Kimmel and M. A. Messner (eds) *Men's Lives*, New York: Macmillan.

Featherstone, M. (1991) *Consumer Culture and Postmodernism*, London: Sage.

Ferguson, M. (1983) *Forever Feminine*, London: Heinemann.

Ferguson, M. and Golding, P. (eds) (1997) *Cultural Studies in Question*, London: Sage.

Goffman, E. (1979) *Gender Advertisements*, London: Macmillan.

Hebdige, D. (1979) *Subculture: the Meaning of Style*, London: Methuen.

Jackson, P., Lowe, M., Miller, D. and Mort, F. (eds) (2000) *Commercial Cultures: Economies, Practices, Spaces*, Oxford: Berg.

Lury, A. (1994) 'Advertising: moving beyond the stereotypes', in R. Keat, N. Whiteley and N. Abercrombie (eds) *The Authority of the Consumer*, London: Routledge.

McRobbie, A. (1994) (ed.) *Postmodernism and Popular Culture*, London: Routledge.

—— (1999) *In the Culture Society: Art, Fashion and Popular Music*, London: Routledge.

Mort, F. (1988) 'Boy's Own? masculinity, style and popular culture', in R. Chapman and J. Rutherford (eds) *Male Order: Unwrapping Masculinity*, London: Lawrence and Wishart.

—— (1989) 'The politics of consumption', in S. Hall and M. Jacques (eds) *New Times*, London: Lawrence and Wishart.

—— (1996) *Cultures of Consumption: Masculinities and Social Space in Late Twentieth-Century Britain*, London: Routledge.

Nava, M. (1997) 'Framing advertising: cultural analysis and the incrimination of visual texts', in M. Nava, A. Blake, I. MacRury and B. Richards (eds) *Buy this Book: Studies in Advertising and Consumption*, London: Routledge.

Nixon, S. (1993) 'Looking for the Holy Grail: publishing and advertising strategies and contemporary men's magazines', *Cultural Studies* 7(3): 466–92.

—— (1996) *Hard Looks: Masculinities, Spectatorship and Contemporary Consumption*, London: UCL Press.

—— (1997) 'Circulating culture', in P. du Gay (ed.) *Production of Culture/Cultures of Production*, London: Sage.

Parsons, T. and Bales, R. F. (1953) *Family, Socialization and Interaction Process*, London: Routledge.

Pumphrey, M. (1989) 'Why do cowboys wear hats in the bath? Style politics for the older man', *Critical Quarterly* 31(3): 78–100.

Rutherford, J. (1988) 'Who's that man?', in R. Chapman and J. Rutherford (eds) *Male Order: Unwrapping Masculinity*, London: Lawrence and Wishart.

Simpson, M. (1994) *Male Impersonators: Men Performing Masculinity*, New York: Routledge.

Southwell, T. (1998) *Getting Away With It: the Inside Story of 'loaded'*, London: Ebury Press.

Spencer, N. (1992) 'Menswear in the 1980s: revolt into conformity', in J. Ash and E. Wilson (eds) *Chic Thrills: a Fashion Reader*, London: Pandora.

Tolson, A. (1977) *The Limits of Masculinity*, London: Tavistock.

Wernick, A. (1987) 'From voyeur to narcissist: imaging men in contemporary advertising', in M. Kaufman (ed.) *Beyond Patriarchy: Essays by Men on Pleasure, Power and Change*, Toronto: Oxford University Press.

Willis, P. (1977) *Learning to Labour: How Working Class Kids Get Working Class Jobs*, Farnborough: Saxon House.

—— (1978) *Profane Culture*, London: Routledge & Kegan Paul.

Winship, J. (1983) '"Options – for the way you want to live now", or a magazine for superwoman', *Theory, Culture & Society* 1(3): 44–65.

—— (1987) *Inside Women's Magazines*, London: Pandora.

5 Producing TV
Consuming TV

Steve Spittle

Introduction

It is probably uncontroversial to claim that national television cultures have undergone rapid and fundamental change in the last decade. We have seen, at least in wealthier nations, the emergence of multichannel television, pay-per-view and the steady erosion of audience share for terrestrial, free-to-air television. This has been accompanied by 'lighter touch' regulation, particularly for the new cable, satellite and digital channels. In fact, it has become unfashionable to talk in cultural terms about broadcasting, and more common for broadcasters and politicians alike to talk about the development of television markets. In this chapter, my primary focus will be on how television has increasingly become a site for the promotion of consumption practices within market capitalism. In order to investigate this market-based promotion of lifestyles I have chosen to use a model of critical discourse analysis that allows me to link media discourse with wider social practice. Before I introduce my analytical method and my analysis, there follows a brief discussion of how contemporary television is produced and consumed within the wider framework of market concerns, even where it is produced within public service structures.

The management of costs and the maximisation of audience share have become key concerns for the producers of television programming. The increasing salience of these concerns has had a number of consequences, but several appear central. The growth of channel space, first with analogue cable and satellite broadcasting, and then with digital television, has given producers a great deal of time to fill but without congruent increases in revenue. Viewers have proved rather unwilling to pay premium subscription rates for anything other than very particular sports and movies, so ensuring that most new channels have to look carefully at programme costs. Even though global television advertising spend has increased dramatically over the last three decades, the proliferation of channels has meant that production budgets are ever more closely scrutinised. Public service broadcasters have also seen fixed or falling revenue from licence fees, and, in the case of British public service broadcasting, attempts to remind producers of the importance of cost management by establishing internal markets. The technological changes that have delivered greater channel capacity have occurred at a time when the governments of many advanced industrial countries have sought to deregulate their broadcasting systems in tune with a neoliberal economic agenda. Deregulation has become a way to secure competitive advantage in the race to attract global media businesses and to develop home media industries as efficient global players. In Britain this is clearly evidenced by the 'lighter touch' regulation applied to new broadcasting entrants. It is also seen in the sympathetic government response to calls by the largest Independent Television (ITV) contractors for the creation of a single, lightly regulated ITV which could compete for audiences and revenue on a global scale.

Broadcasters have sought to minimise costs and maximise revenues in a variety of ways. Four seem to be central:

- *Buy in rather than produce* – *Sky One* and other British satellite and cable channels have pursued this course. While this approach massively reduces costs, audiences tend to be small. Mainstream terrestrial channels have had to use acquired programming carefully, lest they overstep regulatory limits and/or alienate audiences.
- *Produce format TV* – format TV (such as docu-soaps, cookery programmes and talk shows) delivers audiences at relatively fixed costs and so reduces risk. The label 'format TV' is often used pejoratively and broadcasters have carefully to balance predictability and innovation in the production of such programming. Nevertheless, terrestrial broadcasters have made great use of format TV, possibly because much of it contains factual elements. The broadcaster can then claim they are meeting key elements of their public service remit, namely the need to educate and inform, while securing large audiences.
- *Repeats* – used to give the viewers 'another chance to see' or repackaged as theme nights. Again, mainstream channels have to use repeats carefully, whereas some of the newer entrants such as *UK Gold*, *Bravo* and the *Sci-Fi Channel* consist mainly or entirely of repeats.
- *One-offs* – the tendency has been to avoid one-off programmes or short runs, because of the economies of scale available for longer runs.

Most channels will use a mix of the above mechanisms to keep costs down and to maintain audience share, but their position in the ecology of the television marketplace will determine which mechanisms they take advantage of. My concern in this chapter is centrally with mainstream terrestrial television and its role as a site for the promotion of consumption practices within market capitalism. I would argue that mainstream terrestrial television has tended to use 'format television' as its main weapon of cost control and audience maximisation. Since the early 1990s, terrestrial schedules have seen format-driven programming such as docu-soaps, DIY and cookery programmes move out of the daytime schedules and into the traditionally high-cost, high-audience environment of peak-time viewing. For terrestrial broadcasters, such programmes have delivered audiences at minimal costs, while at the same time enabling them to reassure regulators that they are producing increasing amounts of factual programming.

John Corner has argued that in the multichannel environment we currently inhabit the 'cultural character of TV is changing' (Corner 1995: 176). I would suggest that one of the key changes that we are witnessing is the increasing focus on lifestyle issues, particularly in format-driven programming. Of course, television has always sought to represent ways of life in its output, but the focus of many programmes has become on the attainment of lifestyles through an engagement with market-based consumption practices. Cookery programmes may ostensibly tell us how to cook, but they are equally demonstrating how the production and consumption of food is a key marker of distinction, which can be reconstituted as a lifestyle through our own efforts and our engagement with the market. Such lifestyle-oriented format television is of great interest because it alienates neither viewers nor commercial interests. Its implicit promotion of DIY, gardening and beauty products is seen as uncontroversial. This form of programming helps us to interrogate how the changing nature of television has a co-constitutive relationship with the changing nature of the consumer. Just as consumers have sought to express their identities through consumption, television has produced programming that suggests that our lifestyles are expressive of our identities. Just as television has suggested that even the previously utilitarian pursuits of cookery and home decoration are arenas for self-expression, then the markets in these areas have become increasingly fashion-led. I am suggesting here not just that television has become thoroughly marketised, but that its viewers have too. We seem to have less interest in wider social issues and more interest in the consumption-based lifestyles offered to us by television and commercial markets. In this development, we may see something of what Herman suggests has been the 'long trend towards entertainment and gradual marginalisation of the public sphere' (Herman 1998: 133).

I am particularly interested in the emergence of what I want to call 'transformative lifestyle programming'. This is television that foregrounds the possibility of expressing and transforming identity through the active consumption not only of material goods but also of ways of doing things. I will focus on a British manifestation of 'transformative lifestyle programming', but most readers will be familiar with similar forms of programming in their own television markets. Throughout this chapter, I shall argue that lifestyle programming has a role to play in both social distinction and identity construction (Bourdieu 1984). I conclude by suggesting that such distinction and identity construction is implicated in wider shifts in social and economic organisation, such as the perceived change from Fordist to post-Fordist production practices. At this point, some examples and definitions are appropriate.

'Transformative lifestyle programming' is a useful umbrella term that I will use to describe a wide spectrum of television production that has the common feature of seeing lifestyle as something which can be expressed and transformed through the consumption of goods, services, ideas, styles and ways of doing things. This televisual transformation of everyday life into lifestyle seems to be a preoccupying narrative within contemporary television cultures. For example, the British garden transformation programme *Ground Force* differs from earlier gardening programmes, and their emphases on floral identification, seasonal planting imperatives and straightforward instruction. Instead, a televisual *Ground Force* working towards a tight deadline offers us the transformation of an ordinary garden. The programme shows us aspects of garden design and land-scaping, but not in enough detail for us to replicate the process. Anyway, because the team is producing the transformation for an unknowing individual (who will be hopefully surprised and delighted by the transformation), we are encouraged to see the transformed garden as an expression of the person and their lifestyle.

This pattern is repeated throughout lifestyle programming. It is to be used for creative ideas rather than for straightforward instruction. This is particularly true of programmes that take a situation or a person and 'transform' them.

These programmes suggest to us that transforming our homes, gardens, cookery practices and bodies is something we can embark upon for expressive and aesthetic reasons rather than as an activity that is promoted by necessity alone. In the last five years television viewers in affluent countries (USA, Australia, Holland, Britain, etc.) have found themselves increasingly addressed as consumers with an active interest in expressing and defining their identities in terms of the lifestyles that they 'choose' to consume. These expressive lifestyles are closely tied to our roles as consumers. Lifestyle, in this model, is less tied to an organic way of life rooted in tradition and class solidarity (Williams 1981). Instead, it is something that is dynamic and individualised and closely associated with consumer choice and the repertoire of lifestyles available through the market. Featherstone (1991) points to the increasing concentration on lifestyle in consumer culture and distinguishes this from the emphasis on use value and functionality associated with mass culture. Lifestyle, for Featherstone, is concerned with the aestheticisation of reality.

> Rather than unreflexively adopting a lifestyle, through tradition or habit, the new heroes of consumer culture make lifestyle a life project and display their individuality and sense of style in the particularity of the assemblage of goods, clothes, practices, experiences, appearances and bodily disposi-tions that they design together as a lifestyle.
>
> (Featherstone 1991: 86)

Featherstone, following Bourdieu (1984), associates this 'learning mode to life' with a particular class formation, the new petit-bourgeoisie. Members of this group are seen as natural consumers, engaged in consumption that is both positional and distinctive (Lury 1996). Although the new petit-bourgeoisie may be unusually active in stylised, expressive consumption, the broad demographic who watch lifestyle programming suggests a wider interest, if not active engage-ment, with such consumption practices. Bourdieu's (1984) concept of '*habitus*' seems to have particular salience for my discussion, because it simultaneously captures the fixity of our place in the social space and the dynamism of our sense of place in the social space. For Bourdieu, our *habitus* is largely determined in our early years, from such influences as family, education and class position. It is apparent in our socially patterned but taken for granted preferences, the way we move our bodies and the way we talk. Bourdieu defines *habitus* as:

> A system of lasting, transposable dispositions, which, integrating past experiences functions at every moment as a matrix of perceptions, appreciations and actions and makes possible the achievement of infinitely diversified tasks thanks to analogical transformations of schemes, permitting the solution of similarly shaped problems.
>
> (Bourdieu 1984: 83)

Lury (1996) reads Bourdieu as suggesting that classes and class fractions attempt to impose their *habitus* on other classes and class fractions. The success of such impositions is closely related to the cultural, educational and economic capital available to various groups. In the Critical Discourse Analysis that follows I will explore the ways in which the texts of lifestyle programming use the markers of distinction to offer judgements about *habitus*, and by doing so, encourage viewers to make such judgements for themselves.

Analysing *Changing Rooms*

Norman Fairclough's approach to critical discourse analysis (1992, 1995a, 1995b) offers the important insight that language use is a social practice. It is not just socially shaped but also socially constitutive (Fairclough 1995a: 131). What we say is not simply determined by our position in the social space, it is capable of more or less reproducing existing power relations or being socially transformative. In my analysis I will analyse discourse through the concept of *habitus* outlined by Bourdieu and the notion of lifestyle put forward by Featherstone. My analysis seeks to recognise the importance of the urge to classify that is inherent in the symbolic practices surrounding issues of taste, lifestyle and consumption. I believe that such everyday classifications are central to the wielding of symbolic power that attempts to win hegemonic consent for social groups and their practices.

My sample is an edition of the home decoration makeover programme *Changing Rooms* (Bazal Productions) from the 1998 season (1998b). I have chosen *Changing Rooms* because it is, in terms of ratings and profile, the most significant transformative lifestyle show on British television. It is aired at peak-time on BBC1, the second-most-watched television channel available to British viewers. The *Changing Rooms* format has also been successful in other television markets. There are, for example, versions in Holland, New Zealand, Belgium, Germany and Australia. In Great Britain, the show is widely seen as a model for similar programmes such as *Real Rooms*, *Period Rooms*, *Fantasy Rooms* and *Home Front*. Although these clones and spin-offs have all proved successful in their time-slots, they have not proved quite as popular with viewers. *Changing Rooms* may be regarded as the market leader in 'transformative lifestyle programming', so it seems like a suitably representative text from which to draw a discourse sample. The selection of an appropriate sample for analysis is always a subjective and imperfect process, but I offer the following analysis as a series of snapshots of contemporary discursive practice. This chapter uses a necessarily small pool of discourse for analysis; future work will expand the analysis of consumption practices. I would claim that the text that I analyse has something to tell us about shifts in wider social practice and particularly about debates around lifestyle and the penetration of promotional culture into contemporary television programming.

I will begin my analysis by examining *Changing Rooms* in terms of the discursive context of its production and how similar 'lifestyle discourse' is distributed through other texts surrounding the programme. I define 'lifestyle discourse' as discursive practice, which has, at least as one of its functions, the promotion of lifestyles that are at least partly dependent on market-based consumption. I will conclude by making some suggestions about how the discursive practice that I have analysed can be linked to wider changes in consumption practices and the relationship between television and consumer culture.

Production of discourse

'Changing Rooms' *in context*

Changing Rooms is produced by the independent production company, Bazal Productions. It started life on the minority BBC2 channel, but its popularity ensured a move to the mass appeal BBC1 in a peak-time slot. The show's peak-time position (the programme is currently (2001) broadcast at 8 p.m.) means that it has to be produced to appeal to a large and broad audience. It is presented by Carol Smillie, a former fashion model and presenter of such popular programmes as *The National Lottery Show*, *Holiday* and the daytime chat show *Smillie's People*. The choice of Carol Smillie, telegenic interior designers such as Anna Ryder Richardson (also a former model) and the resident DIY expert 'Handy Andy' positions *Changing Rooms* firmly in the cross-generic info-tainment category that has become a central feature of contemporary popular television. The head of Bazal Productions (which is part of the GMG Endemol Entertainment group), Peter Bazalgette, has, as a result of shows like *Changing Rooms*, become an influential figure in the British television industry.

The profusion of 'transformative lifestyle programming' suggests that network executives, programme commissioners and producers believe that the selection of a 'magic format' can be to some extent the guarantor of a successful television programme. Within broadcasting, 'magic formats' are seen as formats that offer a combination of high audiences and relatively low costs. Contemporary British television is increasingly format driven, as evidenced by the colonisation of the schedules by the docu-soap format, reality programming and lifestyle programming. These format-driven programmes have proved popular with audiences and are far cheaper to produce than high-quality dramas or conventional documentaries. Their appearance at a time when ever more television channels are fighting over audience share and revenue that is declining or static is perhaps hardly surprising.

Peter Bazalgette's success in producing successful format television led him to be asked to deliver the prestigious James MacTaggart Memorial Lecture at the Edinburgh Television Festival in August 1998. In his speech, Bazalgette suggested that in a multichannel environment there should be less regulation, more competition and the development of programming funded and directed by commercial sponsors. Bazalgette's call to commercialism is nothing new, but his role as a producer of programmes for Britain's main public service broadcaster, provides an indicator of how far commercial values have penetrated into broadcasting culture. Bazalgette's rhetoric included a definition of the audience rooted in their role as consumers.

> As consumers they're now much more aggressive and more individual. They have less free time – two hours a week less than they had four years ago – and their leisure time is not a treat. It's a fundamental right. So they're going to take their happiness seriously. At the same time they're uninterested in politics and less motivated by religion. It doesn't mean they're any less intelligent. But, as programme makers, we have to understand: consumerism is their religion. They define themselves not by their beliefs but by the cars they drive, the beer they drink and the colour they paint their bedrooms.
>
> (Bazalgette, 28 August 1998: 13)

Peter Bazalgette's speech offers us a view of ourselves as primarily motivated by our new 'religion' of consumption. His view closely accords with Featherstone's assertion that the pursuit of lifestyles through consumer culture is a developing feature of contemporary late-capitalist societies.

It should be borne in mind that Bazalgette is not an isolated proponent of consumer sovereignty (Adam Smith Institute 1984) within the British television industry. He is viewed as a model of success that many in commercial and public service broadcasting are keen to emulate. Clearly the role of Bazal Productions in *Changing Rooms* is likely to privilege discursive practice that fits with the audience-image held by Peter Bazalgette. His language is not that of the Reithian paternalist; it functions discursively to legitimate the colonisation of the lifeworld (Habermas 1984) by the market. I suggest that in programmes such as *Changing Rooms* we see the distillation of these consumerist ideals delivered through a potent mix of information and entertainment. In the text of *Changing Rooms* I suspect that the intentionality of the producers acts as an important frame for how the programme is conceived and executed. It is possible to argue that the world-view of an independent producer may not impact upon the discursive practice of a given text, but in Bazalgette's case, the programmes he produces are rarely in conflict with his belief in the 'religion of consumption'.

Distribution of discourse

Discourses of the market, individualism and choice are emblematic of late-capitalist societies, but they do seem to be penetrating areas previously free of them. For instance, in healthcare the last decade alone has seen the growth of internal markets, competitive tendering and GP fund-holding. More specifically, within *Changing Rooms* a discourse of expressive consumption is in evidence. This has been eagerly distributed into the discourse practice of the producers and retailers of home decoration products and the market researchers who provide them with market intelligence. The Mintel *Home Decoration Survey* of June 1998 highlighted the growing interest in home decoration based on aesthetic concerns, rather than the more functional concerns traditionally associated with DIY (Mintel 1998).

Mintel found an increase in design awareness that they attributed to home decoration television programmes and magazines. As an illustration, 20% of the householders surveyed had used decorative paint techniques. The use of decorative wood-care products had also risen sharply (a 46% increase between 1993 and 1997). Finally, paint producers had reported that coloured emulsions were for the first time outselling white emulsions. Despite this growing market for decorative products, Mintel found that fewer householders were regular home decorators, they just seemed to be spending more on decorative products. Mintel concluded that the participation in home decoration is in slight decline, but its changing nature has meant an increasing demand for decorative products that were previously the preserve of professional interior designers. They attributed this change to the media profile of these products:

> The media has proved to be useful in terms of increasing awareness of what is achievable through decorating and this has had an entirely beneficial effect on the home décor market.
>
> (Mintel, June 1998)

The trade journal *DIY Week* highlighted the same theme, claiming that 'TV shows make Britons fans of home decorating' (6 April 1999: 7). Further distribution of this promotional discourse was offered by *London Metro*, which claimed similarly that 'TV shows are inspiring DIYers' (4 May 1999). Under the headline 'Topps Tiles Rises 27%' the *Financial Times* was even more explicit about the promotional properties of lifestyle programmes such as *Changing Rooms*:

> *Changing Rooms*, the TV programme about DIY helped to boost first-half sales by 27% at Topps Tiles, the specialist retailer of tiles and bathroom furnishings.
>
> (Pretzlik, 2 January 1999: 22)

It is apparent that the financial press, market researchers and those involved in the home décor market believe that shows such as *Changing Rooms* have an important promotional function. The concern with the expressive approach to lifestyle is also distributed through the discourse practice of lifestyle magazines and innumerable newspaper supplements and features. Unsurprisingly, discourse practice aimed at consumers emphasises aesthetic concerns and individual expression over the economic concerns that dominate discourse practice aimed at the home décor trade. The same elision of market concerns is found in the discourse practice of *Changing Rooms*. Beyond briefly mentioning the price of the various products that help to change a room, *Changing Rooms* shares the concern with aesthetics and the expression of identity represented in print-based lifestyle magazines. I would argue that, discursively, the promotional and economic aspects of home decoration are kept at arm's length. Lifestyle trans-formation is presented as something that you acquire by virtue of taste, creativity and decorative skill, rather than a product of market transactions.

In *Promotional Culture* Wernick (1991) argues that promotional discourse is becoming pervasive in contemporary communication. It circulates beyond straightforward advertising into areas such as health-care, education, politics, and with particular relevance to my argument, television programmes. Wernick's thesis is certainly wide-ranging.

> The term [promotional culture suggests that] the range of cultural phenomena which, at least as one of their functions, serve to communicate a promotional message has become, today, virtually co-extensive with our produced symbolic world.
>
> (Wernick 1991: 182)

Although Wernick perhaps overstates the penetration of promotional discourse, I would argue that in settings where it has been previously absent, its ideological force is that much stronger. The appearance of lifestyle programming in the public service order of discourse reflects an increasing trend for viewers to be addressed as consumers. I would suggest that the promotional function of these programmes is enhanced precisely because of the non-commercial nature of the host broadcaster, in Britain's case, the BBC.

Changing Rooms as text

The elevation of *Changing Rooms* to peak-time and the development of related merchandise, are indicative of the popularity of the programme and the wider popularity of 'transformative lifestyle programming'. At a textual level, such programming works by offering a blend of informational and entertainment elements, and perhaps more importantly, conversationalised discourse (Fairclough 1995a, 1995b) that offers viewers access to an accessible sub-set of professional design discourse, provided by designers drawing heavily on everyday speech. The conversationalisation evident in *Changing Rooms* is an important deter-mining frame for the production of identities and relations between participants. *Changing Rooms*, as I mentioned previously, draws on types of discourse associated with both information and entertainment programming, situating it in the cross-generic form of infotainment. It is useful to outline the elements of text structure that seem to be drawn respectively from entertainment and information genres.

Changing Rooms *text structure*

Entertainment elements

These are as follows:

- Time limit for the completion of the task;
- A £500 spending limit for task completion;
- An emphasis on participant reactions;
- Use of music during transformation scenes;
- Use of a host familiar from other entertainment programmes;
- A cast of telegenic helpers and instructors (note the name Handy Andy);
- The construction of a potential conflict.

Informational elements

These are as follows:

- The provision of design and craft knowledge.
- A guide to product pricing.

The two lists, although by no means complete, reveal the preponderance of entertainment over informational elements. As I mentioned earlier, it would be difficult, if not impossible, to use the programme as an informational guide for the replication of the on-screen transformations. The emphasis on entertainment elements importantly influences and circumscribes the identities and relations offered by the text. In establishing identities for participants, the programme draws on two overarching types of discourse, namely the lifeworld discourse (Habermas 1984) of conversational, colloquial speech and the professional discourse most frequently employed by the designers and Handy Andy. *Changing Rooms* is interesting in the way that professional discourse is frequently supplemented by lifeworld discourse to offer accessible, cut-down identities to viewers and so give them access to previously rarefied and recondite professional language. In *Changing Rooms* the reverse is also true, in that lay participants who predominantly use lifeworld discourse also draw upon professional discourse.

Fairclough supports this perception, by arguing that a feature of contemporary orders of discourse is increased conversationalisation of professional discourse (Fairclough 1995a: 137). He suggests that such conversationalisation is an ambivalent development, which may, at differing moments, either help to reproduce social relations or transform them. Although conversationalisation is widely apparent in *Changing Rooms*, particularly in the speech of the two interior designers, there is also, as I have suggested, a synchronous process of the professionalisation of discourse in evidence, particularly in the speech of the four lay participants. In order to engage successfully in expressive consumption, the participants have to display a basic knowledge of design imperatives, taken from professional discourse. I will give some examples of professionalisation a little further into my analysis.

The identities put forward in *Changing Rooms* show considerable discursive fluidity between the lifeworld and professional discourse types. The two designers are the most likely to employ professional discourse. This use of language is most strongly representative of what Clifford (Lury 1996: 55–9) calls the art–culture system, defined as 'the general system of objects within which [aesthetically] valued objects circulate and make sense' (Clifford, quoted in Lury 1996: 55). Although the designers do employ professional discourse it is generally heavily conversationalised and expressed in terms of 'feel', 'look' and 'themes'. The need for discourse to be conversationalised is apparent in the edition in question, which offers an example of what I will call discursive chastisement, when a designer new to the show engages in the production of excessively technical, professional discourse. The resident DIY expert Handy Andy and the host Carol Smillie are shown in the participants' garden seemingly engaged in a spontaneous discussion (although the use of detail shots filmed live suggests that the situation has been set up for the cameras).

HANDY ANDY: Look at this … all right.
(*With Carol's help Andy unfurls a long design plan.*)
HANDY ANDY: Keep going … keep going … This is this fabulous new designer Michael … keep going.
(*Sarcastically*)
ANDY: We've got years to do it in …
CAROL: (*Interrupting*) I tell you what though. That Laurence Llewelyn-Bowen [the show's most prototypically ethereal designer] would have had a couple of scabby bits of paper and a bit of a drawing.
ANDY: (*Drawing random squiggles on a side of A4 paper*)You'd have got that off Laurence.
CAROL: Would you rather have that [Laurence's squiggles] than this [the new designer's plan]?
ANDY: Yes, I would [rather have Laurence's plan]. (*He goes on to throw the new designer's plan away.*)

It is unusual for *Changing Rooms* to feature discussions about the approach of designers. It appears that the identity put forward by the new designer does not support the dominant discursive practice of *Changing Rooms* – that the skills of interior design are accessible to all. The use of a technical chart is clearly an example of straightforward professional discourse, unmediated by lifeworld discourse. This short exchange humorously makes it clear that an acceptable identity for a designer on *Changing Rooms* must largely be constructed from life-world discourse. Handy Andy's imitation of a designer's plan is more closely aligned to the show's conceit that design is about expression and creativity rather than plans, rules and details. The fact that both the designers and Andy draw heavily on lifeworld discourse allows viewers to access professional discourse drawn from both the world of craft skills and the abstractions of the art–culture system outlined by Clifford. If designers must draw on lifeworld discourse, then so must Handy Andy, the resident DIY expert. He makes craft discourse accessible by talking about 'bodging', 'slapping things up' and 'sticking holes in'. Again, we as consumers are offered an identity that we can relate to from our own experiences of home decoration.

The text offers a central opposition between the concrete (Andy's straightforward ability to do things) and the abstract (designers who are creative and 'have ideas'). This opposition gives *Changing Rooms* a potential point of conflict between designer abstraction and concrete craft viability. In this opposition, we can see the playing out of a struggle between aesthetic and practical concerns. This is precisely the struggle that many attempting home decoration will be engaged in. Importantly, the hierarchy of relations within *Changing Rooms* ultimately privileges professional discourse from the art–culture system rather than the craft discourse of Handy Andy. Indeed, Andy, the main proponent of craft professional discourse, has limited power to act, except on the instructions of the designers. In this edition of *Changing Rooms*, and many others, Andy is shown in conflict with the designers. However, discursive equilibrium is generally restored, as Andy repeatedly but reluctantly follows the vision of the designers. Importantly, while the designers are allowed to discuss *their* rooms at the end of each show, Handy Andy is offered no such framing, explanatory role. Perhaps it is unsurprising that *Changing Rooms* should privilege discourse from the art–culture system. If the show is to encourage expressive consumption, then potential obstacles (such as craft concerns about viability) must only be allowed minimal expression.

I have tried to establish that in putting forward identities both the designers and 'Andy' draw heavily on lifeworld discourse alongside a consciously limited professional vocabulary. If the designers offer a version of their professional selves that emphasises creativity and abstraction in the design process, Andy conversely offers a version of himself based on a set of concrete craft skills. He may engage in 'cheeky banter' with the designers and participants but he follows the designers' instructions efficiently. Andy's identity is that of the ideal tradesman, ultimately subservient to those who employ him. Just as the designers offer accessible versions of their professionalism, Andy reassures us that our creativity could be fairly uncomplicatedly turned into reality merely by sketching our ideas on a piece of paper (à la Laurence Llewelyn-Bowen). The idealised and accessible identities offered in *Changing Rooms* seem to be an important aspect of promotional culture. Without them, we might suspect that expressing our creativity through home decoration might be rather too daunting to undertake.

The host of *Changing Rooms*, Carol Smillie, has perhaps the most ambiguous identity. Carol is required to interview both professional and lay participants and also to assist with the work. However, Carol's role is more than that of an interviewer. She discursively sets the tone for the show, attempting to keep the atmosphere light and humorous even if the resultant 'changed rooms' are seen to be unsatisfactory. Carol is required to be a discursive jack of all trades. At one point she will discuss design principles with a designer, and, at another, elicit opinions from lay participants on how their neighbour will react to the ongoing transformation. Effectively, she acts as a bridge between programme participants and the programme and its audience. Carol assists but does not direct the redecoration. This articulation of identity seems to be that of the helpful friend and confidante. This identity is used effectively throughout the programme to elicit possibly negative and emotional reactions and to filter them through the traditional televisual figure of the genial host.

Finally, for this section, I will deal with the identities occupied by the lay participants, who in the sample consist of a mother and son (Cathy and Richard) and a mother and daughter (Jennifer and Deborah). The two sets of neighbours both live in large detached houses in a Leeds suburb. Both Deborah and Richard have returned from university especially to take part in the programme. All the lay participants would seem to fit Featherstone and Bourdieu's classifications of the new petit-bourgeoisie. Lay participants in *Changing Rooms* are rarely drawn from social extremes. For example, those living in poor housing or in housing that signifies considerable wealth are infrequently featured in the programme.

The principal role of the lay participants is reactive. They react to the designers' proposals, to Carol's questions and to Andy's DIY instruction. Their key moment of reaction comes when the rooms are revealed to them at the end of the programme. Importantly, their reactions allow us to assess their *habitus* and to make a judgement based on our relationship to the bundle of tastes and preferences revealed. Increasingly, on *Changing Rooms*, lay participants demonstrate aesthetic consciousness. For example, 19-year-old Richard outlines, prior to redecoration why he wants his room changed.

Richard: There's nothing really in here that matches or blends together. Everyone else has got rooms where they've all had it designed.

Although Richard appears rather uncomfortable and inarticulate during the programme, in the discourse sample above he demonstrates a desire to engage in expressive consumption. He notes that 'nothing really matches or blends' and that his friends have 'all had it designed'. This expressive yearning is perhaps at the margins of art–culture discourse, but it is nonetheless significant despite its conversationalised form. The aesthetic consciousness necessary to make distinctions is more evident in an interview between Jennifer (Deborah's mother) and Carol. The two are sitting in Jennifer's soon to be transformed bedroom. Jennifer reveals that she decorated the room four years previously.

Jennifer: I sponge-printed it because that was an exciting thing to do.

The use of the term 'sponge-printing' alerts us to Jennifer's knowledge of decorative paint techniques. That she did the work because it was an 'exciting' thing to do suggests that she regards redecoration as an expressive rather than a utilitarian activity. The two short discourse samples I have used here seem to support Featherstone's assertion that members of the new petit-bourgeoisie have a 'learning mode to life' (Featherstone 1991: 91). Furthermore, they suggest a heightened aesthetic consciousness, which is 'to be read and classified in terms of the presence and absence of taste' (Featherstone 1991: 86). Further discursive evidence for this view is provided in a behind-the-scenes documentary called *Changing Rooms Stripped Bare* (Bazal Productions 1998a). In it, designer Laurence Llewelyn-Bowen reflects on the changing nature of lay participants.

> They're such bullies these days, they really are. I loved it, the first series. You'd just run in there and say 'I am a designer' and they'd say 'we're not worthy'. These days, really, they've got their opinions sorted out.
>
> (Bazal Productions 1998b)

As a text, *Changing Rooms* appears to work by offering the viewer discursive encouragement to view home decoration as an achievable expression of identity. Perhaps more importantly, it places us in a position of voyeuristic judgement about the *habitus* of others and allows us to locate them in relation to our own. While the informational function of the text could be said to incorporate us into consumer culture, the pleasure of judgement depends very much on our orientation to the aspirational 'learning mode to life' that I believe characterises the text. I would tentatively suggest that it is quite possible to enjoy *Changing Rooms* and be ambivalent about aspirational consumption, or even oppositional to it. Ultimately, however, the text is premised on generating reactions to expressive consumption. In inviting us to make distinctions it offers encouragement for us to engage in expressive consumption to mark out our own *habitus* all the more clearly.

In these moments of judgement we cannot help but reveal our own places in the social space. As Bourdieu suggests, when such distinctions are made they reveal as much about the classifier as the classified.

> Taste classifies, and it classifies the classifier. Social subjects, classified by their classification, distinguish themselves by the distinctions they make between the beautiful and the ugly, the distinguished and the vulgar, in which their position in the objective classification is expressed and betrayed.
>
> (Bourdieu 1984: 6)

The popularity of programmes such as *Changing Rooms* is perhaps partly explicable by their combination of discursive practices drawn from lifeworld and

professional discourses, by their meshing of the informative and the entertaining, and by the opportunity that they give us to assess the tastes and
preferences of others in relation to our own *habitus*.

Conclusion

My analysis raises the question of how the discursive practice of *Changing Rooms*
and the other discourses concerned with expressive consumption are constituted by and are constitutive of wider social practice. In the economic realm,
such discursive practice seems to have had an impact on the nature of the home
décor market (at least according to the industry, the financial press and market
research). There appears to have been a shift from the functionality of DIY to
the development of an interest in fashion-led, aesthetically conscious home
redecoration. At the same time, levels of participation in DIY/home redecoration do not appear to be rising.

The diversity of ways in which discourses such as *Changing Rooms* can be
read might lead us to believe that aspirational expressive consumption is something that we all participate in with varying levels of enthusiasm and
engagement. If these programmes reveal a shift in consumption practices away
from those that emphasise the expressive over the functional, can we make any
tentative links to shifts in wider social and economic organisation? I would
argue that we can begin to make these links. Lury (1996) makes the claim that
the perceived shift from mass consumption to expressive consumption is part of
a wider shift in economic and industrial organisation.

> It is the distinctive use of consumer goods by the developing middle class
> that is seen to play some part in the shift from Fordism to Post-Fordism.
>
> (Lury 1996: 95)

Lury characterises production under Fordism as massified, with centralised
management and strong class solidarity among predominantly semi-skilled
workers. By contrast, post-Fordism is concerned with flexible specialisation, an
expanded service sector and a core of multiskilled workers. These workers, Lury
suggests, demonstrate far less class solidarity and organisation. Commodities
under post-Fordism are differentiated by market segment; they have a limited
shelf life and are linked to fashion-led consumption. This is quite different from
consumption under Fordism, where goods and services had minimal differentiation and were aimed at mass markets. I would like to suggest that when Fordism
was dominant, production and consumption were more reflective and constitutive of minimally differentiated ways of life linked strongly to class solidarity.
It can be persuasively argued that Fordism has not been superseded but simply
exported. The manufacturing geography for the profusion of 'lifestyle' goods has
largely shifted to less-developed countries where production is of necessity the
defining concern and the consumption of lifestyles rather less salient than the
preservation of life. Under emergent post-Fordism, there is evidence to suggest

that fluid and flexible production and consumption practices have begun to replace ways of life based on class solidarity with a repertoire of individualistic lifestyles made available through consumer culture.

I do not claim a revolutionary transition from Fordism to post-Fordism. However, late-capitalist countries in Europe, the Pacific Rim and North America do seem to have undergone considerable shifts in the organisation of production and consumption practices. The dynamism and diversity of lifestyles on offer encourages the view that we can choose our position in the social space, or *habitus*. Although I would concede that the rhetoric of classlessness has some social currency, our willingness to engage in distinction, and our engagement *with* and *in* expressive consumption, suggests that tastes and preferences are still very much both socially constitutive and constituted.

Changing Rooms and similar programmes may reflect a culture, as Peter Bazalgette argued in his speech at the Edinburgh Television Festival, where consumption has become central to our sense of self-worth. However, should we then accept his argument that consumption is the new religion? Like all orthodoxies, Bazalgette's market-led sentiment is open to question. As Robert Bocock has argued:

> More traditional religious, ethnic and political symbols still hold tremendous appeal to many groups in the world, but the symbols surrounding Western consumption often co-exist with these other forms of symbolism.
>
> (Bocock 1994: 182)

At the start of this chapter I suggested that lifestyle programming had something to tell us not just about the marketisation of television, but of ourselves as viewers. These are programmes clearly linked to a wider promotional culture and we have embraced them in large numbers and with little protest. I would suggest that this may be because they tell us a truth about ourselves. We are no longer able to make clear distinctions between our roles as consumers and as citizens. We are not only both of these social phenomena, we are often both simultaneously. In contemporary television, the promotional culture of the market is inseparable from much lifestyle programming. Equally, in our own lives it is hard to define ourselves outside of the lifestyles offered to us by the market. *Changing Rooms* and similar discursive practices seem both to promote and reflect wider changes in production and consumption and illustrate the synergetic relationships between contemporary media culture, promotional culture and the demands of the market. The practices of distinction encouraged by fashion-led promotional culture are complex and often contradictory. At the same moment as we express our individuality through attempting to replicate a decorative paint technique, we can relax in the knowledge that we are part of the fashionable mainstream. There does seem to be an innate conservatism in such a patterning of aesthetic judgements which reinforces rather than transforms existing social power relations. As Joanne Finkelstein points out:

Fashions provide a barrier of protection for the individual against which the unfashionable seems foreign. The sociological significance of this is that a separation between the individual and the group is established and legitimated.

(Finkelstein 1994: 282)

The broad audiences for programmes such as *Changing Rooms* might suggest a widespread engagement with expressive consumption, but this cannot and should not be read off from a piece of discourse analysis. There is a growing body of diverse and interesting work that looks at the everyday reading practices of television viewers, but far less attention has been paid to how television programmes mediate and promote our relationships with market capitalism. A detailed, critical analysis of reading practices is beyond the scope of this chapter, but such work needs to be undertaken if we are to gain any sense of the wider politics of consumption and our place within them. If consuming the products of markets is increasingly tied to the creation of identities, then attention to the texts of promotional culture and to the audiences for those texts must receive far more urgent and critical attention.

References

Adam Smith Institute (1984) *Omega Report: Communications Policy*, London: Adam Smith Institute.

Bazal Productions (1998a) *Changing Rooms*.

—— (1998b) *Changing Rooms Stripped Bare*.

Bazalgette, P. (1998) *The James MacTaggart Memorial Lecture, 28 August*, Edinburgh Television Festival.

Bocock, R. (1994) 'The emergence of the consumer society', in A. Giddens, D. Held and D. Hubert (eds) *The Polity Reader in Cultural Theory*, Cambridge: Polity.

Bourdieu, P. (1992) *Language and Symbolic Power*, Cambridge: Polity.

Corner, J. (1995) *Television Form and Public Address*, London: Edward Arnold.

DIY Week (1999) *TV shows make Britons fans of home decorating*, 6 April 1999.

Fairclough, N. (1992) *Discourse and Social Change*, Cambridge: Polity Press.

—— (1995a) *Critical Discourse Analysis: the Critical Study of Language*, Harlow: Longman.

—— (1995b) *Media Discourse*, London: Edward Arnold.

Featherstone, M. (1991) *Consumer Culture and Postmodernism*, London: Sage.

Finkelstein, J. (1994) 'Fashion, taste and eating out', in A. Giddens, D. Held and D. Hubert (eds) *The Polity Reader in Cultural Theory*, London: Polity.

Habermas, J. (1984) *The Theory of Communicative Action*, vol. 1, London: Heinemann.

Herman, E. S. (1998) 'Privatising public space', in D. K. Thussu (ed.) *Electronic Empires*, London: Edward Arnold.

London Metro (1999) 'TV shows inspiring DIYers', 4 May 1999.

Lury, C. (1996) *Consumer Culture*, Cambridge: Polity.

Mintel Marketing Intelligence (June 1998) *Home Decoration Survey*. Available on the web as: http://www.mintel.co.uk/subscriber/on-line/LS/0/Home_Decoration/Report/10.htm (accessed 12 October 1999).

Pretzlik, C. (1999) *Topps Tiles Rises 27%*, 20 January 1999, London: Financial Times.

Slater, D. (1997) *Consumer Culture and Modernity*, Cambridge: Polity.
Thussu, D. K. (ed.) (1998) *Electronic Empires*, London: Edward Arnold.
Wernick, A. (1991) *Promotional Culture*, London: Sage.
Williams, R. (1981) *Culture*, London: Fontana.

6 Consuming advertising

Consuming cultural history

Liz McFall and Paul du Gay

Introduction

The sets of processes and relations that we refer to as 'the economy' are no longer quite as taken for granted as once they were. Many of the old certainties – both practical and academic – concerning what makes firms hold together or markets work, seem less clear cut and our knowledge of them less secure. Yet, among these proliferating uncertainties has emerged – or re-emerged – a belief that something called 'culture' is somehow critical to understanding what is happening to economic and organisational life in the present. This 'cultural turn' takes many forms depending on context and preferred project. In this chapter we want to focus on just one aspect. This is the claim, often associated with terms such as 'economies of signs', 'the network society', 'the knowledge economy' and so on, that we are living through an era in which economic and organisational life has become increasingly 'culturalised' (Lash and Urry 1994, Leadbeater 1999, Castells 2000). So what does it mean to make such a claim?

One of the most sustained attempts to use this argument is contained in the work of Scott Lash and John Urry. In their book, *Economies of Signs and Space*, they argue that:

> Economic and symbolic processes are more than ever interlaced and inter-articulated; that is ... the economy is increasingly culturally inflected and ... culture is more and more economically inflected. Thus the boundaries between the two become more and more blurred and the economy and culture no longer function in regard to one another as system and environment.
>
> (Lash and Urry 1994: 64)

In attempting to back up their claim that the economy is now more than ever 'culturalised', they point to a number of developments. First, for example, they argue that organisations whose business involves the production and distribution of cultural hardware and software have become amongst the most innovative and creative economic actors in the world. Today, the 'culture' industries broadly defined and other so-called 'soft' knowledge-intensive industries not only represent some of the most important economic growth sectors but offer paradigmatic instances of the de-differentiation of 'culture' and 'economy' in terms of their own business practices (Lash and Urry 1994: 108–9).

Second, they maintain that more and more of the goods and services produced for consumers across a range of sectors can be conceived of as 'cultural'. What this means is that these goods are deliberately and instrumentally inscribed with meanings and associations as they are produced and circulated in a conscious attempt to generate desire for them amongst end-users. This is linked to a growing aestheticisation or 'fashioning' of seemingly banal products to enable them to be marketed to particular groups of consumers as emblematic of certain, desirable 'lifestyles'. These factors are taken as an indication of the increased importance of 'culture' to the production and circulation of a multitude of goods and services. This process, in Lash and Urry's account, has been accompanied by the increased influence of what are often termed the cultural intermediary occupations of advertising, design and marketing. These occupations are regarded as playing a pivotal role in articulating production with consumption by fuelling the association of goods and services with particular cultural meanings and values addressed to prospective buyers (Lash and Urry 1994: 222).

Finally, Lash and Urry suggest that the growing importance accorded to signifying practices in doing business is not only evident in the production, design and marketing of goods and services, but also in the internal life of organisations. Indeed, as we have seen, there has been a distinct 'turn to culture' within the world of business and organisations in recent years. This is premised, in part, on the belief that in order to compete effectively in the turbulent, increasingly internationalised markets of the present, the foremost necessity for organisations is to change the way in which they conduct their business and the ways that people conduct themselves in organisations (Lash and Urry 1994: 108). It is worth noting that advertising, as a cultural industry and as an institution and technique applied to the production and manipulation of meaning, occupies a pivotal position throughout these perceived shifts.

Now, the empirical significance of these claims of 'increased culturalisation' needs careful consideration. Authors working in the social anthropology of economic life, for example, have indicated just how empirically insubstantial the exemplary oppositions – between a more 'use'-value-centred past and a more 'sign'-value-centred present – are that run through these sorts of accounts (Sahlins 1976, Douglas and Isherwood 1978, Miller 1995). Much of the hyperbole surrounding claims of increased 'culturalisation' can be explained, perhaps, by the fact that those taking the 'cultural turn' in the field of economic and organisational analysis are busy finding 'culture' where previously none was thought to exist. However, they also tend, perhaps, to work against the grain of 'cultural economic' analysis. As an emergent form of enquiry concerned with the practical material-cultural ways in which 'economic' objects and persons are put together from disparate parts, they do so by setting up their co-ordinates too far in advance and thus leaving no 'way out' from their terms of reference. This has the effect of rendering certain potentially important, if often seemingly banal, contextual details insignificant or even invisible. After all, techniques of 'economic management' do not come ready-made. They have to be invented, stabilised, refined and reproduced; they have to be disseminated and implanted in practices of various kinds in a range of different locales. This involves much hard tedious work whose success and effects cannot be taken for granted in advance. Thus, the emergence and development of such techniques are probably not best explicated in terms of the large-scale transformative processes beloved of much contemporary social theory but rather cry out for the 'grey, meticulous and patiently documentary' genealogical methods recommended by Foucault among many others (1984: 76). As arguments about 'increasing culturalisation' have attributed particular significance to the role of advertising and other forms of promotion, one way of testing what might be gained from such an approach is to look more closely at the specific production context in which it developed historically.

Advertising and the culturalised economy

Critical theorists like Baudrillard (1988), Featherstone (1991) and Lash and Urry (1994) have understood advertising as a mediative institution with a singular capacity to link and transform the spheres of culture and economy. In the specific study of advertising, this notion is also very much in evidence. In spite of the changes in direction which advertising critique has taken (from the semiotic analysis expounded by Barthes (1977), Williamson (1978) and Goldman (1992), the commodity fetishism thesis of Haug (1986) and Jhally (1987), to the work of authors like Leiss, Kline and Jhally (1990), Wernick (1991), Fowles (1996) and Myers (1998)), there is at least one area of common interest. That is, a preoccupation with advertising's unique potential to disrupt and transgress the relationship between the economic and the cultural sphere. In one of the most explicit and influential recent analyses of this issue, advertising is characterised as occupying a decisive role in effecting a 'mutation' in the relationship between culture and economy (Wernick 1991). In this respect, there is a tendency, evident both in critique aimed specifically at advertising and in certain branches of social and cultural theory, which can reasonably be described as *epochalist*. By this term we refer to a generalised concern to map temporal distinctions in the form of the culture/economy relationship in terms of what Osborne (1998: 17) has called 'overarching societal designations'. In this sense the spirit of the age, including the precise manifestation of the culture/economy pairing, is to be encapsulated in terms like post-industrial society, post-modernity or consumer culture.

The aim of the following discussion is to show that a study of advertising that is both centred in production practice and historically situated is a useful place to begin a reappraisal of the culture/economy dualism. This type of analysis, we suggest, can respond both to the challenge of providing a cultural analysis of the economic and to the epochalist bent in existing theory. Detailed exploration of advertising practices reveals that relatively little is known about the historical development of this sphere of production, yet such evidence raises important questions for critical thinking about production and its relationship to consumption. Further, the epochalist tendency in advertising critique is generally related to the view that contemporary advertisements are increasingly sign-driven, emotional and persuasive in contrast to earlier advertisements that are understood as use-driven, simple, and informative announcements. These perceived changes in form have often been interpreted as evidence of advertising's role in effecting the type of disruption in the culture/economy dualism that has occupied recent theory. Specifically, temporal and periodised changes in advertising format have been understood as related, even causally related, to broader shifts in the fundamental relation between people and objects from a utilitarian, pragmatic and instrumentalist basis to a symbolic, 'dematerialised' and communicative basis.

A historical and contextualised consideration of the development of advertising techniques and styles of appeal suggests that such explanations may be overgeneralised. One way to demonstrate this is to consider the persuasive and emotional dimensions of advertising. This may begin to establish that the use of persuasive and emotional appeals is not the primary or exclusive preserve of late twentieth-century advertising. When the context of production is allowed for, the advertising of earlier periods emerges as a powerful and varied persuasive medium. This however is *not* to suggest that pre-twentieth-century advertising, *as a whole*, was equally, more or less persuasive or emotional than contemporary versions. Rather the argument is that the sheer variety of conditions and circumstances in which advertising has been produced make such comparisons untenable.

The approach to advertising advocated here provides a far more discontinuous, contradictory and varied set of practices than that implied by the teleological and epochal emphasis prevalent in cultural economic reasoning. This type of reasoning is problematic not simply because of the implausibility of teleological explanations but, more significantly, because of the difficulty of finding a fair and objective way of comparing and classifying such fundamentally different entities as eighteenth-, nineteenth- and twentieth-century advertising. The argument here is that the tendency in critical theory to read the *Zeitgeist* of the era from particular cultural forms like advertising produces overgeneralised accounts of its characteristics and functions. In particular, there are issues around the degree of fit between accounts that emphasise the evolution of advertising forms and practices and empirical, historical evidence. A closer look at the historical uses of persuasion and emotion in advertising may begin to make this clearer.

Persuasion, emotion and the production context of advertising

The focus in this section is explicitly on the historical use of persuasive and emotional appeals and the relationship between the production context and the final appearance of advertising. There are pressing reasons for considering these aspects. The substantial differences in appearance between modern advertisements and their historical predecessors are often accepted as immediate evidence of the simpler and more restricted functions of early advertising. The view that early advertising is simple announcement, distinct from the sophisticated persuasion of more recent versions, is almost axiomatic in advertising critique. In many respects, concerns about the increasingly persuasive, emotional or symbolic nature of advertising appeals represent a specific instance of the broader tendency in sociology and cultural studies to understand contemporary patterns of consumption as a corruption of earlier, more pragmatic patterns. Here contemporary consumption is governed by advertising as a new institutional form with an unprecedented capacity to reconfigure the relationships between symbolic meaning and reality. In the following, for example, Leiss et al. question the dominance of the symbol:

> Just because it fits so snugly and comfortably, our thick cloak of symbols seems to be a natural part of our being. The consumer society constructed this field of symbols and implanted it at the centre of marketplace activity, causing a profound transformation in social life.
>
> (Leiss et al. 1990: 285)

Such concerns are usually based on some form of analysis of the changing nature and content of advertising images over a given period of time (Williams 1980, Dyer 1982, Leiss et al. 1990, Falk 1994, Fowles 1996). The question is whether advertisements, by themselves, can really support these types of argument. The apparent simplicity and naïveté of early advertising may be more a function of our profound disengagement from the contexts in which it was produced and received than evidence of the different nature and role of advertising in earlier societies. The argument being put forward here is that decontextualised interpretations tell us little about how specific advertisements operated or were understood at the time of their production. The precise significance, meaning and persuasive or other intent of early advertisements may well be lost to posterity, but a glimpse at these features can yet be gained through considering the specific relations which existed with their fields of production. In the remainder of this chapter, it will be argued that attention to the production context of early advertisements reveals that their final appearance owes far more to operational contingencies than to the characteristics of the epoch.

Debates about the skill involved in the preparation of advertising copy can be traced as far back as the eighteenth century (cf. Addison 1710, Fielding 1741, Johnson 1759). While the preparation of advertising copy may not have been a function performed by specialised staff within the earliest agencies, evidence suggests that the particular properties of effective advertisements, and the skills involved in production, were sufficiently seriously regarded to be the subject of historical debates just as they are debated within the contemporary industry. In 1710, for example, albeit with satirical intent, Dr Addison discusses in *The Tatler* the various devices that advertisers employ to attract attention:

> The great art in writing advertisements, is the finding out a proper method to catch the reader's eye ... Asterisks and hands were formerly of great use for this purpose. Of late years the NB has been much in fashion, as also little cuts and figures ... I must not here omit the blind Italian character, which being scarcely legible, always fixes and detains the eye, and gives the curious reader something like the satisfaction of prying into a secret.

Of particular interest here is Addison's description of italic type, 'the blind Italian'. Addison may not be entirely in earnest but nevertheless this description suggests something of the persuasive impact of even such apparently mundane type effects when they were still a relative novelty. Samuel Johnson also broaches the subject, writing in *The Idler* in 1759:

> Advertisements are now so numerous that they are very negligently perused and it has therefore become necessary to gain attention by magnificence of promise and by eloquence sometimes sublime and sometimes pathetic. ... The trade of advertising is now so near perfection that it is not easy to propose any improvement.

What emerges, in both Addison's and Johnson's essays, is the extent to which they regarded advertising as a strategic and persuasive instrument. McKendrick (1982) argues that the special skill of advertising writing, a process then known as 'puffing', was sufficiently widely practised and recognised to have produced a whole new descriptive vocabulary of the range of different persuasive techniques deployed by the 'puffer' (148–9). The extent to which puffing had entered the consciousness of eighteenth-century England also emerges in Henry Fielding's writing. Fielding is best remembered as a writer, but throughout his career he also put his skills to use as a reformer and publicist. Making his contribution, in a letter signed 'Gustavus Puffendorf', to the often sardonic, contemporaneous debate on the 'Art of Persuasion' as he termed it, Fielding made a rare gesture in its defence:

> An uncommon inveteracy to *Puffs*, of all sorts ... [such that] Every Man who has not forgot to blush trembles to publish the least hint advantageous to himself, for fear of being served up as part of your next Evening's Entertainment ... You would have us likewise to understand that the said Art is but the growth of Yesterday, an upstart Invention ... I must yet insist that the Invention is as old as Time itself.
>
> (*The Champion* 1710, in Elliot 1962: 117)

According to McKendrick (1982: 123), it was fear of the anonymous critic 'Anti-Puffado' that underlay Josiah Wedgwood's publicly stated reluctance to advertise, rather than any real aversion to a technique that he nevertheless used frequently. As a manufacturer who relied heavily on the patronage and endorsement of the upper strata of eighteenth-century society, Wedgwood's fears were well advised (McKendrick 1982, chapter 6). At this time, and throughout the nineteenth century, advertising's status as a legitimate business activity was far from secure and it remained the subject of frequent critical assaults (cf. Macaulay 1830, Burn 1855).

That these debates even took place suggests that, in contrast to the views of Leiss *et al.* (1990), Falk (1994) and Fowles (1996), advertising was already established as a persuasive commercial device by the mid eighteenth century. This view is also supported by evidence which suggests that even at this time the need to produce carefully worded advertising copy was recognised in at least some quarters. The advertisements that follow both originate from the early eighteenth century. The first was singled out in 1710 by Dr Addison as a 'pattern of good writing':

> The highest compounded Spirit of Lavender, the most glorious, if the expression may be used, enlivening scent and flavour that can possibly be, which so raptures the spirits, delights the gusts, and gives such airs to the countenance, as are not to be imagined but by those that have tried it. The meanest sort of thing is admired by most gentlemen and ladies; but this far more, as by far it exceeds it, to the gaining among all a more than common esteem. It is sold in neat flint bottles, fit for the pocket, only at the Golden Key in Wharton's Court, near Holborn Bars, for three shillings and six pence, with directions.
>
> (Advertisement quoted by Dr Addison 1710)

> ·   The Exercise of the Snuff-Box, according to the most fashionable Airs and Motions, in opposition to the Exercise of the Fan, will be taught with the best plain or perfumed Snuff, at Charles Lillie's, Perfumer ... There will be likewise taught The Ceremony of the Snuff-Box, or Rules for offering snuff to a stranger, a Friend, or a Mistress, according to the degrees of Familiarity or Distance; with an Explanation of the Careless, the Scornful, the Politick and the Surley Pinch, and the Gestures proper to each of them. NB The Undertaker does not question but in a short time to have form'd a Body of Regular Snuff-Boxes ready to meet and make head against the Regiment of Fans which have been lately Disciplin'd, and are now in motion.
>
> (Advertisement from *The Spectator* 8 August 1711)

Both advertisements are representative of a style of lyrical exaggeration common in the period, although they may be distinguished as particularly good examples of it. They are interesting in that they suggest a studied rather than a disinterested approach to the wording of the advertisement. Care has been taken to ensure that the appeal is eloquent and articulates with specific prevailing customs and fashions. Neither could be considered simple announcements in the sense usually invoked by critics to classify advertisements of the period. Further, both the Lavender Spirit and the snuff box classes are, by their nature, products calculated to lend 'airs to the countenance'. In essence, these are products and promotional texts aimed precisely at the process of 'continual audience-oriented, self-staging' which Wernick (1991: 193) above, regards as unique to the contemporary 'regime of signification' (Lash 1990: 4–5). This, however, is not what advertising and promotion, pre-industrialisation, pre-mass consumption, is supposed to be about.

While these advertisements, and others like them, may suggest that care was taken in their construction, little is known about precisely how they were produced. Few early business records survive and detailed evidence about early advertising production is therefore remarkably scarce. Nevertheless a range of references in published work and private correspondence suggest it was not entirely unusual for writers and poets to be involved in the preparation of advertising. In the UK by this point James White was one of the first recognisable advertising agents. In contrast to the widespread characterisation of early advertising agents as 'order takers' for newspapers, White was a man with literary ambitions who used his connections to London's literary scene to procure advertising copy from the essayist Charles Lamb (cf. Hower 1939, Turner 1952, Pope 1983 and Lears 1994). White and Lamb had attended school together and a reference to White's persuading Lamb 'to write some lottery puffs' appears in an 1809 letter from his sister, Mary Lamb (RFW 1/6/1, HATa). That this engagement of writers and poets to prepare copy was not an isolated incident seems to be supported by the following comments which appeared in an 1855 issue of the *Quarterly Review*:

> The early part of the present century saw the commencement of that liberal and systematic plan of advertising which marks the complete era in the art. ... Packwood, some thirty years ago, led the way by impressing his razor strop indelibly on the mind of every bearded member of the empire. Like other great potentates he boasted a laureat [sic.] in his pay, and every one remembers the reply made to the individual curious to know who drew up his advertisements: 'La, Sir, we keep a poet!'
>
> (*Quarterly Review* 1855: 211)

There may, be some ironic intent here. McKendrick's (1982) discussion of George Packwood and his shaving empire clearly understands that Packwood himself was the author of the numerous advertisements for his razor strop, which appeared between 1794 and 1796. The impressive range and variety of Packwood advertisements might suggest that more than one author was involved but, given the lack of detailed information on Packwood as 'a plodding lesser man of business' (*Ibid.*: 152), whether this may actually have been the case is most likely lost to posterity. Regardless of who prepared the copy, what the example of Packwood unquestionably shows is that eighteenth-century advertisers, in McKendrick's words, *could* be 'inventive, versatile, remarkably varied in their approach, and irresistibly persistent in their commercial intent' (*Ibid.*: 148).

Another example of the careful construction of early advertising is given in the 1855 *Quarterly Review* article that refers to George Robins as a leading figure in the poetic style of copy. The article cites an occasion, as exemplary of his approach, where he felt it necessary, lest it should appear 'too bright and good' to raise some faults of a property he was promoting in the following terms. He finishes, 'But there are two drawbacks to the property, the litter of rose leaves and the noise of the nightingales!' (p. 211).

These literary flourishes are far from the only strategies that have been used historically to produce more potent and persuasive advertising. Emotional types of appeal also have a long history and are of particular interest because they have, in many theoretical and practitioners' accounts, been directly associated with the advertising of the late twentieth century. Nixon (1996), for example, describes how specific groups of practitioners in the advertising industry in the 1980s understood changes in their techniques and practices as a shift from Rosser Reeve's 'Unique Selling Point' to an 'Emotional Selling Point'. This perceived transition to creative, emotional messages was widely discussed in the trade press and associated with an image-led approach to advertising. For Stuart Bull writing in *Campaign* (24 April 1987), for example, this move took the form of greater ' ... reliance on aural and visual ideas that tap emotion, rather than written proposition, spoken and logical claims which appeal to the head' (cited in Nixon 1996: 87).

There is no question that technological changes in the form and nature of advertising media alone have produced a new range of possibilities for visual and aural communication throughout the twentieth century. A more interesting question to consider is whether these changes in practice and technique can be reasonably understood as a new structure of emotional appeal. The contention here is that emotional aspects of appeal are not specific to particular media techniques but are better understood as relative to the specific assemblage of practices, media and technologies in use at any given historical moment. Understood in this respect, advertisements which make emotional appeals can be identified in the eighteenth century. Concerns about the manipulative potential of advertising date back to its earliest appearances in the press. Johnson (1759) ponders the emotional charge of advertisements with the question of whether they 'do not play too wantonly with our passions?' This play on the emotions could take a number of forms. Advertisements could promise too much, threaten too much, or feature provocative, inflammatory or libellous claims. Johnson cites one of the numerous advertisements for a well-known proprietary treatment of the time, the anodyne necklace, as particularly adept in its use of 'modest sincerity':

> The true pathos of advertisements must have sunk deep into the heart of every man that remembers the zeal shown by the seller of the anodyne necklace, for the ease and safety of poor, toothing infants, and the affection

with which he warned every mother, that she would never forgive herself if her infant should perish without a necklace.

(Johnson 1759)

This advertisement used fear as an appeal strategy. Fear appeals are based on the threat of negative consequences resulting from failure to use the product and have been a common theme in some categories of advertising throughout its history. The strategy was a particular favourite amongst the proprietors of 'quack' medicines. As the following two examples from the nineteenth century demonstrate, advertisers were not shy of making the baldest threats.

> They made her a grave too cold and damp
> For a soul so honest and true.
>   If they had been wise the dire necessity of opening the grave for one so lovely might have been averted, since 'Plantation Bitters', if timely used, are sure to rescue the young and lovely, the middle aged and the ailing from confirmed sickness.
>
> (Plantation Bitters advertisement c.1860, quoted in Rowell 1871: 147)

> What a pity that a young man, the hope of his country and the darling of his parents, should be snatched from all the prospects and enjoyments of life by the consequences of one unguarded moment.
>
> (Perry's Purifying Specific Pills advertisement, c.1830–40, cited in Nevett 1982: 35)

The nature of the threat used in fear appeals varies and their articulation in contemporary advertising can be subtler. A 1996 television advertisement for Michelin tyres, for example, featured the male driver of a car turning around to look 'meaningfully' at his wife and children before setting off. The final copy read only *Make sure it's a Michelin*. The implication that other tyres could not offer the same protection against accident was not stated but nevertheless clear. The argument here is that while the precise format of emotional types of appeal is continually reworked in advertising the underlying structures have remained remarkably stable.

Of particular interest here is the extent to which the choice of particular types of emotional appeal in specific cases appears to be influenced more by production considerations, like precedent, agency practices and the nature of the market and product, than by overarching characteristics of the epoch. Just as nineteenth-century patent medicine manufacturers relied heavily on the tried and tested use of fear in their advertisements, so adaptations of this type of appeal dominate the advertising of particular product categories in the twentieth century. This is well illustrated by the history of deodorant advertising.

Probably the first major advertising for a deodorant was *Odorono's* 1916 campaign, prepared by the agency J. Walter Thompson (JWT). Deodorants at this time were a new untested product and extremely difficult to apply. In an attempt to overcome resistance to the product, the agency conducted research into the deodorant market.

> This investigation developed the facts that Odorono was used by 22% of the women, competing products by 19%, and no deodorant by 59%. Of this 59% of non-users, 47% insisted that they did not need a deodorant. These facts were of the utmost importance. Obviously many of the women were incorrect in their statement that they did not need a deodorant. They did; they simply were not conscious of the fact. It was our task to make them realise it, and this furnished our advertising task with a new objective ... The need for a powerful appeal, yet one that was subtle to an unusual degree.
>
> (Account files, Box 13, JWTa)

It was this perception of the need for a powerful appeal informed by research practices that provided a basis for James Webb Young's 1919 copy appeal *Within the curve of a woman's arm*. The lengthy text, illustrated by a woman dancing in her partner's arms with her arm upraised, revealed how a woman 'may offend without knowing it'. This mild-mannered reference to female perspiration caused outrage at the time but it also had an enormous impact on sales. As a result, playing on fears of olfactory offensiveness became, and remains, standard practice in deodorant advertising. In addition to the importance of precedent in defining the emotional platform from which advertising speaks, this example also reveals the relationship between the appeal type, specific working practices and the nature of the product itself. The results of market research practices and the difficult nature of the product were of crucial significance in the decision to deploy such an adventurous appeal.

The significance of such contextual factors also emerges in the example of JWT's advertising for Chase and Sanborn's tea in the 1930s. The advertisement featured a stylised illustration of an elegant couple, in fashionable evening dress, caught up in a passionate embrace, with the copy: '*Senses aroused, an emotional lift, lifts your sense up, sways the senses, emotions respond to this tea, richer in theol*'. The campaign set out to sell the emotional benefits of the invigorating and stimulating qualities of tea. It is reputed to have increased Chase and Sanborn's sales by several hundred per cent, an achievement of particular note as the company were small players in a reluctant and already saturated market (Fortune 1933). The JWT campaign was a radical departure from the usual emphasis in US advertising on price, brand and flavour. According to agency records, the campaign was informed by product research into the chemical composition of tea. This 'produced' a substance, *theol*, which was emphasised in the advertising. *Theol* was in fact a collective name for the fragrant oils present in tea. As such, it has no chemical properties as a stimulant, but that was not the point. JWT declared that Chase and Sanborn's tea was richer in *theol*, and that Chase and Sanborn's tea 'sways the senses' and provides an *emotional lift*. But nowhere did the agency actually say that the emotional lift was due to the *theol* (Fortune 1933: 38).

The product research helped provide JWT with an alternative and distinctive platform from which to position the campaign. The relationship between the research findings and the campaign, however, is not a straightforward one. The research was not designed to discover the 'truth' about tea, but to generate ideas. These ideas are then filtered through the individuals; their working practices and the culture of the agency and the final campaign reflects all these processes. In this respect, the typography, the artwork and the studied nature of the copy claims are all contributory aspects to the form of the advertisement, but none in isolation can be understood to determine its nature or emotional impact. The emotional appeal then, does not inhere in particular aspects of the advertisement, particular techniques or even the particular media used. The emotional is better understood as a dimension of appeal entirely relative to the historical and production context.

What these examples suggest is the existence of a relationship between the ultimate format and style of advertisements and a specific range of local forces. The impact of such local forces in shaping advertising has tended to be overlooked by more general theoretical explanations that interpret the form of advertisements in terms of teleological shifts in accordance with the priorities of shifting societal forms. The emphasis on contemporary advertising as unique in its use of aural and visual methods to tap into emotion and mood – as opposed to verbal methods to tap into logic and reason – fits neatly into epochal explanations that characterise contemporary society as increasingly consumption-based, dematerialised and symbolic. The argument of this section, however, has been that emotional methods of appeal are not restricted to the visual and aural environment of late twentieth-century advertising. What is new in this advertising is the use of particular visual and aural techniques, facilitated by the changing technological capacities in new media like television as well as in older print-based media. The underlying attempt to communicate through mood and emotion rather than through reason and logic, however, is not a new departure. Both of these structures of appeal have ancient precedents. Thus the choice of method may be more immediately governed by the local forces, mentioned above, than by overarching societal changes.

It is clear that the earlier advertisements featured here are profoundly different from contemporary versions. It is equally clear, however, that it would be entirely inaccurate to characterise these styles of copy as 'simple' informational announcements. This is not to imply that there were not many examples of such simple announcements. Then, as today, a substantial proportion of advertisements make only very straightforward, even mundane statements announcing availability, price or one or two simple product features. Rather the query is with the critical view of advertisements evolving through time into increasingly emotional and persuasive formats, in response to 'epochal' changes in societal structure. A more accurate description may be that the field, at any given historical moment, comprises an array of different forms of appeal, ranging from crude, straightforward, descriptive announcements to subtle, emotional and persuasive messages.

To the extent to which this 'anti-evolutionary' stance may be taken to support a greater degree of stability and continuity in advertising than is commonly supposed, it may seem counter-intuitive. In no sense, however, is the intent here to question the spectacular and well-documented changes in advertising content, style and format which have appeared over the last 250 years. It is immediately apparent that contemporary advertising is characterised by a far greater range of styles and techniques for the manipulation of text, images and sounds, in a broader array of media and supported by a greater range of techniques for researching, profiling and testing consumer reactions than could have been imagined in the eighteenth century. The issue here is not with the existence of profound changes but rather with the way in which such changes are categorised and interpreted as evidence of a teleological progression in the sophistication of advertising's persuasive capacity. Such teleological interpretations of changes in advertising tend to be based around the assumption that the persuasive and/or symbolic dimensions of an advertisement can be judged from a historical analysis of texts alone. The suggestion being made is that these aspects of an advertisement's appeal can only be assessed meaningfully through a consideration of the specific historical context of advertising production.

Conclusion

The types of 'cultural economic' reasoning advanced by writers like Wernick (1991) and Lash and Urry (1994) have, in centre-staging questions of meaning and representation, made crucial advances in the cultural analyses of commercial and economic life. This heightened emphasis on the cultural realm, however, has tended to produce an impulse to engage in 'epochal' or 'caesural' diagnoses, whereby a less-culturalised past is contrasted with an 'increasingly culturalised' present. Such dramatic and abstract thinking – we have argued – disables the explanatory reach of cultural economic reasoning. There is a need for caution in how changes in advertising forms are interpreted as indicative of grand shifts in the contemporary relation between cultural and economic life after the 'cultural turn'. This is not to deny the fact that there have been, over the last quarter century, substantive developments in the economic and organisational arenas – such as the obsession amongst senior managers of large- and medium-sized enterprises with engineering 'corporate culture' – which lend support to an 'increased culturalisation' hypothesis. Rather it is to suggest that substantive claims of 'increased' culturalisation should be assessed on more of a case-by-case basis rather than simply assumed and/or asserted. It is also necessary to draw attention to the difficulties inherent in any project that seeks to extricate the cultural from the economic in an exploration of practices or artefacts which are simultaneously both. As the American sociologist Paul di Maggio has argued in relation to contemporary cultural analysis of economic and organisational life, 'Ironically the price of the insights and explanatory power that a cultural perspective can generate is an enduring scepticism toward "culturalist" accounts that claim too much or generalise too broadly' (di Maggio 1994).

Our short genealogy of the use of persuasion and emotion in advertising has been targeted to counter this expansive tendency in culturalist analyses that seek to explain the development of the industry in terms of fundamental transformations in the systems of economic organisation. Significant as such transformations may be, they cannot reveal the specificity of factors that underlie all the shifts in advertising methods and styles. The desire to understand such stylistic and methodological shifts as a systematic evolution signalling a new epoch, however, should be resisted. Rather than a sensible and legible journey through distinct production epochs, a historicised account of practice provides an array of contradictions: continuities alongside changes, the appearance, disappearance and re-emergence of conflicting trends and subtle, incremental and partial examples of changes in practice. Advertising technique over the last three centuries has regressed as well as progressed at particular moments, and this may be less the function of the teleological unfolding of history and more the result of specific technical, organisational and institutional production arrangements.

References

Addison, J. (1710) *The Tatler* 224: Thursday 14 September.

Appadurai, A. (1986) *The Social Life of Things*, Cambridge: Cambridge University Press.

Barthes, R. (1977) *Image–Music–Text*, London: Fontana.

Baudrillard, J. (1988) 'Consumer society', in M. Poster (ed.) *Selected Writings*, Cambridge: Polity Press.

Bourdieu, P. (1993) *Sociology in Question*, London: Sage.

Buck-Morss, S. (1989) *The Dialectics of Seeing: Walter Benjamin and the Arcades Project*, London: MIT Press.

Burn, J. D. (1855) *The Language of the Walls, a Voice from the Shop Windows or the Mirror of Commercial Roguery*, London: Heywood.

Castells, M. (2000) *The Network Society*, Oxford: Blackwell.

Cousins, M. (1988) 'The practice of historical investigation', in G. Attridge (ed.) *Post-structuralism and Questions of History*, Cambridge: Cambridge University Press.

Davidson, M. (1992) *The Consumerist Manifesto*, London: Routledge.

di Maggio, P. (1994) 'Culture and economy', in N. Smelser and M. Swedberg (eds) *The Handbook of Economic Sociology*, Princeton: Princeton University Press.

Douglas, M. and Isherwood, B. (1978) *The World of Goods*, Middlesex: Penguin.

du Gay, P. (1996) *Consumption and Identity at Work*, London: Sage.

—— (1997) *Production of Culture/Cultures of Production*, London: Sage.

—— (1999) *'Cultural economy', an Introduction*, Seminar given at Goldsmiths College, University of London.

Dyer, G. (1982) *Advertising as Communication*, London: Routledge.

Elliot, B. B. (1962) *A History of English Advertising*, London: Business Publications.

Ewen, S. (1976) *Captains of Consciousness: Advertising and the Social Roots of Consumer Culture*, New York: McGraw-Hill.

Falk, P. (1994) *The Consuming Body*, London: Sage.

Featherstone, M. (1991) *Consumer Culture and Postmodernism*, London: Sage.

Fielding, H. (1741) Letter in *The Champion*, 19 December.

Fleming, T. (1976) 'How it was in advertising: 1776–1976', *Advertising Age*, 19 April, 27–35.

Fortune (1933) 'Tea for sale', August: 34–8.

Foucault, M. (1984) 'Nietzsche, genealogy, history', in P. Rabinow (ed.) *The Foucault Reader*, London: Penguin.

Fowles, J. (1996) *Advertising and Popular Culture*, London: Sage.

Goffman, E. (1979) *Gender Advertisements*, London: Macmillan.

Goldman, R. (1992) *Reading Ads Socially*, London: Routledge.

Haug, W. (1986) *Critique of Commodity Aesthetics*, London: Polity.

Hower, R. (1939) *The History of an Advertising Agency*, New York: Arno.

Jhally, S. (1987) *The Codes of Advertising: Fetishism and the Political Economy of Meaning in Consumer Society*, London: Routledge.

Johnson, S. (1759) *The Idler* 40: Saturday 20 January.

Lash, S. (1990) *The Sociology of Postmodernism*, London: Routledge.

Lash, S. and Urry, J. (1994) *Economies of Signs and Space*, London: Sage.

Leadbeater, C. (1999) *Living on Thin Air*, London: Viking.

Lears, J. F. (1994) *Fables of Abundance*, New York: Basic Books.

Leiss, W., Kilne, S. and Jhally, S. (1990) *Social Communication in Advertising*, London: Routledge.

Macaulay (1830) 'Mr Robert Montgomery's poems and the modern practice of puffing', *Edinburgh Review* April: ci.

McKendrick, N., Brewer, J. and Plumb, J. (1982) *The Birth of a Consumer Society*, London: Hutchinson.

Miller, D. (ed.) (1995) *Acknowledging Consumption*, London: Routledge.

—— (1997) *Capitalism: an Ethnographic Approach*, London: Berg.

Moeran, B. (1996) *A Japanese Advertising Agency*, Surrey: Curzon.

Myers, G. (1998) *Ad World*, London: Arnold.

Nevett, T. (1977) 'London's early advertising agents', *Journal of Advertising History* 1: 15–18.

Nixon, S. (1996) *Hard Looks: Masculinities, Spectatorship and Contemporary Consumption*, London: UCL.

—— (1997) 'Circulating culture', in P. du Gay (ed.) *Production of Culture/Cultures of Production*, London: Sage.

Osborne, T. (1998) *Aspects of Enlightenment*, London: UCL.

Pope, D. (1983) *The Making of Modern Advertising*, New York: Basic Books.

Presbrey, F. (1929) *The History and Development of Advertising*, New York: Greenwood.

Quarterly Review (1855) 'Advertisements', Art Vii–1, unauthored article.

Sahlins, M. (1976) *Culture and Practical Reason*, Chicago: University of Chicago Press.

Sampson, H. (1874) *History of Advertising*, London: Chatto & Windus.

The Spectator (1711) 8 August.

Tudor, B. (1986) 'Retail trade advertising in the Leicester Journal and the Leicester Chronicle 1855–71', *Journal of Advertising History* 9: 2.

Turner, E. S. (1952) *The Shocking History of Advertising*, London: Michael Joseph.

Wernick, A. (1991) *Promotional Culture: Advertising, Ideology and Symbolic Expression*, London: Sage.

Williams, R. (1980) *Advertising: the Magic System. Problems in Materialism and Culture*, London: Verso.
Williamson, J. (1978) *Decoding Advertisements*, London: Marion Boyars.
Winship, J. (1981) 'Handling sex', *Media, Culture and Society* 3: 25–41.

7 Consuming design
Consuming retro

Adrian Franklin

Introduction

The design of things and the consumption of design are important but neglected aspects of consumption. In this chapter I will first investigate the nature of this omission, and second, seek to rectify it through a consideration of the development of design. In the second section of the chapter I will draw on this discussion in order to clarify my recent research on 'retro' consumption. Against those who argue that design and designerism are simply part of the apparatus of capitalist exploitation of consumers, this chapter argues that design is highly sensitive to the aesthetic judgement of consumers and that the history of design includes a strong ideological content that expresses the civilising nature of art and design and also the democratisation of art through industrial manufacture. The case study of retro consumerism argues that part of its appeal is the rediscovery of this aesthetic content; the discovery of design and artistry in the objects of the everyday.

Design and consumption studies: absence and overdetermination

Accounts of the sociological significance of consumption tend to emphasise one of two poles, and both completely avoid the fact that things are designed and that design has a bearing on how and why they are consumed and, importantly, how they arrive as 'things'. The first sort of account, epitomised by Bourdieu (1984), places emphasis on the cultural dimensions of the consumer. Consumption is patterned according to a logic of taste specified by particular cultural locations (*habitus*) in modern societies. What is consumed appears to be driven solely by the cultural condition or '*habitus*' of particular types of people, and they consume particular things in order to mark and 'achieve' social distinction. Under this account, the appearance of precisely the right sort of things to enable the process of social distinction to occur is a somewhat mysterious and happy coincidence. We are to assume that the sheer weight of taste is sufficient to guide producers and manufacturers safely and soundly in the right direction. As Miller argues:

Bourdieu's *habitus* does not spontaneously generate a world of goods, only a set of dispositions. To understand how the congruity between the two is achieved demands an investigation of marketing, designers (as by Forty 1986) and other distributive agencies. It is not sufficient merely to talk of the articulation of two independent spheres.

(Miller 1987: 155)

Bourdieu's analysis of consumption has influenced the production of other *national* studies of consumption, in which nation is implicitly named as an over-arching *habitus* and is implicitly made to carry as much weight as social class and the critical social dimensions of cultural and economic capital, age and gender. So, apart from Bourdieu's foundation study of France there have also been several other national studies of consumption, including one in Britain (Savage *et al.* 1992) and Australia (Bennett *et al.* 1999). The main purpose of Bennett *et al.*'s study of Australian consumption, for example, was 'to show how the tastes that are evident in the cultural choices and preferences of contemporary Australians are pre-eminently social in their organisation and character' (Bennett *et al.* 1999: 1).

Again, design and designers seems to have no role to play; further, 'the population' here is again clearly a national population. It is by no means clear that the things that modern nation states consume are designed or produced exclusively by 'home' markets. Moreover, from a design perspective one sees only too clearly how taste in any one nation was powerfully influenced by leading 'design countries' or regions (e.g. from the 1950s the USA and Scandinavia; from the 1960s UK and Italy) and how dominant tastes emerge within what might be called a transnational design space (Jackson 1998: 13–32). Of course this is very obvious when one thinks about it, but the implicit social spatiality of Bourdieu's *habitus* concept tends towards this fallacy of coherent albeit socially segmented *national* taste cultures. A consideration of design allows that to be opened up.

The second sort of account is the opposite of the first. While the first ignores design, the second gives too much power and determination to producers and singles out design (and advertising) as the means by which consumers are duped into buying what they neither want nor need (Packard 1957, Miles 1998). Some of these accounts buy into a structuralism and reduce the activities of designers to the logic of capitalism, or certain later stages of it. Design is conjured up by the logic to create new markets from the diversification of products. Others relate the emergence of design (*qua* designerism) as especially significant to the late 1980s and 1990s and as symptomatic of post-Fordism and post-modernity: not so much the logic of capitalism now but a 'strategy' related to profound changes in civil society. Collapsing both the stable class segmentations and the mass-production labour processes that they rested on, post-Fordist production strategies involved the re-composition of both work and consumption. Using 'new small batch technologies' designers were able to avoid the unprofitable depths of the mass market by designing things very specifically to lifestyle groups and, in so doing, further defining and redefining the groups themselves. In other words, they not only designed things but also a social identity for the ontologically insecure individuals of late modernity, whose status as consumers was now as critical if not more so than their status as a worker.

In Miles's (1998) review of the role of design he employs both sorts of account. For Miles, the car industry of the twentieth century provides a good example of design being used to create new markets for capitalism in the form of built-in obsolescence. In the first half of the twentieth century, car manufacturers evolved 3–5-year product cycles encouraging consumers to buy new models more frequently than they really needed to or otherwise face the stigma of driving an outmoded model. Miles argues that compulsory obsolescence:

> ... is the foundation stone of the modern design industry and involves the intentional design of products for short-term use. In other words, designers ensure a constant demand for new products by intentionally designing products with limited life spans. This temporality is most noticeably enforced through the creation of intensively designed fashion goods that almost inevitably lose their appeal to consumers within two or three years.
>
> (Miles 1998: 38)

It is not clear whether Miles means limited life *per se* or limited fashion life, but, either way, he argues that this is the explicit purpose of design. While I have some sympathy for this view, it does have some problems. For one thing, it rather problematically casts the consumers as hopeless dupes, whereas in reality they exercise more *judgement* than the compulsory obsolescence design theory allows for. It so happens that the Volkswagen Beetle was a completely obsolete 1930s technology in its heyday and that there were any number of better alternatives offered to the consumer from the 1950s onwards. However, the Beetle was judged to be a pleasing design by consumers who bought it eagerly from the 1950s to the 1980s. So popular was its shape that Volkswagen brought it back in 2000 to boost their ailing market share. One can run the same story with the Mini, voted best automobile of the twentieth century. Here, the designer Alec Issigonis played a somewhat different role (Jackson 1997). In this case the Mini was a design revolution, not an updated version of what preceded it but a radical rethink of what an automobile might be. From its transverse engine that rolled under the car in a head-on crash, to its radical redesign of space and storage the Mini was arguably giving away too much too soon. According to Miles's logic it did not need to introduce such a massive package of improvements and change in one go. Surely such a strategy would undermine the principle of built-in obsolescence? Consumers might want to retain a technologically advanced car for too long. In actual fact, the Mini remained more or less identical from 1959 to 2001. For many years it was a technology leader and for as many years it continued to sell even though its design and technology was well past its 'sell-by date'. Here again, consumer judgement is being exercised. The Beetle and the Mini are not exceptions and their product life is not reducible to a design principle, but involves questions of taste, style, and the assimilation of design into lifestyle. Here one finds a clear case of 'the social life of things' (Appadurai 1986), the idea that things play a role or 'act' in our lives other than as 'unnecessary' or 'necessary' consumer goods. The Mini, for example, was quintessentially modern and new. It embraced new technology rather than feared it. It democratised car ownership, making it possible for more people, especially the young, to have auto-mobility. It was also radical and shocking, somehow mocking the positional status of cars. It also ruptured the backward-looking, tradition-bound nature of British society in the late 1950s. Combined, this *social* character of the Mini assimilated itself into young, modern, intellectual and politically progressive mentalities, holding a special place among them as a car. But it was also a conceptual blueprint for a different type of living. The Mini also ushered in a major transformation of British style in the 1960s – part of what Jackson (1998) calls 'The New Look' – and it marks the beginning of a major change in Western taste.

Miles argues that since the 1980s designers have also exploited the notion of style and lifestyle. Rather than continuing to identify the relationship between things and people and therefore making a positive contribution to cultural and material life, in Miles's account designers merely exploited the segmentary and fluid nature of lifestyle groupings in late modernity. Consumers came to buy products not necessarily for what they did but for what they said about them as consumers. The role of design is therefore not to meet human needs but to create and stimulate those needs in increasingly diverse ways (Miles 1998: 40). He elaborates this argument in relation to the Sony Walkman and Levi-Strauss jeans, and argues that the diversification of product lines through 'design' is unnecessary, superficial and exploitative. Levi-Strauss jeans, he argues, are 'much like any other', but are they? Without doubt the main design concept of Levi jeans in recent years is focused on their 501 pattern. However, Levi 501s were a very old design from the 1950s and became superfashionable not as a result of Levi's marketing but because they were a quintessentially 'retro' look that emerged in hip circles and then became mainstream. Levi's exploited this windfall by using hyperfashionable British advertising, but then even those adverts became hip, especially as they were tied to retro soul hits. I will return to retro consumption later on in the chapter. The Walkman example illustrates his point more clearly: does the world really need all of those (700 worldwide) versions of the Sony Walkman? Was this not exploiting people merely to increase capitalist markets?

Certainly, designers do stimulate new markets, but a final question at this stage hinges on whether or not Miles and others are correct in assuming that design is properly about, or properly restricted to, meeting human needs. I will argue in the next section that the history of design illustrates their slightly different and more complex role. Irrespective of whether they stimulate and create unnecessary consumption, the production and creation of things always involves aesthetic choice and content. At one level, then, they are central to what Welsch (1996, 1997) has identified as an aestheticisation process characteristic of late modernity, by which he means the mantling of aesthetic content on to more and more surfaces of modern life. Welsch and others are scathing of this development, but at another level the aestheticisation of everyday life also relates to the *democratisation* of art. Design and design schools have had a profound influence over consumption by trying to improve and extend the place of art in all levels of society and not simply as a plaything of the wealthy. Designers do not work independently from either producers or consumers, but their origins in the high cultural world of art, as opposed to crafts, can be traced through a process of democratisation that began, in Britain as elsewhere, with the internationally orientated arts and crafts movement at the end of the last century. In other words there is a political, aesthetic, cultural, transnational and economic set of relationships involved in the relationship between consumption and design – aside from the recognition that things (like Mini cars) themselves 'act' within networks of taste formation.

The emergence of 'design' in modernity

The manner by which design emerged in modernity tells us a great deal about its involvement in consumption. In particular, two important historical transformations are worth considering. First, the eighteenth-century evolution of industrial design that resulted principally from the new demands of industrial manufacturing and the expansion of consumer markets. Second, the emergence of national and international design movements that combined industrial design with art-school training institutions and politically led socialist idealism.

Forty's (1986) work on the pottery manufacturer Wedgwood in the eighteenth century illustrates why and how designers first appeared in manufacturing. Wedgwood's ambition as a manufacturer was to achieve high-quality goods combined with advances in the production techniques to increase output from his factories. However, the problems that he faced were not simply those of industrial engineering. Industrial productivity and unit profits were affected by the practice of producing goods prior to their purchase by retailers. A lot of capital was therefore tied up with goods that might or might not sell. Wedgwood therefore adopted the new trend of selling through sales rooms and catalogues. In this way only samples needed to be produced ahead of manufacturing and the manufacturing process was rendered more efficient by producing only what had been ordered. The problem was one of manufacturing accuracy: the goods ordered by catalogue or sales room had to correspond exactly with the sample. Hitherto, whatever had been produced was sighted by retailers and bought on that basis. This expectation was to transform the entire labour process in modern manufacturing. In the older system individual craft workers produced new designs as well as making the finished product. Where several people were all making goods to a single design, individual variations crept into the final output. In order to standardise output three things had to change. First, the design itself had to be of a sort capable of easy replication by workers. Second, the workers themselves had to adjust their work practices to reproduction. Third, the designer had to be in touch with the workers themselves, knowing what they were capable of (re)producing.

Wedgwood found his new expanding markets in the growing industrial towns, where taste was more cosmopolitan and fashion-prone. In these markets the upper and new middle classes established a distinctive self-identity and 'sought to distinguish themselves by exclusive and fashionable tastes of their own' (Forty 1986: 34). In this wealthy but volatile market, Wedgwood was forced to recruit his designers from such centres, but especially from London. Wedgwood realised by the 1770s that 'customers would rate the work of Academicians more highly than that of ordinary plaster-cast makers' (Forty 1986: 36). Wedgwood could never have afforded to use established artists to produce individual wares prior to the mechanisation of production and stan-dardisation of output and advanced sales. But afterwards artists became critical to the entire enterprise by giving products not just a use value but also their name and their aesthetic judgement.

A second critical transformation took this outcome a step further. As a result of the extension and honing of the artistic content to industrial design, international competition grew. The Great Exhibition of 1851 was explicitly organised to showcase British design and industries but it also had 'the inten-tion of improving public taste and educating artisans' (Forty 1986: 58). Thomas Cook's organised tours to the Exhibition for working people composed one of the single biggest mass spectacles of the period (Withey 1997). By the end of the nineteenth century, however, design leadership had swung away from Britain to the continent, and this essentially aesthetic lead-ership was considered to be a major threat to British industry. As a result, rigidly *laissez-faire* politicians were persuaded to intervene in the market in the form of the nationally supported Industrial Design Movement. Whereas the 'things' exhibited in 1851 were still largely manufactured for the upper and new middle classes, by the end of the century, under the influence of Ruskin and particularly Morris, progressive and socialist thinkers argued for the democratisation of art and good design as an edifying and improving aspect of everyday life for all. Medieval art, Morris argued, had been popular art, not the art of palaces:

> rather she fell sick there, and it will take more bracing air than that of rich man's houses to heal her again. If she is ever to be strong enough to help mankind once more, she must gather strength in simple places.
>
> (Thompson 1977: 96)

Morris's famous maxim for domestic interiors in the last quarter of the nine-teenth century reads like a blueprint for the entire twentieth century: 'Have nothing in your houses that you do not know to be useful or believe to be beau-tiful' (Thompson 1977: 97). Morris himself and *Morris and Co* (his production company) were critical but not dismissive of industrial production (Forty 1986: 61). They were caught up in the backward-looking fashion for recovering designs from 'history', particularly those of medieval Europe. However, Morris seemed to glimpse the possibility of marrying industrial techniques with good design and art to make its output more accessible and affordable for all classes, and it is this idea that was carried through by others into the twentieth century.

Socialist values were embraced by the Industrial Art Movement in Britain following World War I, and, according to Lesley Jackson, its key institutional bases, the British Institute for Industrial Art and the Design and Industries Association (DIA) 'recognised the need to direct leading manufacturers to embrace the mass market and to move away from catering exclusively for a wealthy, educated market' (Jackson 1996: 67). Companies such as the glassware producers, James Powell (Whitefriars Ltd.) had close ties to these currents of change. Their design history, which has recently surfaced, demonstrates how these changes impacted on design, production and consumption. Up until the 1920s James Powell and Sons were manufacturing more or less exclusively for the social élite. This was almost self-evident in the highly elaborate and delicate pieces of glassware produced during the arts and crafts period, often based on historical precedents. However, like Wedgwood, this London company was sensitive to changes in art and this is expressed in its design pedigree. Hence designers like William Morris, Dante Gabriel Rossetti, Burne-Jones and Madox Brown all did stained-glass designs for Powell and Sons (Thompson 1977: 136–7). Designs by Christopher Dresser in the 1860s, 1880s and 1890s were seen as contemporaneous, if not in a similar style to those of Powell. Later in the 1920s and 1930s leading British designers Gordon Russell and Keith Murray both approached James Powell Ltd. with a request to design for them.

From the 1920s until the mid 1950s, more and more designs and colourways emerged as modernism gained confidence and popularity. The transition to a mass market from an élite craft market is reflected in their move to a large industrial factory outside London at Wealdenstone. With designer Geoffrey Baxter in place by the mid 1950s, the earlier, plainer designs were phased out in favour of the more organic, abstract and colourful modernism that first of all followed Scandinavian and Italian leadership. However, from the 1960s onwards, Baxter became one of the leading designers of the British *New Look*, and his glass designs from this period in psychedelic colourways and madly eclectic shapes were a successful bid to capture a more youthful and popular consumer society. Baxter's *New Look* was, in turn, exported internationally.

The transnationalisation of design was critical to the development of modern production everywhere. Thus, in the twentieth century, international design exhibitions proliferated, and some, such as the 1951 Festival of Britain are credited with totally transforming consumption and taste: in this case ushering in a modern taste that had barely taken root in Britain before. Jackson's history of Whitefriars glass at this time demonstrates the detailed nature of the relationship between consumers and design. So, for example, Baxter came under direct pressure from buyers at the principal trade fairs, to introduce ever more colourways for his designs. The buyers were in touch with fashions in colours, and so the proliferation of colourways, which often created manufacturing problems, were a result of demand rather than the supply of fresh design. At the same time, with few exceptions, most of Baxter's designs at

Whitefriars remained in production from the 1950s and 1960s through to their closure in 1985, an achievement that was an enormous benefit to the company. Clearly, as Josiah Wedgwood realised some two hundred years earlier, the more you can make with one design, the more profitable that design is. While Wedgwood used the name of Royal Academician artist-designers to sell wares to an élite in 1760, Powell's 1960s Royal Academy-trained designer Geoffrey Baxter went unannounced and his work remained unmarked for a popular mass market. Art had indeed dissolved into everyday life, as Morris would have wished.

In sum, this brief history traces the links between three forms of design–consumption relations; from industrial design through design modernism to designerism. First, it has shown how design did not originate simply as a means of extending markets for capitalist production but as an integral part of the formation of industrial mass production. Second, it has shown how industrial production and marketing favoured the creation of a new professional position of designer. Third, it has illustrated how the modern requirements for design favoured established artists and established a link between industry and art. Fourth, it has shown how, as a result of international competition in which design was held to be critical, design became seen as an appropriate intervention for otherwise *laissez-faire* governments. Fifth, as a result of interventions by organised networks of artists and government, the Arts and Crafts movement at the end of the nineteenth century and the Industrial Arts Movement of the 1920s sought to democratise art – to collapse the distinction between high and low culture. This involved imagining a different sort of society in which machines and factories produce material plenty, but where its output achieves new aesthetic aims, to uplift, improve and beautify everyday life. By the later years of Geoffrey Baxter's work at Whitefriars he was beginning to feel one of the longer-term effects of the historical trajectory sketched out here: consumers who had been brought up in this aestheticised materialism were no longer reliant on industrial and design leadership to identify and judge aesthetic taste. As I have argued, they began to make their own aesthetic preferences known to the designer through the knowledgeability and mediation of commercial buyers. By the 1970s mass markets began to split up and segment along social and cultural (and lifestyle) lines using these newly acquired aesthetic temperaments and tastes. Such a transformation created space for an even more explicitly design-oriented culture, or what Miles (1998) calls designerism.

Design and 'retro' consumption

The preceding discussion of the relationship between design and consumption and the development of design in modern consumption is useful for analysing the consumption of 'retro' goods. For at least twenty years now the consumption of mass-produced 'used' goods from the golden ages of modernism, the 1950s through to the 1980s, has become an established form of consumption. It did not possess a distinctive name until quite recently, but the burgeoning businesses, charity shops, car-boot sales, collectors and authors of its material culture and history have settled upon the term 'retro' as the prefix for the goods and the style of their consumption. Retro is an interesting contrast to a cognate generic commodity, the antique, because it implies the activity of retrospection, thinking about the past, celebrating the past; in this case the industrial production in the period 1950–80. Why has this form of consumption been so popular and enduring, and why has its growth been sustained over so long a period? One might be forgiven for thinking that its consumption might be nothing more than a passing fad. But this is not the case. What is it about these goods and the markets they pass through that make them the object of such a passionate 'leisure consumption' linked as it is to interior decoration, collecting and the formation of explicitly 'modernist' social identities? In Britain the retro market centres on the burgeoning car-boot sales, now reckoned to be the single most popular weekend activity (Gregson and Crewe 1997a). In discussing contemporary theoretical work on the recent fascination with kitsch, Kirshenblatt-Gimblett argues that there is an expressive radical appeal involved in the act of appropriating what others have rejected:

> How is it that objects that attracted slaves to fashion in their first life can be tokens of rebellion in their afterlives? Walter Benjamin noted that the outmoded is a source of revolutionary energy, precisely because to pick it up again, after it has been discarded is a potentially radical gesture ... What some fads lacked in exclusivity during their first life they gain the next time round through the recoding operation that consumers (low riders, punks) produce – through what Umberto Eco calls semiological guerilla warfare.
>
> (Kirshenblatt-Gimblett 1998: 274)

In her essay on kitsch and taste, Kirshenblatt-Gimblett refers to 'stylish arhythmia', literally a stylishnness or coolness that derives its edge from being 'out'. 'What's out for the mainstream is cool for the sub-culture, except that some rejects are cooler than others' (Kirshenblatt-Gimblett 1998: 274). While this seems a plausible account, it needs a performative context and space in which such radical gestures and arhythmias make sense and can be played out. Gregson and Crewe's (1997a, 1997b and 1997c) work on the British car-boot fairs provides at least one ethnographic account. According to Gregson and Crewe, retro shoppers derive at least some of their pleasure from the subversive nature of shopping in these second-hand markets where price, relations between seller and shopper and performance are all subverted within a carnivalesque space. Goods are sold at a uniformly flat, low price (giveaways); bargaining is the rule; shoppers' fortunes are creatively made in performance with sellers; the atmosphere of buying and selling is itself theatrical and playful. Moreover, as Pearce (1995) argues, it is through collecting (one of the more important modes of retro consumption) that the kitsch ('inauthentic art and gift wares') and the world of everyday goods become revalorised. Searching out and collecting such objects and mantling them with an aesthetic content, desirability and rising value is one of the processes by which the distinction between high and low culture is challenged, blurred and dismantled in post-modernity. According to these accounts it would seem very plausible that retro consumption finds its reference point in opposition to contemporary modes of consumption, perhaps, in particular its relatively hierarchical and élitist nature. Whereas in the period of high modernity consumption was modelled on the democratising tendencies of Fordism, contemporary consumption is predicated on and driven by exclusivity and by designerism. Retro goods become radical or cool to the degree that they represent a better past, the past of heroic, democratising modernism. They represent a challenge to the notion of aesthetic judgement because they elevate the everyday and the commonplace; they high-light and celebrate the cultural nature of ordinary lifeworlds. Former advertising posters for soap replace works of art vying for the same domestic space.

The foregoing summarises briefly the sorts of arguments that are made in order to account for retro consumption. These hypotheses are evaluated by taking a closer look at the aestheticisation processes of a small selection of retro goods. The scope and detail of retro-consumption is potentially dazzling and distracting. This chapter is based on a small sample of its most representative or iconic goods, especially those that have generated a cult following (Peat 1994, Jackson 1996, Jenkins 1997). This analysis reveals, first, that the retro good is consumed very differently the second time around. Indeed, retro consumption opposes in many ways the manner in which mass-produced consumer goods were consumed as new goods. However, the main finding is that the consump-tion of retro material culture is not as subversive or radical as it first appears. Far from mounting a challenge to the notion of aesthetic judgement and collapsing the notion of high and low culture, retro consumption focuses on the democrati-sation of art and aesthetic modernism (it is absorbed in an archaeology of industrial art and design) and celebrates its introduction to a mass market.

Second, whereas retro objects were originally purchased for their newness, the shock of the new (new technologies, colourways, designs and so on) and what they presage, they are now bought because of their familiarity (what they represent). This ranges from the nostalgia of older consumers, to the pastiching of the young, for whom the goods were made familiar by TV, film and music. Their original consumers were largely disinterested in their design details, industrial background and provenance. As noted above, the designer Geoffrey Baxter was effectively anonymous until uncovered by retro consumers. However, they are now bought specifically for these reasons, as carriers of artistic and craft backgrounds, traditions, schools and labels as well as signifiers of periods and moments of modernity (see Pearce for the significance of social identity for collectors). This interest in these 'sign value' objects relates to some clearly valued and potentially yearned for values of modernity (collectivism, progress, democracy, equality and so on), as it was expressed in the idealism of the heavily aestheticised discourse of the industrial design movement in the earlier part of the twentieth century, and which found expression and bloomed after 1945 (MacCarthy 1972, 1982).

Third, while they were originally bought in a succession of fast-changing fashions and rendered obsolete after a brief period, they are now, seemingly permanently desirable, even growing in desirability as time and provenance grows about them. Perhaps we are witnessing the creation of a new era of popular 'mass antiques' of the modern period in contrast with the social exclusivity of the arts and craft and art deco periods and before (Collins 1995).

Fourth, the original consumers were among the first generations to experience mass consumption – the proliferation and freely available world of things. These first generations of modern consumers were tied more or less to the new goods markets, to built-in obsolescence and to disposability. These were the generations for which the term 'junk' was relevant as unwanted and/or passé rather than simply broken or unusable things. Junk, being an unwanted good, had to pass into the liminal world of the rag-and-bone men; the dirty secret trades who rendered down junk into recycled raw material. The first generations replaced goods before they accreted sign values other than 'new', contemporary, or technologically current. Typically such modern goods were very rapidly replaced and so had very little time in which to become signs of other social values, times or groups. Consumers were less experienced in recycling the meaning of things and how they can 'contain' the social because in their understanding of goods, their value was associated, almost exclusively, with utility and status, décor and fashion – a symbolic world of the modern present. Thus a light fitting was consumed for its efficient, contemporary or 'latest' technology and for its fashion value as a mode of lighting, rather than its *meaning* as a designed object. But goods produced at any one time become markers, representations and icons of political, social and cultural projects of their period. It is only in retrospect that they become evocative of meaning and it is only as consumers become expert in dealing with these social accretions of meaning, and of their sign values, that the cultural repertoires of goods can extend to have a retro social life (Appadurai 1986).

Retro consumers are experienced in their total immersion in the world of goods and are reflexively interested in them and the contexts of their production. In this sense, retro consumers are tourists consuming a form of cultural heritage. Finally, many of the goods consumed as retro goods were initially purchased not by the final consumers but by gift-givers. As Davis (1972) shows in an important early paper, the gift industry was particularly significant across a broad range of consumer goods. So many of the china, glass and decorative goods were destined to be purchased as gifts in the period 1950–1980 and their principal trade fairs were called 'gift fairs'. It was at these gift fairs that manufacturers received their mainstay orders for each year and, therefore, where manufacturers launched new products and designs. It was the knowledgeable buyers from the giftware trades that determined finally, whether the consumer was ever to be offered new types of article or design, but, as I have argued, they were also in a position to influence design itself. There is considerable scope for more research to investigate the specific nature of such an important period of consumption via what Davis called the gift economy (Davis 1972,

Franklin 1995). However, I will simply note here the potentially significant difference between the manner in which retro goods were initially bought (for others, expressing essentially social relationships and ties; to decorate and to display) and the way that they are bought the second time around (for personal consumption, with a degree of personal self-identification and expression; to collect and to articulate modernist aesthetics).

For Welsch and the modern art movement itself, the aestheticisation of everyday life, the aestheticisation of more and more realms and aspects of daily living was an object of modernity. It was the democratisation of aesthetic tastes, let loose in cultural lifeworlds. However, the typical goods created by mass production were seldom given the aesthetic mantle of say, the arts and crafts movement of the late nineteenth century or the designer boom of the 1980s. Rather, the consumer goods of the 1950 to 1980 period were seen as opposed to aesthetic taste; they were, by their very nature as machine or factory made, less aesthetically pleasing. New derogatory, anti-aesthetic terms came into play, terms like kitsch, gimcrack, trashy, loud, gauche. In this manner, much of this production came into fashion, but when fashion changed it could be trashed because of its inherent lack of aesthetic depth and worth. So, by what process of aestheticisation has the new retro consumer given new worthiness to these goods? Was it by dint of their transgression of the conventions and canons of high-culture aesthetics that they become valued? Was their cheap and cheerful kitsch a loud celebration of the mass consumer revolution? Was it their very democratic and revolutionary position in popular culture and their rejection of 'high'-culture aesthetics that rendered them, second-hand, as icons of social and cultural progress, humanism and equality? All of these formed the hypothesis or assumption that governed the investigation reported here. However, something other than this lies at the heart of retro consumption, even if all of these hypotheses have some truth in them. In the case of all of the key examples that I have chosen, namely, Whitefriars glass (Jackson 1996), Midwinter pottery (Jenkins 1998), and fabric by Whitehead (Peat 1994), it is possible to find, very close to the design and manufacturing projects that gave rise to them, the ideals of modernist aesthetics: that good artists and good design and aesthetically tasteful objects can be produced for the everyday and everyone. Here there is not only the revolutionary means of making large quantities and marketing to mass markets, but also the revolutionary practices of involving top artists to produce an object of art that is at the same time an item of use value. The discovery by consumers of these hitherto hidden aspects of the production of goods in this period is central to their aesthetic appeal in the twenty-first century. Thus retro consumers have found curtain fabrics in car-boot sales and charity shops that were designed by artists in their early careers: these include such names as Henry Moore, Lucienne Day, Jacqueline Groag, Barbara Brown, Bridget Riley and others. As with Baxter's glass, their signature was obscured the first time but revealed the second time – along the selvage edge.

It is possible to regard retro consumption perhaps as the triumph of modernism rather than its subversion or collapse into style. In the consumption of the goods selected here to represent retro consumption, there are all the hall-marks of – and intellectual connections to – those early pioneers of aesthetic modernism. These leading companies ensured that their products, along with those of their rivals, were not what Welsch calls 'surface aestheticisation'. To find and to possess almost any piece of Whitefriars or Midwinter is to discover and own a work of art with a guaranteed provenance. Even companies with fewer claims to aesthetic pedigree were heavily influenced by modernism, and they disseminated a sophisticated aesthetic content to the most modest consumers. A good example of this was a series of everyday plates produced by Ridgeway Potteries and designed by Enid Seeney. The *Homemaker* plate was produced between 1955 and 1967 and sold exclusively through Woolworth's. 'The black and white pattern provides a ceramic catalogue of modern home furnishings including: boomerang-shaped table; Gordon Russell-style sideboard; Robin Day-influenced armchair; two-seater Bernadotte sofa; leggy plant stands; and tripod lights' (Marsh 1997: 59). Another good example is the range of handkerchief vases made by the volume glass producers, W. E. Chance and Company. Their handkerchief vase emulated that of the élite Murano glass makers Venini and, although clearly a cheaper, lesser version, it has very obvious value among retro collectors for introducing this icon of modernist art to the British masses. These examples show in vivid detail how design continues to exert an aesthetic and ideological role in modern consumerism. This chapter has identified how and why artists were originally called upon to replace craftsmen in the manufacturing process and how, through visionaries such as William Morris and others involved in the industrial arts movements, design entered manufacturing and marketing as an improving aesthetic and as the democratisation of art. The case study shows that whereas ordinary consumers were not always aware of the art hidden in everyday objects from the 1950s to 1980, retro consumption offers the chance to appreciate it the second (or more) time around. The designerism of the 1980s made consumers aware that all objects have to have some design provenance and that this is an impor-tant part of consumption and, indeed, an important aspect of the experience of the changing consumer.

References

Appadurai, A. (ed.) (1986) *The Social Life of Things: Commodities in Cultural Perspective*, Cambridge: Cambridge University Press.

Bennett, T., Emmison, M. and Frow, J. (1999) *Accounting for Tastes*, Melbourne: Cambridge University Press.

Bourdieu, P. (1984) *Distinction: a Social Critique of the Judgement of Taste*, Cambridge, MA: Harvard University Press.

Collins, J. (1995) *Architectures of Excess*, London: Routledge.

Davis, J. (1972) 'Gifts and the UK economy', *Man* 7(3): 408–29.

Forty, A. (1986) *Objects of Desire – Design and Society since 1750*, London: Thames and Hudson.

Franklin, A. S. (1995) 'Family networks, reciprocity and housing wealth', in R. Forrest and A. Murie (eds) *Housing and Family Wealth*, London: Routledge.

Gregson, N. and Crewe, L. (1997a) 'Excluded spaces of regulation: car-boot sales as an enterprise culture out of control?', *Environment and Planning A*, 29: 1717–37.

—— (1997b) 'Performance and possession: rethinking the act of purchase in the light of the car boot sale', Mimeo, from N. Gregson, Department of Geography, University of Sheffield.

—— (1997c) 'The bargain, the knowledge, and the spectacle: making sense of consumption in the space of the car-boot sale', *Environment and Planning D: Society and Space*, 15: 87–112.

Jackson, L. (1996) *Whitefriars Glass*, London: Richard Dennis.

—— (1998) *The Sixties*, London: Phaidon.

Jenkins, S. (1997) *Midwinter Pottery*, London: Richard Dennis.

Kirshenblatt-Gimblett, B. (1998) *Destination Culture – Tourism, Museums and Heritage*, Berkeley: University of California Press.

MacCarthy, F. (1972) *All Things Bright and Beautiful: Design in Britain: 1830–Today*, London: George Allen and Unwin.

Marsh, M. (1997) *Collecting the 1950s*, London: Miller's.

Miller, D. (1987) *Material Culture and Mass Consumption*, Oxford: Basil Blackwell.

Miles, S. (1998) *Consumerism as a Way of Life*, London: Sage.

Packard, V. (1957) *The Hidden Persuaders*, Harmondsworth: Pelican.

Pearce, S. (1995) *On Collecting*, London: Routledge.

Peat, A. (1994) *David Whitehead Ltd: Artistic Designed Textiles 1952–1969*, Oldham: Oldham Leisure Services.

Savage, M., Barlow, J., Dickens, P. and Fielding, T. (1992) *Property, Bureaucracy and Culture*, London: Routledge.

Thompson, P. (1977) *The Work of William Morris*, London: Quartet.

Welsch, W. (1996) 'Phenomena, distinctions and prospects', *Theory, Culture and Society* 13(1): 1–24.

Withey, L. (1997) *Grand Tours and Cook's Tours: a History of Leisure Travel, 1750 to 1915*, London: Aurum.

8 Consuming alcohol
Consuming symbolic meaning

Simone Pettigrew

Introduction

Most studies of consumer behaviour have focused on the decision-making processes involved in the purchasing of goods and services. A change towards a more macro orientation is currently occurring in the field of Consumer Behaviour, a change that is enabling researchers to obtain a greater understanding of both the cognitions and emotions involved in the entire consumption process. Part of this process is the analysis of the symbolic meanings of products, particularly the relationship between product meanings and consumers' sense of self. Examining alcohol consumption in the Australian context, this chapter explores the relevance of symbolic consumption and discusses the implications for current conceptualisations of the process of self-construction as achieved through consumption.

Changes in the field of Consumer Behaviour

The sub-discipline of Consumer Behaviour evolved as an offshoot from its parent discipline of Marketing (Sheth and Gross 1988). As a result, interest in consumers has remained largely dependent upon the generation of meaningful data for practising marketers, with the emphasis placed heavily on buying – as opposed to consuming – behaviours (for a full discussion of this point see Holbrook 1995). In turn, the emphasis on the purchase component of consumption has resulted in much attention being given to the cognitive problem-solving activities of consumers, and in particular to the way they process information (see, for example, Jacoby *et al.* 1976, Wright 1979, Creyer and Ross 1997). Theories were borrowed from psychology to assist in the understanding of purchase decisions, a prominent example being the multi-attribute models that remain popular in current studies of consumer behaviour. Due to this emphasis on acquisition behaviours, there has been relatively little consideration of the emotional component of consumption, particularly where these emotions are experienced outside of the actual purchase event.

In more recent years, the field of consumer research has come to incorporate both micro and macro approaches to consumption activities. The information processing approach that dominates micro studies of buyer behaviour has been increasingly recognised as inadequate in facilitating an understanding of many forms of consumption (Mick 1986, Belk 1987, Clarke *et al.* 1998). A growing number of consumer researchers are now adopting a macro approach that, among other things, takes into consideration the broad societal effects of marketing and consumption activities (see, for example, Kilbourne *et al.* 1997). In particular, there is an increasing appreciation of the influence of the social and cultural contexts in which individuals live and consume (Bourdieu 1984, McCracken 1987, Manning and Cullum-Swan 1994). The analysis of these environments and their implications for consumption represents an alternative research approach to the dominant micro orientation of traditional consumer research characterised by an almost exclusive focus on the acquisition process.

A macro approach to consumption includes consideration of the symbolic relevance of products and consumption. In the last two decades there has developed a significant body of literature dealing with the symbolic aspects of consumption as they impact both consumers and marketers (Solomon 1983, McCracken 1990a, 1990b). The symbolic meanings found in products are now recognised to be very important in the consumption decisions of consumers (Holbrook and Hirschman 1982, Englis and Solomon 1995, Belk and Costa 1998). According to McCracken (1990a, 1990b), consumers have a considerable degree of latitude in their use of objects and the symbolic meanings they hold. He views the determination and employment of symbolic meaning as being at least partially in the control of individual consumers, who can employ these meanings to assist them in achieving their social and consumption objectives.

Through their employment of symbolic meanings in their consumption decisions, consumers are thought to be able actively to produce and maintain their self-concepts (Csikszentmihalyi and Rochberg-Halton 1981). The role of objects in the process of self-definition is a result of their ability to provide a source of stable information for consumers to use in their assessments of others (Cushman 1990, Hormuth 1990). Some suggest that consumers are now highly dependent on consumption for self-concept development and maintenance, to the point that they have no choice but to employ products for this purpose in their social interactions (Hormuth 1990, Kleine *et al.* 1992, Firat 1994, 1995, Firat and Dholakia 1998). In other words, self-definition in consumer societies is now perceived to be at least partially reliant on consumption (Belk 1984, Wallendorf and Arnould 1988).

Due to the tendency for consumers to employ products in the process of self-definition, an important aspect of symbolic consumption is the use of consumption as a communication tool between consumers. Every individual in consumer societies is both a source and a subject of judgements made according to product ownership (Douglas and Isherwood 1979). Belk *et al.* (1982) describe stereotyping as part of the symbolic process that allows consumers to express themselves non-verbally via consumption. They suggest that the tendency for people to assess others based on their consumption choices is a culturally universal phenomenon (Belk *et al.* 1982: 4). Stereotyping works on the principle that as people's consumption decisions are considered part of their selves, others can monitor consumption to gauge the nature of an unknown individual (Belk 1988, Firat 1995). Visible consumption thus enables personality traits to be attributed to unknown persons, assisting in the formation of opinions and impressions relating to that individual (Belk 1988, Kleine *et al.* 1992). The communication of social class membership is a particularly important stereotyping function that is performed by consumer goods (Solomon 1983, Fenster 1991), and through their consumption of goods and services, consumers can consciously or unconsciously convey their social standing to others (Bourdieu 1984, Arnould 1989, Englis and Solomon 1995).

An appreciation of the symbolic importance of consumption leads to the recognition of the emotional relevance of consumption. Given the importance of emotions to human existence, the anthropologist Clifford Geertz (1975) suggested that researchers should view human behaviours as being centred around a need to assess the emotional significance of their surroundings, rather than being directed purely towards information gathering. It is this focus on emotions that has been noted as lacking in much consumer research. Holbrook (1995) notes that most of the limited attention given to emotions has focused on the role of affect in the formation of attitudes relevant to purchasing behaviour. According to Holbrook, feelings are typically of interest to marketers only when they impinge directly on the purchase decision. Holbrook and Hirschman (1982) posit that the outcome of this narrow view of emotions in consumption has been a tendency to focus on consumers' likes and dislikes towards products, rather than on the experience of more complex emotions throughout the consumption process. They argue that while there remains a place for the information-processing approach in consumer research, the incorporation of an experiential perspective that places importance on emotional outcomes holds great potential for enhancing our understanding of the consumption process. They list the range of emotions relevant to consumption as 'love, hate, fear, joy, boredom, anxiety, pride, anger, disgust, sadness, sympathy, lust, ecstasy, greed, guilt, elation, shame, and awe' (Holbrook and Hirschman 1982: 137).

Alcohol consumption

Alcohol is a product category that has been associated with both positive and negative emotional outcomes for consumers, and thus represents a useful consumption good to study for insight into the emotional significance of consumption. Other than the pleasurable physical sensation of inebriation, the positive outcomes of alcohol consumption can include a reduction in stress and anxiety for the drinker while intoxicated (Heath 1987). Alcohol consumption also has the potential to assist consumers in their objectives of obtaining social approval, alleviating peer pressure, and reducing inhibitions (Dichter 1964, Plant *et al.* 1990, Beck *et al.* 1993, Pavis *et al.* 1997, Parker 1998). The negative consequences of alcohol consumption, however, can include hangovers, violence (including suicide and homicide), injuries from motor vehicle accidents, exposure to heavier drugs, long-term health problems, foetal abnormalities, and family disintegration (Brady 1992, Pavis *et al.* 1997, Garretson and Burton 1998).

Douglas (1987) and Heath (1987) have performed anthropological analyses of alcohol consumption across cultures, concluding that the ingestion of alcohol is an important social occurrence in human communities. It provides structure to social life by reflecting categories such as age, gender, and social standing (Levy 1986). Initiation to alcohol is often associated with the celebration of special events, with parents often guiding their children in the use of alcohol for this purpose (Hughes *et al.* 1997). The other symbolic association of alcohol is that of male labour (Douglas 1987). Barr (1995) traces heavy alcohol consumption to the development of a cash society, which is characterised by a separation of the places of home and work. This produces a situation where workers are able to go to drinking venues on the way home from work, with workers in this sense typically being males (Heath 1987). Current accounts of the cultural role of alcohol continue to note the symbolic relationship between work, masculinity, and alcohol consumption (Gough and Edwards 1998, Parker 1998).

The Australian context

In the 1995 Australian National Health Survey (Australian Bureau of Statistics 1995), with a sample size of approximately 54,000 people, the average daily quantity of absolute alcohol consumed across all types of alcoholic beverages among those who reported consuming alcohol in the previous week was 47.3 ml per person. When broken down by gender the consumption rates were 57.6 ml per day for males and 32.8 ml per day for females (ABS 1995). These consumption rates are high given that medical researchers warn that 46.4 ml and 26.4 ml are the maximum recommended daily doses of alcohol for males and females respectively (Holman *et al.* 1996). However, in terms of alcohol consumption per capita, Australians rank only nineteenth in the world (Productschap Voor Gedistilleerde Dranken 1999), and thus are not heavy drinkers by international standards.

Beer is the most popular form of alcohol in Australia, as indicated by frequency of consumption and total consumption volumes (ABS 1995). Social commentators have nominated beer as being an important component of self-definition among Australians (Mackay 1989), describing it as an important social text that is highly symbolic of Australian culture (Fiske *et al.* 1987). Despite high average levels of consumption across the Australian population, beer as a product category is characterised by a degree of masculine symbolism that ensures that the majority of beer drinkers in Australia are male (ABS 1990, 1995). This tendency for beer to be associated with masculinity also occurs in other cultures (Gough and Edwards 1998, Levy 1986). In the week prior to the 1989 National Health Survey (ABS 1990, *n* =16,999), 65% of Australian adult males had consumed beer compared to only 14.3% of adult females. Beer consumption is also segmented by age, with younger males consuming much larger volumes of beer than other segments of the population. Australian females exhibit a preference for wine over beer, with the average incidence of wine consumption among females in the week prior to the 1989 National Health Survey registering at 30.5% (ABS 1990).

Mackay (1989) has described beer consumption in Australia as a mechanism that communicates group membership, giving drinkers a way of differentiating themselves from some social segments and aligning themselves with others. He notes that while the use of beer consumption to achieve social interaction is usually associated with Australian males, it is increasingly being employed as a means by which females can communicate their desire for equality. This development is a reflection of the changing social dynamics within Australian culture, where an increasing female presence in the workplace and changing roles within the family home are combining to redefine male/female relationships (Mackay 1993). As one result of this social re-positioning of gender roles, the masculine association with beer consumption is gradually fading in intensity (Fiske et al. 1987).

Should Elle McPherson drink beer?

To explore the symbolic significance of a form of consumption that is recognised to have significant emotional outcomes for consumers, a study of the feelings and emotions involved in the changing sphere of alcohol consumption was conducted in the Australian context. As the symbolic meaning of alcohol consumption is currently in a state of flux due to changing gender relations in Australia, an analysis of males' and females' attitudes towards female alcohol drinkers had the potential to shed light on the role consumption can play in making shifting social norms more tangible and concrete. Also, as such social change is a highly value-laden and emotion-charged process (Mackay 1993), it was of interest to explore the extent to which reactions to these changes are embedded in consumers' attribution activities.

The attributions that are allocated to female drinkers based on the type of alcohol consumed were examined through the use of a projective technique that was designed to elicit the reactions of observers to female consumption of wine and beer. Projective techniques have been recognised as capable of generating rich data that can offer new insights into consumption behaviours (McGrath et al. 1993). Sixty-five interviews were conducted with Australians possessing varying demographic profiles (age, gender and social class) from three Australian states (New South Wales, Victoria and Western Australia). Most of the interviews were conducted in pubs and clubs, although other interviews were held in a variety of locations, including schools, retirement villages and participants' homes. Approximately 70% of participants were male, due primarily to the tendency for pub environments to house more males than females.

Participants were asked to visualise twin females who both exactly resembled Elle McPherson (an Australian model/actress/celebrity). In the exercise, the two females were described as sitting at either ends of a public bar, with the only difference between them being their choice of alcoholic beverage – one was described as drinking wine and the other as drinking beer. Elle is a media-created personality who is representative of a range of physical and symbolic attributes to Australians, particularly the feminine. As such, she was a useful subject to explore attributions made about females who consume beverages that have been imbued with masculine versus feminine symbolism. All those approached to participate in this study were found to be familiar with Elle and the attributes that she represents.

Male participants were asked which of the two Elles they would prefer to ask out on a date, while female participants were asked which Elle would be approached to request change to be used to make a call on a public telephone. Female participants were also asked to guess what the likely response from males would be if asked to choose between the two Elles for a date. The responses were coded according to the demographic characteristics of the participants and by the nature of the responses provided.

The process of triggering consumers' attributions with the use of the visualisation exercise was successful in exploring the ways in which gender and social class meanings are assigned to individuals according to the consumption of particular products. Most participants made well-formed and consistent attributions of the wine-drinking Elle and the beer-drinking Elle. On the basis of this one difference in consumption, they generally viewed the two females as being very different in personal characteristics and social standing.

Masculinity and femininity

The polarisation in attitudes pertaining to appropriate alcohol consumption based on gender became quickly apparent in the interviews. In effect, the choice of alcohol to consume appears to be pre-made for many Australians according to their gender. With the use of the visualisation exercise, participants communicated their understandings of the rights and wrongs of alcohol consumption in Australia, which were typically centred around the appropriateness of different forms of alcohol for different types of people. Males are expected to consume masculine beverages such as beer and spirits, and to consume them in relatively large quantities. By comparison, females are expected to be more restrained in their alcohol consumption, and to limit their drinking to those alcoholic beverages considered more feminine in nature, particularly wine. These interpretations were very consistent across age groups, illustrating the extent of socialisation relating to alcohol that occurs throughout life.

Both male and female participants recognised that femininity is expected in an Australian female. This femininity is expressed in numerous ways, including the choices made among different products. Even though Elle McPherson was generally viewed as being very feminine, her association with the consumption of beer in the projective exercise was enough to make her significantly less feminine in the eyes of many participants:

SP: Do you have a feeling for which Elle you think men would prefer?
Female: Oh yes. They would go for the wine drinker.
SP: Why do you suppose that would be?
Female: I don't know. I think men probably think a beer drinker, a female beer drinker, oh she is just one of the boys, she just wants to have fun. The wine drinker would be feminine – yes.

One way in which the perceived differences in femininity between the two Elles were made evident was through descriptions of the clothing that the two women were likely to be wearing. The wine-drinking Elle was often assumed to be wearing a dress, while the beer-drinking Elle was considered more likely to be wearing jeans. Such assumptions reflect both the more feminine associations of wine relative to beer, and the association of beer with casual drinking situations and wine with more formal social gatherings. The wine-drinking Elle was also generally perceived to be more physically attractive, with the beer drinker described by some as being more overweight and less image conscious than her wine-drinking sister. Some female participants who drank beer opined that it should not be the case that women are judged to be less physically or socially attractive if they consume beer. However, they acknowledged that such attributions are still very common, and they often made these same attributions during the course of their interviews.

While the beer-drinking Elle was usually considered to be less feminine, this did not always prevent male participants from finding the beer-drinking Elle attractive. Some referred to the ease and comfort of drinking with someone who was consuming the same beverage as themselves. They felt that the beer-drinking Elle would be more approachable, more likely to say yes to an invitation, and more fun while out on a date. However, while the beer-drinking Elle was deemed by some to be acceptable for going out on a date, it was often pointed out that it was the wine-drinking Elle who would make the better prospect as a long-term partner, due to her higher levels of social propriety as communicated through her choice of alcohol. Thus while the beer drinker was perceived by some to be suited to enjoyable social activities in the short term, the wine-drinker represented a more desirable marriage partner and was therefore usually considered the more appropriate Elle to approach to request a date:

SP: If you were going to ask one of the Elles out on a date, which one would you ask?
Male: The one with the wine.
SP: Tell me more.
Male: Because when you go to a restaurant you don't want everyone seeing you going out with this girl who will have a tinny [can of beer]. You want to be with a nice one.

Not all participants were comfortable verbalising their attributions on the basis of alcohol consumption, with differences in openness of response often being associated with the age of the participant. Younger participants were much more likely to state immediately that they expected a difference in femininity to exist between the two Elles, while a number of older participants took much longer to disclose such thoughts. It became apparent that they felt that it was not appropriate to stereotype people on the basis of 'superficial' evidence such as alcohol consumption behaviours. It was not until rapport had been established with these participants that they felt comfortable sharing their feelings regarding the relative femininity and masculinity of the two drinkers. Once this point of disclosure was reached, the attributions made by older participants were very similar to those expressed by younger participants.

Class attributions

Depending on the beverage being consumed, participants made consistent assumptions about the social standing of each drinker. They often used terms such as 'sophisticated', 'snob', 'posh', and 'refined' to describe the wine-drinking Elle, while they were more likely to use descriptors such as 'down to earth' and 'easygoing' when discussing the beer-drinking Elle. Relatively few participants directly mentioned the word 'class', instead choosing other terms that convey the same meaning while being less socially contentious. This tendency was not surprising given the recognised Australian aversion to acknowledging explicitly the existence of social differences among the population (Horne 1988, Mackay 1993).

It became apparent that the variables of social class and gender were confounded in the minds of many participants. For example, to be sophisticated is to be more feminine, as well as to belong to a higher social class. By comparison, males are expected to be more relaxed in demeanour, as are members of the lower classes. The confounded nature of these variables is manifest in the symbolic meanings that are attached to wine and beer in Australian culture. Beer is associated with both masculinity and a lower social standing, although these are not mutually exclusive categories. An upper-class male can still consume beer, albeit in lesser quantities, and when a male consumes wine he is assumed to be of a higher social standing than his beer-drinking equivalent. By comparison, when a female consumes beer it is assumed that she derives from a lower social class than her wine-drinking equivalent.

While an immediate association between the beer-drinking Elle and a lower social class was very common among participants, they were generally hesitant to recognise any relationship between the class status they ascribed to the two drinkers and their general attitudes towards them. For example, while male participants generally selected the wine-drinking Elle to be the most desirable, they were reluctant to attribute this preference to her higher perceived social standing. Similarly, female participants preferred to account for their choice of the wine-drinking Elle to approach on the basis of assumed differences in personality rather than perceived social standing. Participants in general appeared to want to believe that their overall assessments of the two women were independent of their assumptions regarding their social status.

As well as being frequently categorised as unfeminine and lower class, the Elle drinking beer was also subject to other negative attributions. These included a general lack of desirability and social acceptability:

Male: The question pops up in your head, why is this chick drinking beer? Has she got some kind of social problem? Is she is trying to drown her sorrows quick smart or what? It is not a good image, I suppose, as far as women are concerned. I know it is stereotypical but that is just the way you are brought up to look at it. You get this beer image which just isn't female.

The assumption can be that a female drinking beer is socially undesirable and may have emotional problems, making her appear pathetic to observers. As the norm is that females do not drink beer in Australia, observers of beer-drinking females can attempt to rationalise these behaviours as being disturbed or abnormal in some way. Ascribing masculine, lower socio-economic, and pathetic characteristics to female beer drinkers were some of the ways by which participants in this study came to terms with exposure to a consumption behaviour that through their cultural conditioning they considered inappropriate and unnatural.

The ability of beer-drinking females to attract such negative attributions from others makes the consumption choices of these consumers complex and difficult. Those females interviewed who drink beer stated that they are aware of the negative attributions that can accrue to beer-drinking females, but that they consider the benefits to be gained from accessing the masculine symbolism of beer to be worth incurring other undesired attributions. For them, the ability to communicate their equality with males is of great importance, and they are willing to accept the negative stereotyping of others in order to enable them to achieve this one objective. They consider current interpretations of female beer drinking to be outdated and due for review amongst the general population. As such, they perceive themselves to be social leaders, showing other females the way to equality and liberation.

Conclusion

Most participants made well-formed and consistent attributions regarding the two Elle McPhersons according to the beverage they were depicted to be drinking. On the basis of this one difference in consumption, participants generally viewed the two females to be very different in personal characteristics and social standing. The consistency in attributions accruing to the two Elles indicates the extent to which the symbolic meanings of products are culturally determined, as opposed to being determined by the individual as postulated by McCracken (1990b). Rather than freely attaching meanings to the various forms of alcohol and their drinkers, participants exhibited a relative uniformity in the meanings they assigned to wine and beer and to female consumers of these products. This suggests that these symbolic meanings are typically accepted rather than contested by individuals, although further research is required to explore the appropriateness of this conclusion to other categories of consumer goods. It is likely that the importance of communicating aspects of the self through consumption is such that individuals cannot risk assigning different meanings to products, as this may result in unwelcome decoding by observers as they carry out their routine stereotyping activities. This finding thus provides an alternative viewpoint to McCracken's position concerning the ability of individual consumers to determine and selectively employ the symbolic meanings resident in objects.

The results of this study also support the position that the construction of identity in consumer societies is achieved to a great extent through the consumption of products, and that the ways in which self-construction is accomplished can be socially specified. By utilising the symbolic meaning resident in products, consumers communicate to others information about themselves. However, the self that they choose to communicate may be a primarily social construction. The definition of what constitutes a 'proper' female in Australian culture is socially determined, leaving female consumers to try to consume 'correctly' to ensure that they communicate the right image to others. Thus, both the nature of the desired self and the ways in which this self is constructed and communicated appear to be heavily socially influenced.

In answer to the question 'Should Elle McPherson drink beer?', the answer depends largely upon her objectives. If she wants to communicate a feminine image, as is generally required of females in Australian society, then beer consumption is likely to result in unwelcome attributions. Alternatively, if she wishes to communicate her liberation from traditional female stereotypes, then beer consumption may be a useful tool to achieve this objective. However, should she choose to consume beer, she may be subject to a range of attributions other than the desired message of equality, including being stereotyped as lower-class, masculine, and socially inept. Through her choice of beverage, Elle would be willingly or unwillingly communicating information about herself. Aware of the probable stereotyping outcomes of her consumption behaviours, her decision will take into consideration the way that others will decode her product choices. To fail to anticipate the attributions of others would have implications for her ability to achieve the level of social integration that she desires.

To conclude, by exploring consumers' feelings relating to their acts of consumption, it is possible to gain insight into the important role of symbolism in these acts. An emphasis on consumers' cognitive decision structures relevant to the choice between different types and brands of alcohol would fail to explicate the complex range of emotions surrounding this apparently simple and pleasurable form of consumption. By accessing the emotions involved in alcohol consumption, it was possible to explore the ways in which such consumption behaviours reflect and reinforce the prevailing social order, as well as provide a possible avenue for change. In this study, the pleasurable act of alcohol consumption was found to be a form of communication where drinkers signal their gender, their social class, and their satisfaction or otherwise with current social norms. Similarly, alcohol consumption provides an ongoing barometer for consumers to observe in their daily acts of 'reading' the social environment to assess their place and role in a constantly changing milieu.

References

Arnould, E. J. (1989) 'Toward a broadened theory of preference formation and the diffusion of innovations: cases from Zinder Province, Niger Republic', *Journal of Consumer Research* 16(2): 239–67.

Australian Bureau of Statistics (1990) 'National health survey: health risk factors', Catalogue No. 4380.0, Canberra.

—— (1995) 'National health survey: summary of results', Catalogue No. 4364.0, Canberra.

Barr, A. (1995) *Drink*, London: Bantam Press.

Beck, K., Thombs, D. L. and Summons, T. G. (1993) 'The social context of drinking scales: construct validation and relationship to indicants of abuse in an adolescent population', *Addictive Behaviors* 18: 159–69.

Belk, R. W. (1984) 'Cultural and historical differences in concepts of self and their effects on attitudes toward having and giving', *Advances in Consumer Research* 11: 753–60.

—— (1987) 'ACR Presidential address: happy thought', *Advances in Consumer Research* 14: 1–4.

—— (1988) 'Possessions and the extended self', *Journal of Consumer Research* 15(2): 130–68.

Belk, R. W. and Costa, J. A. (1998) 'The mountain man myth: a contemporary consuming fantasy', *Journal of Consumer Research* 25(3): 218.

Belk, R. W., Bahn, K. D. and Mayer, R. N. (1982) 'Developmental recognition of consumption symbolism', *Journal of Consumer Research* 9: 4–17.

Bourdieu, P. (1984) *Distinction: a Social Critique of the Judgement of Taste*, London: Routledge and Kegan Paul.

Brady, M. (1992) 'Ethnography and understandings of aboriginal drinking', *Journal of Drug Issues* 22(3): 699–712.

Clarke, I., Kell, I., Schmidt, R. and Vignali, C. (1998) 'Thinking the thoughts they do: symbolism and meaning in the consumer experience of the "British Pub"', *Qualitative Market Research: an International Journal* 1(3): 132–44.

Creyer, E. H. and Ross, W. T. (1997) 'Tradeoffs between price and quality: how a value index affects preference', *The Journal of Consumer Affairs* 3(2): 280–302.

Csikszentmihalyi, M. and Rochberg-Halton, E. (1981) *The Meaning of Things, Domestic Symbols and the Self*, New York: Cambridge University Press.

Cushman, P. (1990) 'Why the self is empty', *American Psychologist* 45(5): 599–611.

Dichter, E. (1964) *Handbook of Consumer Motivations: the Psychology of the World of Objects*, New York: McGraw-Hill Book Company.

Douglas, M. (1987) 'A distinctive anthropological perspective', in M. Douglas (ed.) *Constructive Drinking: Perspectives on Drink from Anthropology*, Cambridge: The Press Syndicate of the University of Cambridge: 3–15.

—— (1979) *The World of Goods: Towards an Anthropology of Consumption*, London: Allen Lane.

Englis, B. and Solomon, M. R. (1995) 'To be and not to be: lifestyle imagery, reference groups, and the clustering of America', *Journal of Advertising* 24(1): 13–28.

Fenster, M. (1991) 'The problem of taste within the problematic of culture', *Communications Theory* 1(2): 87–105.

Firat, A. F. (1994) 'Gender and consumption: transcending the feminine', in J. A. Costa (ed.) *Gender Issues and Consumer Behavior*, Thousand Oaks, CA: Sage.

—— (1995) 'Consumer culture or culture consumed?', in J. A. Costa and G. J. Bamossy (eds) *Marketing in a Multicultural World*, California: Sage Publications: 105–25.

Firat, A. F. and Dholakia, N. (1998) *Consuming People: from Political Economy to Theaters of Consumption*, London: Routledge.

Fiske, J., Hodge, B. and Turner, G. (1987) *Myths of Oz*, Sydney: Allen and Unwin.

Garretson, J. A. and Burton, S. (1998) 'Alcoholic beverage sales promotion: an initial investigation of the role of warning messages and brand characters among consumers over and under the legal drinking age', *Journal of Public Policy and Marketing* 17(1): 35–47.

Geertz, C. (1975) *The Interpretation of Cultures*, London: Hutchinson.

Gough, B. and Edwards, G. (1998) 'The beer talking: four lads, a carry out and the reproduction of masculinities', *The Sociological Review* 46(3): 409–35.

Heath, D. B. (1987) 'A decade of development in the anthropological study of alcohol use: 1970–1980', in M. Douglas (ed.) *Constructive Drinking: Perspectives on Drink from Anthropology*, Cambridge: Cambridge University Press.

Holbrook, M. B. (1995) *Consumer Research*, Thousand Oaks, California: Sage.

Holbrook, M. B. and Hirschman, E. C. (1982) 'The experiential aspects of consumption: consumer fantasies, feelings, and fun', *Journal of Consumer Research* 9: 132–40.

Holman, C. D., English, D. R. and Winter, M. G. (1996) 'Meta-analysis of alcohol and all-cause mortality: a validation of NHMRC', *Medical Journal of Australia* 164(3): 141–5.

Hormuth, S. (1990) *The Ecology of the Self*, Cambridge: Cambridge University Press.

Horne, D. (1988) *The Lucky Country*, Melbourne: Penguin Books Australia.

Hughes, K., MacKintosh, A. M., Hastings, G., Wheeler, C., Watson, J. and Inglis, J. (1997) 'Young people, alcohol, and designer drinks: quantitative and qualitative study', *British Medical Journal* 314(7078): 414–18.

Jacoby, J., Chestnut, R. W., Weigl, K. C. and Fisher, W. (1976) 'Pre-purchase information acquisition: description of a process methodology, research paradigm, and pilot investigation', *Advances in Consumer Research* 3: 306–14.

Kilbourne, W., McDonagh, P. and Prothero, A. (1997) 'Sustainable consumption and the quality of life: a macromarketing challenge to the dominant social paradigm', *Journal of Macromarketing* 17(1): 4–24.

Kleine, R. E., Schultz-Kleine, S. and Kernan, J. B. (1992) 'Mundane everyday consumption and the self: a conceptual orientation and prospects for consumer research', *Advances in Consumer Research* 19: 411–15.

Levy, S. J. (1986) 'Meanings in advertising stimuli', in J. Olson and K. Sentis (eds) *Advertising and Consumer Psychology*, New York: Praeger.

Mackay, H. (1989) *The Hugh Mackay 1989 Beer Report*, Appendix 4, Sydney, Australia.

—— (1993) *Reinventing Australia: the Mind and Mood of Australia in the 90s*, Sydney: Angus & Robertson.

McCracken, G. (1987) 'Advertising: meaning or information?', *Advances in Consumer Research* 14: 121–4.

McGrath, M. A., Sherry, J. F. and Levy, S. J. (1993) 'Giving voice to the gift: the use of projective techniques to recover lost meanings', *Journal of Consumer Psychology* 2(2): 171–91.

—— (1990a) 'Culture and consumer behavior: an anthropological perspective', *Journal of the Market Research Society* 32(1): 3–11.

McCracken, G. (1988) *Culture and Consumption*, USA: Indiana University Press.

Manning, P. K. and Cullum-Swan, B. (1994) 'Narrative, content, and semiotic analysis', in N. Denzin and Y. Lincoln (eds) *Handbook of Qualitative Research*, Thousand Oaks: Sage Publications.

Mick, D. G. (1986) 'Consumer research and semiotics: exploring the morphology of signs, symbols and significance', *Journal of Consumer Research* 13: 196–213.

Parker, B. J. (1998) 'Exploring life themes and myths in alcohol advertisements through a meaning-based model of advertising experiences', *Journal of Advertising* 27(1): 97–112.

Pavis, S., Cunningham-Burley, S. and Amos, A. (1997) 'Alcohol consumption and young people: exploring meaning and social context', *Health Education Research: Theory and Practice* 12(3): 311–22.

Plant, M. A., Bagnall, G. and Foster, J. (1990) 'Teenage heavy drinkers: alcohol-related knowledge, beliefs, experiences, motivation and the social context of drinking', *Alcohol and Alcoholism* 25(6): 691–8.

Productschap Voor Gedistilleerde Dranken (1999) *World Drink Trends*, Oxfordshire: NTC Publications.

Sheth, J. N. and Gross, B. L. (1988) 'Parallel development of marketing and consumer behaviour: a historical perspective', in T. Nevett and R. A. Fullerton (eds) *Historical Perspectives in Marketing*, Canada: Lexington Books: 9–33.

Solomon, M. R. (1983) 'The role of products as social stimuli: a symbolic interactionism perspective', *Journal of Consumer Research* 10: 319–29.

Wallendorf, M. and Arnould, E. J. (1988) ' "My favorite things": a cross-cultural inquiry into object attachment, possessiveness, and social linkage', *Journal of Consumer Research* 14(4): 531–47.

Wright, P. (1979) 'Decision process theory and research', *Advances in Consumer Research* 6: 218–21.

9 Consuming home technology

Consuming home computers

Elaine Lally

Introduction

All consumption activity has increasingly become technologically mediated over the past few decades. The shopping experience has been transformed by its technological infrastructure: barcode scanners have in some cases completely displaced interaction with human retail staff. Customer service is no longer seen in terms of the quality of the interpersonal interaction between the consumer and the commercial organisation but can instead be a quantitative measure of efficiency: the length of time the customer spends standing in the queue at the bank, or the time they spend on hold at the call centre. At the same time, technological innovations have profoundly transformed payment methods: the introduction since the 1980s of electronic funds transfer and ATM facilities, and the growth of credit-card use have shifted the emphasis away from cash and cheques as the media of transaction. When workers were paid in cash there was a direct experiential articulation between earning money and spending it. The electronic transfer of a salary payment directly into a bank account interposes a layer of abstraction into the process of being paid for the work that we do and disengages the activities of earning and spending. While the growth in the ready availability of credit (particularly through credit cards) has facilitated a rapid growth in consumer debt levels, this may also be a sign of our increasingly abstracted relationship to money (Miller and Slater 2000: 167). Indeed, our use of money in consumption activities is being transformed into a modality of data-processing: personal information and spending patterns are a valuable commodity in themselves (in exchange for which corporations are prepared to reward us as consumers).

It is generally anticipated that the Internet and e-commerce will again transform the nature of consumption. However, the changes involved may simply be extensions to the longer-term trajectory of developments in the technologies of consumption and in the consumption of technologies. This chapter examines the home computer as a high-technology commodity. The development of discourses and representations of home computing throughout the 1990s is described, followed by an exploration of how these developments are received by consumers (drawing on interviews with home-computer owners). Novel commodity forms, it is argued, can only be taken up by consumers on the basis of understandings and forms of practice which they are already familiar and comfortable with. The chapter concludes with some speculation on the future of technologies of consumption.

As highly technological commodities, computers are of particular importance because of their close association with and integration into processes of globalisation. The acquisition of a home computer is clearly identified for consumers with a faith in the inevitability of techno-social progress, and a resulting belief that these are changes which must be kept up with, because inaction carries a risk of being 'left behind', a pressure which is particularly acutely felt by parents on behalf of their children. There is therefore both fear and risk of failure in these technologies and also promise and hope for the future.

The first computers which could be bought and owned by consumers were self-assembly microcomputer kits which became available in the mid 1970s. However, it was not until the late 1980s that developments in the technology and its marketing led to a shift in the portrayal and use of the home computer. The computer as a 'software player' for the home became more of a family activity and less one concentrated in the hands of the (typically male) hobbyist (Haddon 1988). These developments paved the way for the transformation of the personal computer into a sort of 'information appliance' for the home. During the 1990s, representations of home computing drew both on the computer's legacy as a business and educational tool, but also on traditions in the design, marketing and use of household technologies such as the television, VCR, CD player, and even the microwave oven. This cultural reconstruction of the technology was oriented towards reshaping it to the aesthetic and functional parameters appropriate to the commodity culture of the modern Western household. From the mid 1990s onwards, for instance, images of computers in the kitchen or in shopping trolleys appeared widely in advertising and magazine articles. The common juxtaposition of computers and food, despite the almost universal injunction against food and drink around computers in actual contexts of use, is clearly a strategy of representation which is meant to be read symbolically rather than literally. This strategy of taming and reshaping a highly technological object in order for it to fit into the domestic context, has been referred to as a process of 'domestication'.

Domesticating the information appliance

Innovative goods, such as new high-technology commodities, pose a problem for producers and marketers because consumers' understandings of novel goods can only be based on what they already know and understand (although this can be based on imagined expectation rather than direct experience (Campbell 1992)). Consumers draw on an established repertoire of knowledge and cultural competence when contemplating the acquisition of a consumer good (Glennie and Thrift 1992). Commodification processes – including advertising and cultural discourses around consumer goods – therefore must present novel goods within contexts which are already culturally familiar, so that their potential to fit into the contexts of everyday life will be understandable to consumers (Carrier, 1990). Novel technological commodities are therefore integrated into the everyday life of households through complex processes, which Silverstone has termed *domestication*:

> Domestication is a process both of taming the wild and cultivating the tame. ... One can think of domestication too, as both a process by which we make things our own, subject to our control, imprinted by, and expressive of, our identities; and as a principle of mass consumption in which products are prepared in the public fora of the market. In a sense the commodity is already domesticated, and it is in this 'anticipation of domesticity' which the commodity embodies that we must understand the context of our own domesticity.
>
> (Silverstone 1994: 174)

Novel goods are created within social contexts of production, but must be positioned within the marketplace in ways which match the understandings and expectations of consumers. The personal computer's place in the home is therefore anticipated and built into the design of the object itself and incorporated in representations of home computers in advertising and other discourses about home computing.

Information technology is particularly in need of these processes of domestication to condition their uptake by consumers. Discourses about technological progression are characterised, at the extremes, by a similar mixture of utopianism and dystopianism as followed earlier innovations, such as the telephone and television (Spigel 1992). There is simultaneously both great hope for a better future through technology, and a fear of technologies out of human control. For consumers, these competing discourses about technological progression naturalise the inevitability of the deepening penetration of information technology into everyday life (both within and outside the domestic sphere), and generate a sense for them that these are changes which they must keep up with or be left behind.

Home computing was domesticated during the 1990s through its integration into the domestic commodity culture of the Western industrialised world. By the late 1980s the identification of the personal computer as a consumer electronics item was strengthened by the broadening of its distribution base: it became possible to purchase personal computers in department stores and electrical goods chains selling consumer electronics items ('brown' as well as 'white' goods), and computer equipment started appearing in advertising catalogues alongside VCRs and televisions. Consumers with little first-hand technical experience might be expected to be more willing to consider buying a computer from one of these stores rather than from a specialist computer retailer, where there is a common perception that the sales people speak in a jargon-laden foreign language.

While retaining both the legacy of its history as a business and educational tool, and the computer's powerful symbolic resonance with futurity, the home computer's pattern of representation resonated also with those of other household technologies such as the television, VCR, CD player, and even the microwave oven. A 1994 advertisement for an *Apple Macintosh* computer showed a father and daughter making muffins, with the computer sitting on the kitchen bench top beside them. The caption for this advertisement emphasised the computer as an everyday household object: 'It has 101 household uses, but it doesn't slice, dice or julienne'. The text accompanying the image implied that a computer would soon become indispensable to the contemporary home: 'personal computers are quickly becoming as popular in homes as microwave ovens and VCRs'. The range of household functions potentially undertaken by the personal computer was indicated by the text's subheadings: 'give your kids an edge in school', 'organise your household', 'improve your home business', 'make more of your spare time'.

The integration of home computers into domestic lifestyle consumer markets is also illustrated by the appearance from the mid 1990s onwards of computing magazines aimed at the inexperienced home user, and of computer-related material in mainstream family magazines. For example, a pull-out section in the September 1996 issue of *Better Homes and Gardens* magazine, entitled 'Home technology: how your home computer can help you', appeared particularly to encourage non-computer owners to acquire the technology. It was suggested that some people might still be holding back because they were not sure what the computer would do for them:

> If you don't already have a computer, you are probably part of a large group which is planning to buy one … It's especially hard to choose the right model when you're still unsure what you will do with your home computer. A home computer can be used to access the Internet, to play games, and to teach yourself a foreign language. You can write a letter, or a book, design a personalised Christmas card or a poster for your home business. It can schedule your appointments and help balance your home accounts.
>
> (Harden 1996: 196)

The supplement included articles on 'making a home for your computer', 'what to look for when buying a PC', 'making an income from the home computer', 'home banking and balancing personal finances', 'getting connected' to the Internet, a section on home automation, and 'things you never knew you could do on a computer'. This latter article included suggestions which integrated well with the staple *Better Homes and Gardens* content: gardening, craft, cooking, home video editing, and obtaining entertainment and travel information.

These popular forms of representation of domestic computer technologies construct a powerful normative image of the technologies, their appropriate functions and the cultural values with which they are associated. Many of the representations seem to appeal directly to a population which has internalised the need to achieve for themselves and for their children and the importance of the application of technological and economic resources to this project. In the case of personal computers, it is commonly believed that a computer at home is an advantage to children in their education, and conversely, that the absence of a computer in the home disadvantages them. Many advertisements play on this belief. The following slogan for Interactive Electronic Publishing's software products Teddy's Big Day (for one- to four-year-olds) and Teddy's Hide'n'seek (for three- to seven-year-olds), for example, appeared in the November/December 1994 issue of *Family PC*:

> In 25 years when your kid is pulling 200K a year after graduating top of the class at Harvard and you're lucky enough to catch her on the cell phone, you might want to remind her where it all started.

'Educational' computer software is favourably compared with playing games: one piece of music software used the slogan 'marking time or killing time', juxtaposing one of their own screen shots with one of a 'street fighting' computer game. Other computer software advertisements take advantage of parental concerns about the harmful effects of too much television. Computer use is presented as interactive and therefore better than more passive activities; the television, as 'babysitter in a box', is contrasted with computer use – 'creativity in a box'. Indeed, the concepts of education and entertainment tend to become conflated around computer use: there is a widespread belief that even game-playing is computer use and thus beneficial for children, assisting them to acquire generalised 'computer literacy' skills.

Promotional discourses around home computing have long presented home computing as a form of 'rational recreation', in which 'domestic space becomes an extension of the classroom and the office, and the user practices "useful" skills' (Murdock *et al.* 1992: 153). A further strategy in the process of domesticating information technology products for household consumption is that of using brands which are associated with children's toys and educational products (such as Disney, Time Warner, Crayola, Fisher Price, Virgin) to produce computer software products. This product placement strategy functions to legitimise products for which many parents may have no pre-existing 'brand awareness', and defuse the intimidation that people without prior experience with these technologies might feel towards shopping for such products.

In addition to these trends in the symbolic and functional reshaping of personal computing for the home, a number of attempts were made during the 1990s to reorient the physical appearance of home computers. A number of computer manufacturers introduced – largely unsuccessfully – computers with the look and feel of consumer electronics items (in charcoal grey or matt black finishes, and with styling more like CD players and VCRs) rather than the office 'boxy beige' look. One such computer was the Olivetti Envision, released in late 1995, which was matt black and looked rather like a VCR with floppy disk and CD-ROM drives, and was controlled with a remote control and cordless keyboard. The Acer Aspire line, released at about the same time, included models in dark emerald green and charcoal grey. These models were designed to make the home computer conform to the traditional differentiation of household goods into 'white' and 'brown' goods, but their lack of commercial success suggests that consumers were not ready to accept the complete re-categorisation of the computer as a home media and entertainment device. For consumers, perhaps, the significantly higher cost of computers as compared to televisions, CD players, VCRs and other consumer electronics items meant that they needed to be clearly associated with more serious uses than mere entertainment, and that therefore the home computer needed to retain its beige 'office equipment' physical image.

The success of Apple's iMac, then, with its curved styling and translucent casing in vibrant colours, seems perhaps to have been in moving entirely beyond the 'brown goods'/'white goods' dichotomy. The iMac not only challenges this distinction, but does so by moving into symbolic dimensions occupied by objects of personal consumption, such as food (a range of iMac colours took the names of fruit), and appealing to more individualised and bodily pleasures than has previously been the case for computer advertising. This trend may indicate that the battle to naturalise the personal computer's place as a domestic information appliance has largely been won.

The process that I have been describing as one of the domestication of the personal computer is paralleled by the way that the Internet has been represented during the latter half of the 1990s. The World Wide Web can be seen as a domestication of earlier perceptions of the Internet as 'information superhighway'. Although in the mid 1990s the 'information superhighway' was widely talked about and understood as an innovation which would have profound effects on everyday life, its cultural and commercial potential as a new mass medium (which seemingly exploded within a few short years) was still unexplored. The 'highway' seemed appropriate as a metaphor for this sense of potentiality: the new electronic infrastructure would facilitate getting from one place to another, but it was not clear what kinds of places one would be able to reach. The Internet is, indeed, perhaps now better thought of as a kind of 'information utility' for the home. The concept of an 'information utility' was referred to as far back as 1992 by a former CEO of Hewlett Packard. It would be: 'a public infrastructure as widespread as electricity, an intelligent network of networks stacked with services, such as intelligent directories, the Library of Congress online, the expertise of the world's best doctors'. The information appliance would 'plug into the information utility as easily as a lamp into an outlet. ... it'll be intuitive; users can plug into the information utility and get it to work without ever reading a manual' (Young 1992: 7).

The considerations discussed above texture consumers' expectations by providing a domesticated image of the computer as a convenient and useful 'information appliance'. In the following section, the experiences of consumers themselves are explored, as they engage with these important contemporary developments. The discussion draws on interviews conducted with home-computer owners in western Sydney (Lally 2000). In the interests of anonymity all respondents are referred to by pseudonyms.

The consumer's perspective

The computer is a technology which is particularly closely linked with futurity and with accelerating processes of globalisation, and these associations form the cultural context for home-computer acquisition. Here is Peter Richards, a university administrator, describing the justification for the family's first computer purchase in 1990:

> We felt there was an increasing need for the kids to be computer literate, and we also saw a need for them to be able to type up basic things like letters or assignments ... At that point the primary schools were just starting to build up their computers too, and we thought what's the point of learning them at school if you can't do it at home. Another factor, just thinking back, most of my work use was on mainframes, so I also felt the need to upgrade my own skills. I could see that PCs were becoming more important, but I didn't work directly with them ... And also, I thought that if I needed to learn that, then my children would need to learn it more than me.

The Richards' reasoning is paralleled in the accounts of many of the households in my study. In particular, the close integration of instrumental discourses (that they are able to do certain things on the computer and that it will have certain effects on their lives), with expressive or affective discourses (about not wanting to be left behind by rapid sociotechnical change or about achieving a sense of personal empowerment through mastery of the technology) is quite typical, and makes it clear how interdependent ideological and instrumental logics are in these narratives.

Parental hopes for children's future career prospects tend to be one of the most powerful motivators for home-computer purchases (Murdock *et al.* 1992). The hope that a home computer will be a benefit for children is often expressed in more generalised and abstract terms than it is for adults, who tend to specify particular concrete benefits and uses rather than describing a generalised 'computer literacy' as the important benefit for their children of having a computer at home. For many parents it is a question of maximising their children's career options. This necessarily means that they need to gain computer skills and knowledge, since it is universally believed that computers are going to be even more important in the workplaces of the future than they are today.

For many adults a home computer contributes to their engagement in the world of work on a number of levels: at the abstract level of idealised hopes and fears for the future, in the development of a general familiarity with personal computers ('computer literacy') or of particular work-related skills (such as word-processing or database skills), and in their ability to be able to bring work home from their employment or establish a small business working from home. A home computer is justified by giving flexibility in the use of work time: having a home computer is more convenient and 'family-friendly' than spending longer at work.

Although it certainly seems to be important to people that a computer is a tool which performs certain functions, computers are also highly evocative cultural artefacts. For many people, therefore, there' is a fascination with the computer as a thing in itself, as a symbol of futurity. Doug Fowler, who is unemployed, calls himself a 'futurist':

> Computers have been a passion of mine ever since I knew that computers were around. To me it's part of technology and I'm interested in technology, science, so it was just one thing that I could have. It was my access to technology... I am a science fiction fanatic ... and you read stories with computers so to own a computer is my way of being in science fiction.

The association of computers with futurity and the seeming inevitability of technological progression provide a powerful sense for consumers that these are changes that they must participate in or they will be excluded, in a sense, from parts of contemporary culture itself (Haddon 1992: 83). There is, however, both promise and fear in these technologies, and they therefore hold out not just the threat of being left behind but also the promise of privileged access to the future through them. Goods can 'help the individual contemplate the possession of an emotional condition, a social circumstance, even an entire style of life, by somehow concretising these things in themselves', and can thereby 'become a bridge to displaced meaning and an idealised version of life as it should be lived' (McCracken 1988: 110). Indeed, one of the engines of consumption in modern society is that which regularly declares 'certain purchases obsolete (when they can no longer serve as bridges) and demands the purchase of new goods' (p.115). This effect is particularly strong in the case of new technologies such as the personal computer.

For older people, in particular, keeping pace with changing technology can be an integral part of keeping up with a rapidly changing world. The inevitability of techno-social progression is linked to the inevitability of the ageing process itself. Ruth Bourke, a retired high-school teacher makes the point:

> It makes me feel as though I've got a handle on the future ... I'm no longer engaged in day-to-day work, so this makes me feel as though I'm still in the workaday world in a way. That I can keep up with the technology – oh, I'm not into toys for toys' sake – but I do like to know what's happening in the world, and I don't like to feel that I've been left behind.

As Haddon and Silverstone (1996) also recognise, the newly retired are of particular interest in showing how information technology may contribute to personal projects of self-development. These technologies may be able to 'enhance and improve the quality of life of the elderly, through increases in the control of the physical and symbolic environment that they are believed to be able to provide' (Haddon and Silverstone 1996: 155). For Ruth Bourke, it is clear that the computer's powerful symbolic association with futurity gives just such a sense of control over a rapidly changing cultural environment.

Consumption decisions do not only involve, however, a simple intention on the part of the purchaser. For consumers, there is a need to maintain a sense of control over the incorporation of such technological innovations into the life of the household (Silverstone and Haddon 1996: 60). Inexperienced computer consumers must navigate a minefield of conflicting messages in negotiating this new cultural terrain, which is clearly highly stressful but is often seen as a necessary parental responsibility. The practices and institutions of consumption are organised to provide defences against such anxiety (Robins 1994), but consumers must draw on an established repertoire of knowledge and cultural competence, which can, to some extent, be transferred to novel cultural territory (Glennie and Thrift 1992). Stress and anxiety in the process are reduced through following comfort, familiarity and trust in individuals, institutions and situations. Consumers learn from their experiences in unfamiliar situations and through them develop new skills, competence and dispositions (such as brand preferences).

With a purchase like a computer, the size of the investment is greater than many households will have available at one time. There is variability in people's willingness to go into debt for a computer purchase. As Lunt and Livingstone (1992) point out, consumers in general will only borrow money for the purchase of goods which are judged to be necessities or investments (although credit-card purchases are an exception to this generalisation). For the Richards family, the easy availability of cheap finance for the purchase through a low-interest finance offer was a factor in both the timing of their purchase and the dealer that they bought it from. Other study participants bought their computers on '6 months interest free' deals with a department store credit card. One of these computers came with 12 months' hotline support and a small portable television. Such 'sweeteners' seem to be a common (and successful) way in which the market acts to make the decision as simple as possible for the consumer, by reducing the risk involved in purchase, and thereby reducing the amount that is at stake for the consumer.

Consumers of innovative goods like personal computers must gather information on which to base a purchase decision even once they have been convinced of the need to acquire one. People often follow the market for some (sometimes considerable) time before purchasing. Print advertising and magazines were particularly important for participants in shaping their interest in home computers and giving them a sense of what is available in the marketplace and at what cost. Other methods of familiarisation were also used: using friends' computers, experiences at school and in the workplace. It is necessary to minimise the risk, and consequently the confusion and frustration involved in the acquisition: owners talk of the stress of 'making the right decision' in what is perceived as a rapidly changing environment. This is particularly acute for first-time purchasers: those who trade up to a second or subsequent computer generally have a clearer idea of what they want.

Consumers' sense of control over the acquisition process often depends on a sense of trust in the people who are dealt with as part of the process. In many cases people rely on friends, relatives and other acquaintances for advice, but this generally also entails distinguishing between the people in computer retailers who can be trusted to give accurate and unbiased information and advice on the purchase, and those who seem to be simply interested in closing the sale. The choice of computer is not, then, based on some instrumentally rationalised calculation, but often comes down to a choice between potential social and cultural relationships. There is often also the expectation that the purchase itself will initiate an ongoing relationship between the consumer and either the retail organisation (perhaps in the form of ongoing support services) or in more abstract terms with brand loyalty or a continuing association with the manufacturer of the product (so that some consumers identify themselves as 'Macintosh' people or 'MS-DOS' people). Through the purchase of a commodity the consumer may therefore enter into an ongoing social and cultural relationship.

These issues are illustrated through the experiences of computer purchase of some of the study participants. Although Patricia Collins visited the major chain stores, she settled on buying locally, from a small specialist computer retailer because she thought she would get better after-sales service from them, but also because she had a more personalised sense of trust in them. The purchase may also involve the establishment of an ongoing relationship with the producers of the computer. The Coopers, with little prior direct experience to base a decision on, bought an IBM because:

> I guess we thought IBM was a name. If machines were IBM-compatible that must have been for a reason. So if everything is IBM-compatible, well why not get IBM. Maybe in reality it's not that logical but it seemed it to us.

It is not, however, a question of whether such decisions are logical or not, but that they obey different logics to the dominant instrumental, rational model of such decisions. The Richards family, for example, felt that having a 'name' brand machine, bought from a reputable company, was important. The impression made by the salesman at a large electrical goods and furniture retailer and Peter Richards' consequent feeling of trust in the advice he was being given was important in determining where they bought their computer:

> They were very helpful there, and I found that the salesman there was very good. He really seemed to speak with a level of authority, which was the

thing I was impressed with. I went there several times, at different times, and spoke to different sales people, and I'd look around the store and ask the questions. I pretended I didn't know anything, which was pretty close to the truth.

Here we see the strategy of asking the same questions of a number of different people, to establish a consistent picture. People will often 'triangulate' the information received from a variety of sources: sales people, friends and relatives, and printed materials.

There is a common perception that sales people are not to be trusted without further corroborating evidence that the advice they are giving is sound, since it can be assumed that their primary motivation will be making the sale. At one store which had recently opened:

> they had a couple of sales people in there, one of them looked barely older than my daughter and he looked like he was supposed to be the expert on the subject, and he explained what you were getting for your money, but didn't strike me as being very professional ... I thought 'at least I've checked this place out'. I only went there once.

The Richards finally bought their computer where they found a sales person who seemed to be an 'authoritative' source of information – one who could be trusted. Both domestication – as a process of presenting novel technological commodities to consumers in terms that are familiar and understandable to them – and the kinds of strategies on the part of consumers which have been described in this section, may be seen as means of minimising risk and anxiety within a novel domain in which consumers have imperfect knowledge and immature cultural competence. Perhaps there are lessons from the experience of home computing which might give some insight into future trends in the consumption of technologies, and into the acceptance of new technologies of consumption, such as e-commerce.

Conclusion

Consumer strategies for exploring novel cultural terrain must draw on what the consumer knows and is familiar with. The market assists in this process through the kinds of domesticating activities which have been described here. However, it is always the case that cultural forms, including technological innovations, may be taken up in unanticipated and creative ways by consumers (Miller 1987). The development of the MP3 compression technology, for example, is undoubtedly set to revolutionise the distribution of music. Although the potential for distributing music digitally over the Internet has been clear for several years, as illustrated by the availability of samples of music on the web sites of record companies, it has taken the grass roots 'revolution' of the Napster controversy to bring the industry to a realisation that it will inevitably be transformed. Further, spaces of consumption, and here e-commerce spaces will undoubtedly be no exception, are often co-opted for social purposes other than consumption. Just as shopping malls become places for hanging out and sites for performing social identities, so new technologies of consumption may be used for other purposes. The Amazon.com site, for example, is used by many academics as a general bibliographic resource: it contains information on many more books than are available in any library, including those not yet published, and its 'recommendations' feature makes it a useful resource for browsing.

It is early days to make predictions about how e-commerce and other new technologies of consumption will transform the activities of consumers, since it is clear that, at the time of writing, e-commerce is still in its infancy. Western industrialised countries like the United States and Australia can still count only on approximately 50% of their populations being online at home, the most likely site for e-commerce (ABS 2001: 3). Home Internet access is expanding rapidly, however. In Australia at least, more people now access the Internet from home than from any other site, including the workplace (ABS 2001: 7; although this may not translate into other cultures: see for example, Miller and Slater (2000) for a study of Internet use in Trinidad). As the Internet becomes an established part of the everyday life of the majority of householders, e-commerce will inevitably become something that consumers feel more comfortable engaging in. There is evidence that the longer consumers are online, the more likely they are to shop there and spend more money when they do (Burton 2000). In the twelve months to November 2000, only 10% of Australian adults purchased or ordered goods or services over the Internet, but this was an increase of 66% over the previous twelve months (ABS 2001: 11). Books, magazines and music were the most popular items bought. It is estimated that in 2000, the Australian online sector accounted for 1.5% of total retail spending, almost three times the 1999 level. Sectors which are doing well online include travel and ticketing, computers and electronics, groceries, flowers and alcohol, and books and entertainment products (Howarth 2000).

Products likely to succeed will be 'digital' goods such as music, video, pictures, e-books, games and so on, where it is possible to deliver the goods online rather than relying on physical fulfilment systems. Items which rely on or can benefit from the provision of information to support them are also likely to succeed online, for example, health and beauty supplies. Pharmacy items are mostly non-perishable, easy to ship and generate many repeat purchases, and are therefore ideally suited to this medium. There is an appealing anonymity in shopping online for products which it might be embarrassing to ask for in a high-street pharmacy.

Ultimately, consumers' attitudes towards online shopping will be coloured by their early experiences: if a consumer orders online and the web page takes their credit-card details and then freezes, or the item is out of stock, not delivered on time, damaged in transit and so on, they may be reluctant to try the experience again. Consumer acceptance of e-commerce must also contend with (quite justified) concerns about the preservation of privacy on the Internet. At

Amazon.com, for example, every click a user makes or page a user browses is recorded and used to respond almost instantly with recommendations for related items to buy. While some users may see this as the ultimate in automated personal service, for others the amount of personalised information which can be aggregated in this way is a cause for concern. Indeed, it is likely that escaping the attentions of direct marketers will become ever more difficult for consumers in the future. Falling revenues for online advertising and growing uncertainty about the effectiveness of simple banner advertising on web pages are driving Internet marketers to develop more sophisticated and better targeted models. Commentators suggest that we are likely to see more use of email for direct marketing, while technologies for sending marketing messages to mobile phones are under development.

After the dot com failures of 2000, most analysts now agree that the most successful business models for e-commerce will be those with both physical stores and web sites: what is known as the 'clicks and mortar' model. Traditional retailers are increasingly developing e-commerce strategies, a trend likely to strengthen as household names make use of their brand recognition to increase their online customer base. Online-only businesses are finding that it is not possible to build a brand on the Internet: traditional channels, such as television and print advertising, must be used for building brand awareness. The increasing profile of e-commerce players on traditional media channels is also, however, an important conditioning influence for consumers who are not already online, or who have not so far ventured into online shopping. When it seems like everyone else must be doing their shopping online, consumers are more likely to try it themselves.

References

Australian Bureau of Statistics (2001) *Use of the Internet by Householders*, February, catalogue number 8147.0, Canberra: Australian Bureau of Statistics.

Burton, T. (2000) 'Traffic is still building up', *Sydney Morning Herald*, 5 December: 28.

Campbell, C. (1992) 'The desire for the new: its nature and social location as presented in theories of fashion and modern consumerism', in R. Silverstone and E. Hirsch (eds) *Consuming Technologies*, London: Routledge.

Carrier, J. (1990) 'The symbolism of possession in commodity advertising', *Man* 25(4): 693–706.

Glennie, P. D. and Thrift, N. J. (1992) 'Modernity, urbanism, and modern consumption', *Environment and Planning D – Society & Space* 10(4): 423–43.

Haddon, L. (1988) 'The home computer: the making of a consumer electronic', *Science as Culture* 2: 7–51.

Haddon, L. and Silverstone, R. (1996) *Information and Communication Technologies and the Young Elderly*, SPRU CICT Report Series No. 13. Brighton: Science Policy Research Unit, University of Sussex.

Howarth, B. (2000) 'The dinosaurs are fighting back', *Business Review Weekly*, 15 December: 70.

Lally, E. (2000) *The Computer at Home: Material Culture and the Relationship of Ownership*, Unpublished Ph.D. thesis, University of Western Sydney.

Lunt, P. K. and Livingstone, S. M. (1992) *Mass Consumption and Personal Identity*, Milton Keynes: Open University Press.

McCracken, G. (1988) *Culture and Consumption: New Approaches to the Symbolic Character of Consumer Goods*, Bloomington and Indianapolis: Indiana University Press.

Miller, D. (1987) *Material Culture and Mass Consumption*, Oxford: Blackwell.

Miller, D. and Slater, D. (2000) *The Internet: an Ethnographic Approach*, Oxford: Berg.

Murdock, G., Hartmann, P. and Gray, P. (1992) 'Contextualizing home computing: resources and practices', in R. Silverstone and E. Hirsch (eds) *Consuming Technologies*, London: Routledge.

Robins, K. (1994) 'Forces of consumption: from the symbolic to the psychotic', *Media, Culture & Society* 16: 449–68.

Silverstone, R. and Haddon, L. (1996) 'Design and the domestication of information and communications technologies: technical change and everyday life', in R. Mansell and R. Silverstone (eds) *Communication by Design: the Politics of Communication Technologies*, Oxford: Oxford University Press.

Spigel, L. (1992) *Make Room for TV: Television and the Family Ideal*, Chicago: University of Chicago Press.

Young, J. A. (1992) 'Business 2001', *Financial Executive* 8(6): November/December: 56–7.

10 Consuming youth
Consuming lifestyles

Steven Miles

Introduction

In considering the emergence of 'Consumer Studies' as a discipline in its own right, there may well be an argument for suggesting that research, and most markedly, theory, has become somewhat preoccupied with the more melodramatic aspects of the 'changing consumer'. In this chapter, I want to suggest that this is particularly the case when you consider discussions of young people as consumers. Many social scientists, marketeers and consumer researchers in general have recognised the significance of young people both as an emerging consumer market and as a barometer of social change. However, the social scientific tradition, in particular, has tended to focus on melodramatic expressions of youth. As such, conceptions of youth consumption have, in turn, tended to degenerate into little more than stark generalisations and stereotypical portrayals of youth sub-cultures. The intention of this chapter is to discuss the core role that consumption plays in the everyday construction of young people's lives and how that role may be even more fundamental in a world where youth sub-cultures appear to have dissipated. The contention here which I develop further elsewhere (Miles 2000a) is therefore that the notion of 'lifestyle' may play a particularly invaluable role in Consumer Studies' efforts to address the impact of consumption on young people's lives and vice versa, but also as a means of coming to terms with young people's relationship with social change.

Historical dimensions of youth consumption

In considering the emergence of a consumer society, it is worth noting that young people's experience of a consumer society, at least in a sense, puts them at the forefront of recent social change. In this respect, the work of Osgerby (1998) which I want to discuss in some detail, is of particular interest. Osgerby points out, for instance, that it was in the image of the 'teenager' that post-war mythologies of affluence found their purest manifestation. In this sense, young people have long been at the 'sharp-end' of consumer culture, '... distinguished not only by their youth but by a particular style of consciousness, leisure-oriented consumption' (p. 35). Osgerby goes as far as to argue that the 'teenager' emerged as an ideological terrain upon which post-World War II social change in Britain was constructed. It was in the aftermath of the war that young people began to establish themselves as their own distinct cultural entity and were therefore emerging as an increasingly attractive prospect to the market. In particular, as Osgerby (1998) notes, improved economic prospects saw a growth in demand for unskilled and semi-skilled labour and young people therefore constituted an increased proportion of the workforce. In the post-war years, as Osgerby points out, young people became increasingly associated with affluence, an association that was popularised by Abrams' (1959) work on the teenage consumer, in which he identified a 100% increase in discretionary spending amongst young people. Despite the various problems that Osgerby (1998) identifies with Abrams' (1959) methodology, there is considerable evidence to suggest that young people's earnings did rise in the post-war era and that they were at least experiencing relative prosperity (Osgerby 1998: 26). What is perhaps most interesting about these broad trends is that they constituted what was largely a working-class phenomenon, as ironically at the time the middle classes were taking advantage of longer periods in secondary education and were therefore in some respects excluded from the opportunities that consumption might have afforded them.

By the 1950s and 1960s the youth market was really coming to fruition, as Gaines (1991) suggests, and young people were thus able to exploit a situation where they had increasing spending power, but none of the responsibilities of their parents. Davis (1990) notes that by the 1950s average teenage earnings had increased by over 50% in real terms in comparison to the pre-war years. It was during this period that fashions, entertainments, foods and drinks, specifically aimed at satisfying the 'needs' of the young consumer came on to the market (Stewart 1992). Although young people's spending did not account for a large percentage of overall consumer spending at this time, the fact that their spending tended to be concentrated on non-essential sectors made them an especially attractive proposition to the market. Young people found themselves, as Stewart (1992) points out, in a unique position. They benefited from the newly found affluence of their parents and yet had none of their financial burdens. Within the boundaries provided by the culture industries young people were actively able to carve out their own autonomy – an autonomy that was expressed through distinctive purchasing styles and patterns of consumption (Furlong and Cartmel 1997). In effect, young people continued to take advantage of an economic situation in which manufacturers and service industries demanded their labour, as well as the money being earned by their parents.

Regardless of the class implication of changing patterns of consumption, the 1950s and 1960s undoubtedly witnessed a revolution in consumer youth industries most vocally expressed through the growth of pop music, which went hand in hand with television programmes such as *Ready, Steady, Go!* in transmitting youth lifestyles through forms of consumption. As Ehrenreich *et al.* (1997) point out, rock 'n' roll became the most potent commodity to enter teen consumer culture. Music provided a vehicle through which young people could express themselves according to their musical taste, alongside the appropriate forms of dress and fashion. In this context, the media played a key role in broadening and popularising forms of youth consumption that would have been impossible without it (Osgerby 1998).

Fashion clearly played an important role in the emergence of consumer-based lifestyles during the 1950s and 1960s, notably through sub-cultures such as the Mods, who prioritised notions of style and smartness. But an interesting point here is that consumption played a key role in constructing young people's lives in a negative as well as a positive way. That is, alternative sub-cultures, and most notably rockers, rejected the 'effeminacy' of conspicuous consumption in favour of a sturdy image of masculinity, paradoxically legitimising dominant ideologies of consumerism by operating within those ideological parameters, as Osgerby (1998) suggests. But perhaps the most significant point to make in this respect is as Ehrenreich *et al.* (1997) argue, consumption appeared to provide young people with a resource which allowed them to solidify their identities separate from both child and adult worlds. No longer obliged to take on the façade of little adults, young people could set about expressing their teenhood through their own products, tastes and modes of self-expression.

The commercial expression of teenhood continued throughout the 1970s and by the 1980s it was almost as if consumerism had emerged as a way of life for young people. Not only did it represent a valuable means of self-expression, but it provided a resource for the construction of everyday life. This was very much a two-way relationship in the sense that youth consumption not only solidified young people's relationships, but it also provided economic benefits. For instance, Côté and Allahar (1996) describe the way in which teenage magazines are dominated by advertising beauty-care products, fashion, clothing and other items designed to enhance young people's appearance and popularity. Going on to discuss the work of Evans *et al.* (1991), Côté and Allahar (1996) point out that while overtly these magazines promote self-improvement they do so by suggesting that conforming to fashion trends (via consumption and more specifically self-beautification) is the only legitimate way of pursuing such an improvement.

Despite the above trends and the apparent freedoms they provided for young people, sociologists of youth have tended to be preoccupied with the fact that although from the late 1970s onwards and during a period when the media-driven portrayals of consumer lifestyles were at their most vivid and the pressures to conform to modes of consumption as a form of self-expression were at their most persuasive, in both practical and economic terms young people were actually more vulnerable than they had been for decades. As several authors have noted, young people were beginning to experience increasingly extended transitions, both into employment and adulthood, than was previously the case, thereby undermining their ability to partake in consumerism as a way of life (Jones and Wallace 1992, Roberts 1995). Ironically, in an environment where the British Conservative government were keen to promote an ideology of consumer sovereignty and enterprise, as symbolised by young upwardly mobile professionals, or 'yuppies' as they became known, and at a time when the pressures to consume were intensified, for a lot of young people their freedom to consume was becoming increasingly constrained. But, despite such reservations, young people emerged as an increasingly important market, as at least in broad terms, the disposability of their income became increasingly obvious, until by 1990 research carried out by BMRB found that two-thirds of 15–19-year-olds had some form of a current bank account (Stewart 1992).

The 1990s and 2000s have been no easier for young people in balancing the contradictory offerings of a consumer culture. Indeed, the pressures on young people to consume appear to be in force at an earlier and earlier age. As such, Gunter and Furnham (1998) devote an entire book to a psychological analysis of the young people's market, pointing out that young people are socialised as consumers at an early age, through the simple act of parents taking their children grocery shopping, for instance. Children are 'consumer socialised' not only by their parents, but also by their peers. As such, Gunter and Furnham go on to report some research conducted by McNeal (1992) in which child consumption was found to be influenced by peers at the age of seven. The peer-related pressures on children and young people to consume are clearly massive as Middleton *et al.* (1994) point out, and this can have grave financial implications for less affluent parents struggling to keep pace with the demands of a consumer culture.

Despite the above developments and from a sociological point of view, a broader concern with 'youth culture' in recent years has arguably underestimated the impact of consumption on young people's lives, in so far as it hasn't always considered the nature or significance of that consumption for the individual consumer. To this end I am very sympathetic to an approach that calls for a focus on the consumer as the prime mode of an analysis in this respect. As far as young people are concerned then, there has been a tendency to look at youth culture for youth culture's sake. Research has often focused on youth sub-cultures which have been perceived to be deviant or debased, but also low down the social ladder due to differences in class, race, ethnicity and age (Thornton 1997: 4). Although sociologists and sub-cultural researchers have in effect, used youth as a vehicle for the systematic study of the cultural, by doing so they have labelled and therefore framed, shaped and delineated social formations to the extent that the relationship between the subordinate and the dominant culture (and those that might actively abide by that culture) have become increasingly blurred. As a result, the potential value of addressing the question of consumption as a means of bridging the gap between structural and cultural aspects of young people's lives appears to have been underestimated.

Youth cultural 'transitions'

In the above context youth sub-cultures have been too readily identified as an indicator of social change (and in particular of social ills) by sociologists, and as a result they 'have been given significance and prominence within much broader sociological debates, and beyond the lives of the minority of adolescents who are involved' (Widdicombe and Wooffitt 1995: 7). More specifically, Widdicombe and Wooffitt argue that sociologists have been too theoretical in their treatment of youth sub-cultures and have failed to accommodate actors' own accounts or experiences. This might well be because the methods that sociologists traditionally used to understand youth sub-cultures were bound up with notions of class and resistance. The process of commodification appears to have undermined this analysis in the sense that the oppositional force constituted by young people has arguably been incorporated into the dominant order. Sub-culture, in effect, has arguably been commodified and '... made palatable for popular consumption' (McRobbie 1993: 411). Young people have apparently been subsumed into dominant power structures, but the means by which social scientists have addressed such changes have not been as adaptable as the object of their study. The danger with a sub-cultural approach to youth, then, is that sub-cultural analyses of young people's experience simplify what being a young person is all about and, by doing so, focus on specific spaces in which young people can be themselves at the expense of many other such spaces. More often than not this has tended to involve the media in particular portraying young people as harbingers of moral panic, to the extent that the creative possibilities and the real problems experienced by young people are neglected (Hollands 1995). Most recently there has been a tendency to generalise from discussions of young people's involvement in dance culture from which the current state of youth is 'read off' often without recourse to the complex social contexts in which young people consume (or more likely do not consume). Youth cultures such as dance may not provide the well-entrenched lifestyles that we associate with the sub-cultures of the 1960s and 1970s, and as such may be better conceptualised through the lenses of consumption, which may help us understand more about their everyday significance (Thornton 1997, Miles 2000a).

It is also worth noting, at the other end of the spectrum, that when addressing the nature of young people's lifestyles many commentators have focused on the notion of 'transition': the process by which young people somehow manage to reach 'adulthood'. This reflects the broad concern that in recent years traditional routes into adulthood have apparently become increasingly problematic. The concept of transition therefore focuses on the way that structures affect how young people grow up. However, this overemphasis by sociologists of youth on the 'transition debate' has tended to blinker them from equally important concerns about youth lifestyles and in particular how such lifestyles actively engage with the structural constraints that young people have to contend with from day to day. In some respects the tendency for sociologists to adopt a structural perspective on transitions has been counter-productive, primarily because of its failure to prioritise the actual views, experiences, interests and perspectives of young people as they see them, in favour of bland discussions, most commonly, of trends in employment and education patterns (Roberts 1995, Miles 2000a). The most damaging problem with the 'transition debate' is that it has tended to take young people out of the youth equation.

In other words, the sociology of youth has tended to treat young people as troubled victims of economic and social restructuring without enough recourse to the active ways in which young people negotiate such circumstances in the course of their everyday lives. In this context, 'youth' becomes little more than a term describing an undifferentiated mass of people of similar age experiencing similar things, when what it should be describing is a highly differentiated group of people of similar age subject to a whole variety of experiences depending upon a diverse range of personal circumstances. In effect then, I am suggesting that a social scientific analysis of young people's consumer lifestyles may well help us bring young people back into the study of youth while extending the parameters of consumer research that prioritises *consumers*.

Lifestyles

In the above conceptual context, it could be argued that the apparently declining value of the notion of 'sub-culture' and 'transition' as outlined by Muggleton (1997), demands the use of an alternative conceptual focus, and that that focus should be youth *lifestyles*. In effect, as Chaney (1996) points out, lifestyles can be described as 'functional responses to modernity' (p. 11). Lifestyles then, are an active expression of not only the relationship between the individual and society and structure and agency, but also people's relationship to social change.

In a world where individual lifestyles appear to have more salience in young people's everyday experiences than specific sub-cultural agendas, it is necessary to define exactly what is meant by the term 'lifestyle' and to identify more precisely what sociological value it has as a conceptual tool. It is worth noting for instance, that a lot of the social scientific work on lifestyles has tended to be associated with health, that is, the degree to which people, and quite often young people, are healthy (e.g. Prokhorov *et al.* 1993). This chapter incorporates a broader definition of lifestyles which is more concerned with young people's active expression of a way of life. Perhaps the key concern here then as Reimer (1995) points out is:

> how people act and create meaning in everyday life, especially in those areas where one can act more independently. Lifestyle is ... the specific pattern of everyday activities that characterizes an individual. Each individual's lifestyle is unique: it is not identical to anyone else's. But at the same time, lifestyles orient themselves towards the common and the social .... We choose lifestyles in relation to other people ... Analyses of lifestyles should therefore often address similarities and differences between groups of individuals rather than towards similarities and differences between groups.
>
> (Reimer 1995: 124–5)

In addition, part of the appeal of the notion of lifestyle therefore lies in the way in which it actively addresses the duality of structure and agency; that is the idea that life is actively constituted by the contrary feeling that the individual is both free and yet somehow simultaneously constrained. It is arguably this feeling that lies at the heart of young people's experience of social life and therefore arguably plays a key role in the construction of their identities, something which has perhaps been most effectively discussed by the Swedish researchers, Johansson and Miegel (1992). There may well be a valid argument for suggesting that the notion of lifestyle should be closely bound up with the question of identity. As individuals, people appear to be concerned with establishing a sense of who it is they are, both individually and as part of the wider world (Plummer 1981). In this context, a lifestyle can be described as the outward expression of an identity. Lifestyles are, in effect, lived cultures in which individuals actively express their identities, but in direct relation to their position as regards the dominant culture. Most importantly, the construction of lifestyle is an active social and control process to the extent that, '... each individual may be viewed as a producer of his or her lifestyle, and it is through this creative participation in the normative order that individuals may generate status, meaning and self-esteem' (Plummer 1981: 521). In this context many authors have discussed the ways in which the emergence of a so-called risk society has particularly profound implications for young people's lives, which are increasingly uncertain (Beck 1992, Furlong and Cartmel 1997). Qualifications and training provide no guarantee of a career and the apparent breakdown of traditional support mechanisms alongside the rise of individualism seem to suggest to young people that every decision they make is increasingly significant and more importantly falls on their shoulders and their shoulders alone. Any strategic mistake made in this respect becomes that young individual's personal disaster and he or she is forced to live with the consequences.

In this sort of pressure-cooker environment young people's roles as consumers are arguably increasingly important as a means of escape. This, in turn, reflects broader social changes within which consumerism has come to enjoy a higher social profile, particularly amongst young people who are often at the cutting edge of cultural change. In effect then, lifestyles are constructed *through* consumption, which is in itself the primary indicator of lifestyles in a changing world. Consumption, as Sobel (1981) notes, is 'the activity that best captures what is meant by lifestyle' (p. 47). Perhaps the only study to present a comprehensive discussion of what constitutes young people's lifestyles is that conducted by Johansson and Miegel (1992), who argue that youth culture as a resource for youth lifestyles is both conformist *and* creative, as part of a broader process of identity construction during which they become aware of themselves as autonomous cultural beings. Going on to point out that lifestyle is at least partly an individual phenomenon that cannot necessarily be defined according to limiting conceptions of group taste, Johansson and Miegel argue that lifestyles are 'complex systems consisting of a multitude of relations between individuals' values, attitudes and actions' (p. 292). The argument presented here then is that young people are in actual fact very reflective about their lifestyles and adapt those lifestyles in a self-consciously mobile and yet instrumental fashion.

A particular concern here is that young people are actually more conservative than they may have been in the past precisely because they no longer appear to have anything to protest against, and that consumption may actively reinforce such 'conservativeness'. Indeed, it has been argued, by authors such as Calcutt (1998), that everybody is alienated and, as such, young people do not have anything particularly rebellious to say any more. Young people are, in effect, looking for self-definition, but have nothing to define themselves against. From this point of view, even if the term 'counter-culture' ever existed then it is pretty much redundant. Any expression of subversiveness has effectively been transmuted into a commodifiable form. However much young people may believe that they can change the world they appear to have very little opportunity to do so, because the political world in which they live is apparently a grey non-committal world with little substance, which can barely be defined itself. In this context who can a young person possibly define him or her self against? Sociologists have in recent years failed to come to terms with such contradictions, largely as a result of an apparent reluctance to address the actual life experiences of the people they are studying, but at times do not appear to be studying closely enough partly because they seem unable to comprehend the changing nature of the world which young people inhabit (see Wyn and White 1997). The first step should involve moving beyond a mind-set in which young people's identities are necessarily oppositional. From this point of view, consumption can be used in all sorts of ways and, as such, young people's patterns of consumption can just as easily buttress the status quo as rebel against it.

In light of the above discussion it is tempting to concur with Drotner's (1991) contention that young people amount to a sort of 'avant-garde' of consumption in the sense that in many ways they appear to be the most pioneering sector of consumers, inasmuch as at times they even go as far as to consume the 'unconsumable', or rather they commodify virtually anything. It is also worth noting Drotner's (1991) point that young people in the 1990s appear to be preoccupied with creating themselves and therefore have particularly well-developed needs for aesthetic consumption, needs transmitted to them via television and the media, for instance. They are indeed 'the pioneers of consumer society' (Drotner 1991: 49). This reflects a paradoxical situation where young people are increasingly culturally independent in terms of the free time and money at their disposal and yet they are increasingly dependent upon adults economically, as a result of delayed transitions into the workplace. This point in itself serves to reiterate the key role played in the construction of social life by the relationship between structure and agency. In this context, young people simply cannot afford to consume entirely individualistically. I do, however, agree with Stewart's (1992) suggestion that what characterises young people in terms of their core values is that, above all, they are being incorporated into the mainstream. For the majority of young people, as Stewart (1992) points out, there appears to be very little left for them to rebel against. Give a young person the opportunity to drive his or her first car and he or she will be more than happy (Veash and O'Sullivan 1997). In this context, young people are independent of mind and yet conformist in a world where 'the individual experiences and the influences individuals are exposed to are becoming increasingly homogenous' (Stewart 1992: 224). In essence then the study of consumer lifestyles provides a measure of the ways in which the experience of 'youth', assuming we can even begin to contemplate the existence of any such period in an individual's life, has been subsumed into the mainstream.

There are all sorts of factors involved in an assessment of young people as consumers, such as gender, ethnicity, disability, sexual orientation, geographical location and social class (Morrow and Richards 1996). In this context, as I suggested above, Paul Willis's (1990) influential discussion of the culturally creative experience of young people as consumers provides an invaluable insight into the nature of youth consumption. His attempt to come to terms with the meanings with which individuals endow consumer culture represented a significant advance in the field of youth studies. However, Willis (1990) undoubtedly overestimated the degree to which young people can assert their own agency within the frameworks that consumption provides. Young people do not have the advantage of complete freedom of access and cannot freely construct meanings. Youth consumption is far more complex than this sort of approach tends to imply. Consumption is not always an ordered and easily explained activity. Having said that, lessons can be learned from Willis's situated analysis of young people's experiences of consumption and in this context it is important to consider how various groups of young women (and men) are represented in specific contexts as consumers, and especially as disordered consumers, and the ways in which such representations and the associated regime management and treatment are gendered, sexualised, racialised and class-specific (Griffin 1997: 16).

Consumers in context

In calling for an emphasis on consumers as opposed to consumption, my particular concern is that consumer lifestyles are addressed in context and that forms of consumption are of particular interest in so far as what they tell us about consumers' lives beyond the act or experience of consumption. For instance, I have recently been involved in a European Union funded project on 'the performing arts and risky transitions into adulthood' with colleagues from Germany and Portugal (Banha *et al.* 2000). This research was primarily concerned with evaluating the benefits of three unconventional youth training programmes, the aim of which was to give young people some of the necessary skills to be able to operate in the workplace. It soon became clear, however, that these training programmes were about more than the straightforward acquisition of skills. They provided the foundations upon which young people could, in effect, 'find themselves'. But what was interesting about this research from a consumption point of view was that patterns of consumption actually played a key role in facilitating young people's negotiation of their 'transitions'. In other words, these young people used everyday forms of consumption to develop communal aspects of meaning. In struggling to find who it is they are, young people use consumption as a resource that actively constructs broader patterns of social and power relationships.

This research involved the evaluation of two theatre-based performance projects and a circus school. We found that as young people became acclimatised to these training programmes, they, in effect, developed communally appropriate lifestyles. They therefore consumed and behaved in particular ways that befitted both the group as a whole and the 'secure space' in which that group operated. The training that the young people received actively engaged with their lifestyles and in doing so reaffirmed those lifestyles. For these young people, fashion and leisure were clearly not trivial activities but provided an important background in which young people make key decisions about their futures. These young people therefore created a niche that was both integrative and individual. In this sense, youth lifestyles provided an arena within which young people can at least attempt to assert their own agency. This agency is a reflection of young people's broader relationship with social structures and the transition process in general (Miles 2000a). In this context, young people participate in education and training, they make decisions, while trying to keep their options open. And they engage in youth cultures in order to stylise and symbolise the decisions that they take, as a means, in turn, of finding meanings through which they can cope with life in general. These 'solutions' may not always lead to social integration and can equally be one-dimensional or counter-productive. Young people may, for instance, feel insulated from broader structural conditions by partaking in a particular 'sub-cultural' lifestyle. But, by doing so, they may simply be prolonging their own exclusion. The point is, however, that they are using aspects of consumption as a means of at least *trying* to take control (Banha *et al.* 2000). Chapitô, the circus school based in Lisbon, Portugal, for instance, provided a social space within which a specific lifestyle was made available to young people. Those young people attending the school therefore dressed in a particular way as a means of visibly asserting their membership of the group, and at another level as a means of illustrating their ability to cope, as individuals, with the demands of complex transitions. Young people at Chapitô use hair-styles, clothes, body-piercings and tattoos as a means of identifying themselves as 'belonging' to Chapitô, but also as a means of demonstrating their ability to cope with the rapidity of social change. In this sense, forms of consumption provide a means by which young people can begin to 'find themselves' within the broader structures to which they have to respond.

In the above context, I want to suggest that the ideological impact of consumer lifestyles plays a key role. Regardless of the creative nature of the meanings that young people invest in their consumer lifestyles, the suggestion here is that social change has created a particular form of consciousness amongst young people which legitimises consumerism as a way of life (Miles 2000b). Young people may get as much as they want out of what they consume, but, by its very nature, such consumption will inevitably buttress the status quo. Consumer capitalism thrives inasmuch as it suggests that consumers can endow meaning in consumer goods completely freely. A young person can only be accepted as an individual within the cultural contexts laid down for him or her, bearing in mind the limitations laid down on those contexts by broader structural inputs. It is almost as if an individual can offset the risks of everyday life by consuming in similar ways to their peers; the only alternative being to face those risks head on. Consumerist ideology works because it infiltrates our everyday common-sense world. Ideology has in effect become materialised, most visibly perhaps in young people's lifestyles, and as such, Žižek (1989) believes that we are living a lie which, and because we live it, becomes real (Hawkes 1996). This, then, relates to what Thomas and Thomas (1928) say about reality amounting to what the individual *perceives* to be reality, and in turn to what Dittmar (1992) refers to as the materialism–idealism paradox; that is the commonly accepted idea that every individual has a unique personality independent of material circumstances, alongside the paradoxical notion that material possessions are central regulators, not only of large-scale social processes, but also of interpersonal relations and impressions. In a so-called post-modern world an individual may lose his or her subjectivity amidst a plethora of lifestyle choices, and yet the society in which he or she lives puts considerable emphasis on the uniqueness of each and every person. This contradiction underlies young people's everyday experience of rapid social change.

As an ideology, consumerism has, in a historical sense, increasingly come to affect mundane and everyday aspects of young people's lives, and young people will subsequently and inevitably reproduce dominant power structures, while often, as a result, feeling a sense of social exclusion. After all, 'The commercial links are inescapable and trenchant. All symbolic materials are supplied under determinant conditions – not from the voice of God' (Willis 1990: 130). At one level this means that young people at the turn of the century are actually more about continuity than they are about change. Rebellion appears to have given way to conformity to the extent that 'youth cultures' arguably no longer stand for the same principles as they did in the past.

But the more important point here is that – regardless of the above power dimension – at the everyday level, ideology is a negotiated ideology, and it is the way in which such ideologies are negotiated in everyday settings that is of broader interest to 'Consumer Studies'. Ultimately, the personal factor, as Swingewood (1991) notes, is a constitutive factor of every social occurrence, 'social science cannot remain on the surface ... but must reach the actual human experiences and attitudes which constitute the full, live and actual reality beneath the formal organisation of social institutions' (Thomas and Znaniecki 1927: 1834).

The essential argument underlying this paper as a whole is that young people are having to deal with the dilemmas of rapid social, cultural and structural change as a routine part of their everyday lives, and that a primary means by which they deal with this situation is through the maintenance of consumer lifestyles. Consumer lifestyles effectively provide a vehicle or a currency through which fluid identities are constructed. A consumer imperative has therefore emerged as a fundamental means of stabilising young people's lives at the turn of the century. Such stability is not manifested in the form of a deep-rooted sense of sameness, but in a flexible, mutable and diverse sense of identity within which consumerism appears to present the only viable resource. Young people's lifestyles are therefore concerned with the *continuity of change*. This assertion has significant implications for the future of consumer studies. In particular, it raises doubts about the legitimacy of a 'post-modern' conception of consumption which, I would argue, often appears to be more concerned with being 'post-modern' and in fulfilling some notion of what it means to write in a post-modern fashion than addressing the actualities of post-modern consumption as they exist in everyday life (Miles 1999).

As far as youth consumption is concerned, young people may not have 'real' economic power, as Jones and Martin (1999) suggest, but what power they do have they use in the active construction of their own lives and their own everyday relationships. At least from this point of view the degree of power they impart on the marketplace is virtually irrelevant. I would not for one minute dispute Bynner *et al.*'s (1997) contention that the experience of many young people is characterised by an increasing sense of anxiety, depression and even despair. But when he asks whether or not young people have the necessary human and social capital to succeed in a post-modern world, I would have to say, yes, they most certainly do, and consumer lifestyles have an important role to play in dealing with social change in this context. Young people do not play simply for fun but to feel that they belong in a world which often appears to legislate actively against such a feeling.

Consumption isn't or at least shouldn't be about the melodramatic. Consumers often consume for the most instrumental of reasons. These reasons may amount to a complex interplay of ideology and identity construction, but at their core lies the need for a sense of stability. Young people use consumption as a means of establishing lifestyles that make the world a manageable place. In a sense then, 'Consumer Studies' has itself created a world in which the object of its studies, the consumer, has been made unmanageable (Gabriel and Lang 1995). We may perceive forms of consumption to be diverse, fragmented and 'post-modern', when the opposite may actually be true. But one thing is for certain: there is a need to move away from amorphous discussions of consumer culture in order to develop a more grounded focused study of how consumers consume and why. Consumer lifestyles are of interest not purely for their own sake, but perhaps more importantly, as a 'way in'; as a means by which broader questions of social change can begin to be addressed. A study of young people as consumers illustrates the paradoxical nature of consumption. Only when the consumer is placed at the heart of Consumer Research, in its broadest sense, will the extent of that paradox be fully realised.

References

Abrams, M. (1959) *The Teenage Consumer*, London: Press Exchange.

Banha, R. B., do Carmo Gomes, M., Miles, S., Pohl, A., Stauber, B. and Walther, A. (2000) '"Coming out of the shell ...." Advantages of performing arts in the context of risky youth transitions', Unpublished report submitted to the European Union.

Beck, U. (1992) *Risk Society: Towards a New Modernity*, London: Sage.

Bynner, J., Ferri, E. and Shepherd, P. (1997) *Twenty-Something in the 1990s: Getting On, Getting By, Getting Nowhere*, Aldershot: Ashgate.

Calcutt, A. (1998) *Arrested Development: Popular Culture and the Erosion of Adulthood*, London: Cassell.

Chaney, D. (1996) *Lifestyles*, London: Routledge.

Côté, J. and Allahar, A. L. (1996) *Generation on Hold: Coming of Age in the Late Twentieth Century*, London: New York University Press.

Dittmar, H. (1992) *The Social Psychology of Material Possessions: to Have is to Be*, Hemel Hempstead: Harvester Wheatsheaf.

Drotner, K. (1991) *At skabe sig – selv. Ungdom, æsteik, pœdagogik*, København: Glydendsal.

Ehrenreich, B., Hess, E. and Jacobs, G. (1997) 'Beatlemania: a sexually deviant consumer culture?', in K. Gelder and K. Thornton, *The Subcultures Reader*, 532–36, London: Routledge.

Evans, E., Rutberg, J. and Sather, C. (1991) 'Content analysis of contemporary teen magazines for adolescent females', *Youth and Society* 23: 99–120.

Furlong, A. and Cartmel, F. (1997) *Young People and Social Change*, Buckingham: Open University Press.

Gabriel, Y. and Lang, T. (1995) *The Unmanageable Consumer*, London: Sage.

Gaines, D. (1991) *Teenage Wasteland: Suburbia's Dead End Kids*, New York: Pantheon.

Griffin, C. (1997) 'Troubled teens: managing disorders of transition and consumption', *Feminist Review* 55: 4–21.

Gunter, B. and Furnham, A. (1998) *Children as Consumers: a Psychological Analysis of the Young People's Market*, London: Routledge.

Hawkes, D. (1996) *Ideology*, London: Routledge.

Hollands, R. (1995) *Friday Night, Saturday Night*, Newcastle: Newcastle University Press.

Johansson, T. and Miegel, F. (1992) *Do the Right Thing: Lifestyle and Identity in Contemporary Youth Culture*, Malmo: Graphic Systems.

Jones, G. and Martin, C. D. (1997) *The Social Context of Spending in Youth*, Centre for Educational Sociology Briefing, University of Edinburgh, No. 11, June.

Jones, G. and Wallace, C. (1992) *Youth, Family and Citizenship*, Buckingham: Open University Press.

McNeal, J. U. (1992) *Kids as Customers*, New York: Lexington Books.

McRobbie, A. (1993) 'Shut up and dance: youth culture and changing modes of femininity', *Cultural Studies* 7: 406–26.

Middleton, S., Ashworth, K. and Walker, R. (1994) *Family Fortunes: Pressures on Parents and Children in the 1990s*, London: CPAG.

Miles, S. (1999) *Consumerism as a Way of Life*, London: Sage.

—— (2000a) *Youth Lifestyles in a Changing World*, Buckingham: Open University Press.

—— (2000b) 'Post-modern consumer research at the crossroads: a pluralistic seduction?', *CMC: Consumption, Markets and Culture*, 3(2): 135–64.

Morrow, V. and Richards, M. (1996) *Transitions to Adulthood: a Family Matter?*, York: York Publishing Services.

Muggleton, D. (1997) 'The sub-culturalist', in S. Redhead, D. Wynne and J. O'Connor, *The Clubcultures Reader*, Oxford: Blackwell.

Osgerby, B. (1998) *Youth in Britain Since 1945*, Oxford: Blackwell.

Plummer, K. (1981) 'Going gay: identities, life cycles, and lifestyles in the male gay world', in J. Hart and D. Richardson (eds) *The Theory and Practice of Homosexuality*, London: Routledge.

Prokhorov, A., Perry, C., Kelder, S. and Klepp, K.-I. (1993) 'Lifestyle values of adolescents: results from Minnesota Heart Health Youth Program', *Adolescence* 28: 111.

Reimer, B. (1995) 'Youth and modern lifestyles', in J. Förnas and G. Bolin (eds) *Youth Culture in Late Modernity*, London: Sage.

Roberts, K. (1995) *Youth Employment in Modern Britain*, Oxford: Oxford University Press.

Sobel, M. (1981) *Lifestyle and Social Structure: Concepts, Definitions, Analyses*, New York: Academic Press.

Stewart, F. (1992) 'The adolescent as consumer', in J. C. Coleman and C. Warren-Anderson (eds) *Youth Policy in the 1990s: the Way Forward*, London: Routledge.

Swingewood, A. (1991) *A Short History of Sociological Thought*, London: Macmillan.

Thomas, W. I. and Thomas, D. S. (1928) *The Child in America: Behavior Problems and Programs*, New York: Knopf.

Thomas, W. I. and Znaniecki, F. (1927) *The Polish Peasant in Europe and America*, vol. 2, Chicago: Chicago University Press.

Thornton, S. (1997) *Club Cultures: Music, Media and Subcultural Capital*, Cambridge: Polity.

Veash, N. and O'Sullivan, J. (1997) 'Forget about Swampy. All they want is their own car', *The Independent* 19 November: 5.

Widdicombe, S. and Wooffitt, R. (1995) *The Language of Youth Subcultures*, London: Harvester Wheatsheaf.

Willis, P. (1990) *Common Culture*, Milton Keynes: Open University Press.

Wyn, J. and White, R. (1997) *Rethinking Youth*, London: Sage.

Žižek, S. (1989) *The Sublime Object of Ideology*, New York: Verso.

11 Changing consumer

Changing disciplinarity

Russell W. Belk

Introduction: the changing consumption setting

I used to wonder at the changes that my grandmother, born in 1900, saw in her life. She went from going to grade school on horseback to riding in automobiles and aeroplanes. She and her generation saw the introduction and adoption of radio, movies, television, home photography, telephones, electricity, jets, rockets, atomic energy, world wars, space exploration, the rise and fall of Communism, the rise of consumerism, modern art, credit cards, hi-fidelity, computers, and the considerable shaping and reshaping of the world's nations. Yet with all the change she saw before she died at age 94, my grand-daughter, born in 1999, will undoubtedly see far, far more change during her lifetime. And more and more of this change will involve and be understood through consumption.

Today's consumer faces a world of unprecedented consumption opportunities. More of us than ever before can almost instantaneously call up information, people and places that for practical purposes were inaccessible only a decade ago. If a person or place that we call up on our computer screen looks interesting, we can press a few more buttons and procure airline tickets so we can physically visit them. Ordering the material ingredients that define a consumer lifestyle (increasingly conflated with a human lifestyle), has also never been easier. We can manage finances and investments, borrow money, pay bills, gamble, and find jobs from the comfort of our home computers. We can work, educate ourselves, and shop without leaving home. We can meet mates, enjoy works of art and music, download pornography, and go to online sites where we can chat and exchange information and opinions with those who share common consumption interests with us. We can follow our favourite sports team, sing the praises of our favourite automobile, play a computer game with someone in Bangkok, or get mutual support for a consumer boycott without getting up from our chairs. We can play with virtual pets that convincingly imitate neonatal features, learn and respond favourably to our attentions. We can drive bikes or cars equipped with electronic maps that show us where we are and tell us where to go. When these devices fail us, we may wonder not only where we are, but who we are.

Stepping outside the comforts of home we can increasingly travel anywhere we wish. World travel is faster and more affordable to more people than ever before. There are more entertainments, festivals, concerts, sporting events, theatres, museums, shopping malls, theme parks, and potential tourist destinations than were previously imaginable. If we are hungry then there are more restaurants with more diverse and more global cuisines than at any prior point in human history. Religious choices also abound, and they too are becoming increasingly involved with consumption. For example, the Caprice resort hotel in Turkey caters strictly to Islamists, and features separate swimming pools for men and women. Material Christianity is nothing new, but it has proliferated in recent years (Brouwer, Gifford and Rose 1996, Sherman 1997, McDannell 1998).

The landscape of our world also seems to be becoming increasingly branded and commoditised. We need not go to Las Vegas to realise that experiences are increasingly based on grand spectacles. Neither do we need to do much more than step outside our doors to realise that the world is becoming more multicultural and global. If we step a bit father outside our doors we soon realise that the world is also becoming more polarised between haves and have-nots, both within and across cultures and nations. The current era is not only one in which we have been faced with dramatic changes in consumption opportunities, but the pace of these changes is unprecedented and continues to accelerate.

Yet all of these changes are really changes in our environments and societies rather than necessarily changes in us as consumers. So it is as well to ask how the consumer, faced with such momentous choice, affluence, polarisation and fragmentation, adapts to these changes. What do we do with these opportunities, burdens of choice, or illusions of choice (see Warde, Chapter 2)? What freedoms and costs do they entail? And how do we benefit or suffer from living in a world of abundant choices? The answers to questions such as these will emerge from the growing number of researchers, analysts, businesses, artists and scholars who are devoting themselves to the study of consumption. Some of these answers will in turn affect the consumption choices that increasingly define our world. These changes in our consumption environment will then further impact on us as consumers. And this will no doubt lead to further changes in our enquiries about consumption.

So consumers, consumption theory and the practices of marketing and consumption are all increasingly interdependent as well. One example of this is a new online journal edited by Simone Pettigrew entitled the *Journal of Research for Consumers* (http://www.jrconsumers.com). The journal is targeted at both consumers and consumer researchers. Businesses likely will also make use of it as well. Another example of the increased inter-penetration of consumption in our lives is the increasing number of museum exhibits and special exhibitions devoted to the topic. Just one illustration is the recent highly popular Brand.New exhibition at the Victoria & Albert Museum in London (Pavitt 2000). The show included conferences involving academics, designers, business firms and museum personnel. The popularity of the show also offers further testimony to the importance of branded consumption in our lives. There was a show of brands in modern art of the twentieth century at the Museum of Modern Art a decade earlier (Varnedoe and Gopnik 1990), but the V&A show moved brands themselves – rather than art featuring advertising and brands – to centre stage. Brands have become culture.

Advertising has become our source of myths. And consumption has become our focus of rituals through which we search for the sacred (Belk *et al*. 1989).

In order to summarise some of the changes taking place in this interrelated set of phenomena, my point of entry is to focus on the changing role of academic disciplines studying consumption. By identifying some of the major trends surfacing in the academic study of consumption, we should be able to see evidence of the changing consumer and the changing consumption environment more clearly.

Trends in Consumer Research

Consumer Research is growing in appeal to many disciplines

The last two decades of the twentieth century saw the demise of serious opposition to the spread of global capitalism. As Eastern Europe turned to capitalism, the Soviet Union dissolved, China turned to 'market socialism', and India discarded protectionism and reopened its markets, the world saw market capitalism become the way of the world. These fundamental changes in the world marketplace were caused in no small part by the consumer desires stimulated as the world grew smaller and global communications made consumption the frame through which more and more of us assess our relative places in the world. Despite the subsequent decline of material well-being for most of Eastern Europe and the former Soviet Union, the bursting of the Asian economic bubble, and the warfare and ethnic violence in Eastern Europe, the Middle East, Africa, and parts of Asia and South America, the past decade has also brought unprecedented affluence and peace to most of the Western world. Thatcherism, Reaganism, Dengism, World Bank structural readjustment programmes, and other political and economic policies helped make free-market economies an inevitable force in the world. The hidden engine of this force was expanding consumer desire.

Within this global rise of consumer desire and market economies, it is not terribly surprising that a growing number of academic disciplines have begun to devote a growing amount of research and analyses to consumption. In addition, as Alan Warde demonstrates for sociology in the present volume, there has been a dramatic shift away from Marxist, neo-Marxist, and critical perspectives on consumption and marketing and toward much more positive views. A large number of disciplines have adopted a consumer behaviour research agenda, including sociology, marketing, psychology, anthropology, communications, sports studies, history, women's studies, queer studies, semiotics, political science, economics, art history, tourist studies, museum studies, popular culture, architecture, family studies, media studies, geography, leisure studies, technology studies, design, philosophy, religion, American studies, advertising, psychiatry, psychoanalysis, culture studies, literary criticism, and others. Within marketing departments, a majority of doctoral theses are now focused on consumer behaviour (Folkes 2001). In anthropology, Miller (1995b) argues that consumption may be replacing kinship as the field's central conceptual focus. In addition to the current interdisciplinary volume on consumption, there are a variety of others including Benson (2000),

Brown and Turley (1997), Falk and Campbell (1997), Edgell *et al.* (1996), Hearn and Roseneil (1999), Miller (1995a), Sherry (1995) and Sulkunen *et al.* (1997).

Arguably such shifts in the centrality of consumption in the social sciences and the humanities reflect the increasing centrality of consumption in our societies. A speculative historical path has led from a central human focus on religion in life, to the apotheosis of science, technology, romantic love, and the cult of the child within the family. But during the late twentieth century, the gradual ascendance of discretionary consumption eclipsed all of these for the average consumer. The locus of our identities has at the same time shifted from production to consumption. Verbally we still regard it as more socially acceptable to ask someone 'What do you do?' rather than 'What do you own/what have you experienced?'. But non-verbally, few if any of us fail to notice and predicate our judgements of others upon such consumption goods as clothing, cars, homes, grooming, electronic products (witness pagers, cell phones, PDAs, digital cameras, and so forth), movies seen, places visited, foods eaten, type of computer, athletic equipment brands and models, preferences in art and music, and any number of other elements of consumption. And, in a largely anonymous society, the inferences we draw about others based on consumption are less about their social classes than their consumer lifestyles, gender identities and ages (Costa 1994, Sparke 1995, de Grazia and Furlough 1996, Wardlow 1996, Martinez and Shapiro 1997, Kates 1998, Lukenbill 1999, Scanlon 2000). This point is borne out in the present volume in the chapters by Simone Pettigrew on Australian images of men and women based on choice of alcoholic beverages, Steve Spittle on expressive aspects of room design seen in a popular British television series, Ben Crewe on the rise of glossy men's magazines and Steven Miles on young people's consumption lifestyles. At the same time, Alan Warde (this volume) provides an insightful argument that consumer goods are now far less able than they once were to demarcate class and group boundaries. But while goods themselves may be less able to demonstrate and define class, the cultural capital that comes from knowledge about these goods may nevertheless remain significant in the way we relate to others (Holt 1998).

We can also detect the rising importance of consumption in analyses of lifestyle advertising in the chapter by Janice Winship. While the chapter by Paul du Gay and Liz McFall demonstrates that emotional advertising appeals are nothing new, the emphasis on constellations of products as the primary basis for defining styles of living is (Solomon 1988, McCracken 1991). The importance of advertising in people's lives and lifestyles is further emphasised in a study by Mark Ritson and Richard Elliott (1999) of product-related conversations in a British high school. They found that brand advertising was not only a frequent topic producing conversational capital, but also was incorporated in social interactions, group rituals, and as a metaphor for understanding daily life. Other recent work has focused on what Daniel Boorstin (1973) called consumption communities – groups that identify with each other on the basis of their shared loyalty toward a certain brand. For instance, Muniz and O'Guinn (2001) found that Saab automobiles, Macintosh computers and Ford Broncos were cult brands in a community of American consumers and that as community markers these brands were keys to a shared consciousness involving rituals, traditions and even a sense of moral responsibility.

A good example of the insinuation of consumer goods into the fabric of our lives is the chapter by Elaine Lally, documenting the 'domestication' of computers so that they have become a familiar part of our home environment. Other studies have examined how life on the Internet allows us to adopt new identities (Turkle 1995) and new fantasy lives (Pesce 2000). As Miller and Slater (2000) find in Trinidad, these uses of the Internet are not restricted to the more affluent world, although there remains a 'digital divide' in the world (Silverstone and Hirsch 1992, Miles 1998). While Lally (present volume), I think correctly, argues that the replacement of the concept of the information superhighway with the concept of cyberspace has aided the domestication of the computer and its increasing acceptance in our lives she also argues that besides their hope for a better future through technology, computers provoke our fear that we will lose control to these machines. One possible reaction is to show that we can successfully battle the computer within the competitive arena of the computer or video game (Sutton-Smith 1986). Computer and video games no doubt serve other purposes as well (Fine 1983), but it is telling that they have become a bigger business than the film industry (Pesce 2000).

Another very different reaction to the increased presence of computers in our lives is to seek transcendence through our interaction with these machines. While our awe of the personal computer *per se* (Park-Curry and Jiobu 1982) may have dissipated, various recent analyses have provocatively explored the search for God in cyberspace (Heim 1993, Cobb 1998, Davis 1998, Noble 1999, Wertheim 1999). Thus do we see the cycle of our deepest beliefs coming full circle from the sacred in religion, romantic love, and the family, to the profane in science, technology, and consumption, and back to the sacred through our deification and sacralisation of certain aspects of our consumption (Belk *et al.* 1989).

Consumer Research is becoming more global

As the world becomes smaller and transnational corporations become larger and more ubiquitous, Consumer Research has also become more global. Consider some of the recent volumes presenting Consumer Research from Africa (Burke 1996, Weiss 1996), China (Davis 2000), Japan (Tobin 1992, Clammer 1997), Russia (Boym 1994, Barker 1999), Eastern Europe (Shultz *et al.* 1994, Stan 1997), Asia (Robison and Goodman 1996, Jiny 2000, Pinches 1999, Beng-Huat 2000), and elsewhere (Costa and Bamossy 1995, Miller 1995b, Howes 1996, Steerns 2001). Clearly, it is not just the more affluent world that has come to recognise consumption as a fundamental social process (Ger and Belk 1996b). Consumption studies find that, if anything, concern with consumption may be more critical in the less affluent world. In a quantitative study of materialism in a dozen countries in the early 1990s, Güliz Ger and I found that Romania scored ahead of the US and all Western European countries and that the Ukraine was only slightly behind (Ger

Belk 1996a). Consumer desires in the so-called Third World sometimes ironi-
result in sacrifices of 'necessities' like food in order to afford 'luxuries' like
erators, which remain empty due to lack of funds for stocking them (Belk
19..). Having a television is frequently a higher priority than health care.

Besides growing recognition and study of consumer culture around the world,
an increasing focus of study is how consumer desires are changing as a result or a
part of globalisation. For instance, a volume by Miller (1993) argues that
Christmas is becoming our first global holiday. It is not the Christian aspects of the
holiday that are gaining salience. Rather it is the consumption aspects of the
holiday that are driving its popular acceptance in places like Tokyo, Hong Kong,
Singapore, and Istanbul. As a result, Santa Claus and Ronald McDonald are now
more widely known than Christ. The forces of globalisation are also played out in
increasingly common and far-flung international tourism. Urry (1990) calls the
consumption practices of global tourism 'post-tourism', a term by which he means
to emphasise the phenomenon of playfully consuming the world's cultures,
knowing full well that they represent only a hyper-real and staged authenticity
(MacCannell 1999). But from the point of view of locals, foreign tourists from the
more affluent world are walking billboards for global consumption-based lifestyles.

Even without an influx of foreign tourists, few places in the world are now out
of reach of the influences of television, films, and radio, and, increasingly, the
Internet. Television is being adopted much more rapidly in the less affluent world
than it was in the more affluent world. The penetration rate of colour television in
the larger Chinese cities is now virtually 100% (Li 1998). Thus far, it appears that
the spread of the Internet will be even faster. While it is wrong to assume that
global media and diffusion of Western films and programmes necessarily lead to a
globalisation of consumer ideologies and desires (Liebes and Katz 1990, Miller
1990, Wilk 1993), it cannot be denied that there is movement in this direction.

It may have seemed for a while in the early 1990s that global consumer
lifestyles were an inevitability. Nevertheless, subsequent experiences suggest
that various forms of resistance, creolisation and localism are likely to oppose
such a possibility. Although some of the branded ingredients may be the same,
they are construed and used differently in different cultures. As Watson's (1997)
book on McDonald's restaurants in East Asia demonstrates, while McDonald's
influences local cultures and lifestyles, it must also adapt to these cultures in
order to be successful. This makes scenarios like the following implausible:

A tale of archaeology in the year 3001

Archaeologist Gucci Toyota Rolex, a recent graduate of Ralph Lauren
University (once Karl Marx University) in Budapest, sits in his IBM sensato-
rium seeking clues that will help him understand the obscure origins of the
major World holidays. He believes that some of these holidays, including
Coke Day, Elvis Day, Saint Johnny Walker Day, the Day of the Levi's, Sony
Feel-Man Day, and the Feast of the Seven-Eleven, may have originated almost
a millennium ago in the 20th or 21st century. But the evidence is far from

clear. No major catastrophe or war has obliterated the relevant data. In fact, the period since the likely origin of these holidays is now known as the Pax McDonald's, due to the extended period of world peace that was ushered in after McDonald's first entered what were then known as China, the Soviet Union, and Eastern Europe. This signalled the peaceful global conquest by Saint Ronald McDonald, at a time when McDonald's still sold only food products and the people of the earth spoke a variety of languages. No, the lack of data is instead because at some point after the development of United World Government and Entertainment Incorporated, history simply lacked any tension to make it interesting. There was also convincing evidence that history was a source of discontent and neuroses. So when people learned to stop recording the trivia of daily and yearly events, history stopped as well.

As a result, even the details of Saint Ronald's birth and life are lost in the mists of antiquity, along with the biographies of lesser deities such as Colonel Sanders, the Michelin Man, and Mickey Mouse. Although he accepts the catechism that history is bunk, Gucci hopes that if the roots of current celebrations and their patron saints can be pieced together, this proof of divine inspiration will help stop a strange sociopathology spreading among a growing number of the people of the earth: heretic asceticism! Not only does this barbaric and nihilistic cult refuse to worship Saint Ronald, they reject all of our major holidays and refuse to consume the associated products and services to which they are constitutionally entitled. Recently they have also begun to boycott such sacred sites as Marlboro Country, Ford Country, Sesame Street, Disney Universe, and even McDonaldland. What is worse, they fail to show any enthusiasm for the games, even when such arch rivals as Nissan and the Toyota contest. Obviously, such hereticism is dangerous and threatens not only the economy but our essential values. Gucci has no desire to kindle nostalgia for a long dead past, but by returning to the origins of our major world holidays, perhaps the non-believers can be made to accept the legends celebrated by these holidays and their apathetic and sacrilegious behaviour can be stopped before it spreads farther.

(after Belk 1996)

Just as the force of global corporations seems to move us in the direction depicted in this scenario, these corporations also wish to seem local and familiar by adapting to local cultures in such a way that resistance and opposition are minimised (Belk 2000). This, together with the opposition that does emerge, help to make the scenario above a highly unlikely fantasy.

Consumer Research is becoming more socially focused

While sociology and anthropology have recognised for a long time that consumption is not simply about person–thing relationships, consumer studies within commerce and business schools have only recently begun to realise that consumption is about relationships between people as mediated by things. Due to the influence of economics and psychology, marketing academics have focused on understanding consumption by investigating individual attitudes, needs and perceptions without appreciating that all of these are socially constructed. If consumer behaviour were simply about people satisfying themselves by acquiring and consuming things, our meals would be little more than what Douglas and Isherwood (1996) describe as 'a class of solitary feeding, where the person wolfs or bolts his food, probably standing by his refrigerator in his overcoat' (p. 44). But the fact that instead we prefer to savour our food at a set table or expensive restaurant in the company of others, suggests that there is much more to eating than merely consuming individually nutritious bodily supplements (Finkelstein 1989, Slater 1997, Warde 1997, Warde and Martens 2000). Likewise our uses of smells and tastes are not biologically predetermined, but are largely socially and culturally constituted (Corbin 1988, Classen *et al.* 1994).

If consumption experiences were purely about the individual and the product being consumed, then stage plays and cinema would have been replaced by television, videotapes and DVDs; concerts and musical performances by radio, records, tapes, CDs and MP3; and religious services, confessions, weddings and funerals by the Internet. Sporting events are probably better seen and interpreted by a hearing or viewing broadcast of them rather than by sitting in the stands, but the group experience of being a fan in the stands would be missing (Miles 1998). Canned TV laughter tries to simulate this group feeling for a comedy, but somehow it is not quite the same. Likewise, if gift-giving were simply about economic exchange or redistribution of wealth, it would not exist. We could far better satisfy our material desires by using the money and gift-selection effort we expend on others to instead acquire things for ourselves. But gift-giving is a symbolic and social exchange that conveys feelings of belonging, love, support and mutual indebtedness; it is about relationships mediated through objects. Shopping too is rarely a solitary act of provisioning a household in order to satisfy individual needs. Instead, it has recently been construed as a sacrificial act that transforms accumulation into expenditure through ritualised acts designed to convey love (Miller 1998).

Even within social psychology, there has been some recent interest in a 'social identity approach' which uses group membership to predict behaviour rather than relying on characteristics of the individual (Hogg and Abrams 1988). So, while positivist marketing researchers and consumer psychologists may continue to try to understand consumer behaviour by measuring individual orientations toward consumer goods and the goals they fulfil (Ratneshwar *et al.* 2000), other consumer researchers are now working with a more social understanding of consumption. A case in point is the resurgence of interest in contemporary gift-giving (Cheal 1988, Carrier 1995, Komter 1996, Otnes and Beltramini 1996, Godbout and Caille 1998, Berking 1999, Godelier 1999). This interest also extends to contemporary gift-giving in non-Western cultures (Miller 1993, Hendry 1995). And it overflows into studies of contemporary consumption holidays (Clark 1995, Santino 1994a, 1994b, 1996).

Consumer Research is becoming more historical

With the sudden awakening of many disciplines to the realisation that consumption is perhaps the key feature defining contemporary life and constitutes our primary secular source of hope, it is perhaps inevitable that scholars have sought the origins of contemporary consumer culture in the past. Recent efforts, for example, have sought to further enlighten the conflicting ideologies of Christmas with attention to the evolving invented tradition of this holiday celebration (Miller 1993, Waits 1993, Restad 1995, Schmidt 1995, Gillis 1996, Nissenbaum 1996, Marling 2000). Some of the debates ongoing in this area focus on the degree to which Christmas is primarily a holiday of familial nurturing and communion or a holiday that celebrates greed, materialism and excess (Miller 1993). Both of these opposing ideologies seem entwined in celebrations of Christmas in both Christian and non-Christian countries. For instance, in Schor's (1998) view, Christmas gift-exchange has become little more than placing orders with family and friends rather than directly with merchants. Nevertheless, as Marling (2000) demonstrates, the Christmas holiday remains a celebration of family and kinship.

More generally, historians and social scientists have turned their attention to the history of consumer culture (Susman 1984, Schama 1987, Brewer and Porter 1993, Jardine 1996, Goodwin *et al.* 1997, Slater 1997, Strasser *et al.* 1998, Glickman 1999, Cross 2000, Schor and Holt 2000, Steerns, 2001). Specifically, researchers have traced the rise of the department store (M. B. Miller 1981, Williams 1982, Reekie 1990, Leach 1993), the shopping mall (Kowinski 1985, Miller *et al.* 1998), advertising (Lears 1994, Goldman and Papson 1998), merchandise display (Culver 1988, Leach 1993), the *flâneur* and window shopping (Friedberg 1993, Buck-Morss 1991, Tester 1994, Benjamin 1999), collecting (Muensterberger 1994, Belk 1995), the pleasure beach (Walton 1998, Bosker and Lencek 1999), cosmetics (Peiss 1999), fashions (Roach and Eicher 1965, Bayley 1991, Miles 1998), automobiles (Sachs 1992, Richards 1994, Eyerman and Löfgren 1995), shoes (McDowell 1989, Rossi 1993, Benstock and Ferriss, 2001), and many more aspects of our commodity fetishism. Franklin's chapter on design history is a further contribution in this vein.

One recent thesis variously emphasises the experiential nature of our purchases, their fantasy character (Hannigan 1998), the commercial theming of culture (Gottdiener 1997), the potential of goods to enchant (Ritzer 1999), or the triumph of materialism (Twitchell 1999). Each of these themes suggests that we have winked and given in to spectacle rather than substance. The idea is that we have been seduced and that there is something dissipating and decadent about this state of affairs. Yet this is not a new criticism, and it echoes the condemnations of luxury that have been with us for thousands of years (Berry 1994). Perhaps what is new is the pervasiveness and immodesty of contemporary consumer hedonism. If so, it is well that historical accounts of consumer culture are seeking to trace the histories of consumer cultures and offer comparisons to prior frenzies of consumption.

Some issues for future Consumer Research

The trends affecting Consumer Research are generally quite encouraging. More scholars studying more areas of consumption, recognising global as well as historical aspects of consumer life and attempting to explicate the social bases for consumption, are all positive signs. At the same time, there remain neglected or limited areas of research that are in need of attention. While the conference on which this book is based has taken some steps toward addressing some of these issues, much remains to be done.

Gender and consumption

During most of the nineteenth and twentieth centuries, talk about producers referred to males and talk about consumers referred to females. This is changing, but women continue to dominate routine shopping, gift selection, and self-help groups for compulsive consumption. As a result, women continue to be disparaged as consumers. We have still not shaken the Judaeo-Christian–Islamic (and earlier) story of Eve in the Garden of Eden as being the weak one who gives in to the temptation to consume. Yet we need only consider areas of consumption like electronics, automobiles and gadgets to realise that men exemplify every bit as much of this tendency. Recent attention to gay and lesbian consumption issues may be helping to shake up the age-old assumptions that men produce and women consume, but considerably more attention can be addressed to such issues. The chapters here by Janice Winship and Ben Crewe represent positive steps in this direction.

Have-nots in a world of haves

A twofold outcome of the globalisation of media and marketing and the rise of global capitalism is that the gap between rich and poor in the world continues to expand, while the recognition of how the more affluent live is far more evident and immediate today than it was in earlier generations. Never before has there been so much concentration of wealth, as dozens of the largest multinational companies have more money than dozens of the poorest nations in the world. Coupled with global television, films, advertising and tourism, the result is sometimes desperate attempts to achieve a level of luxury consumption through sacrifices of health and welfare, but more often feelings of bitterness, resignation and loss of hope. The split between rich and poor is not only across nations and cultures, but within nations and cultures (Chin 2001).

Basing feelings of beauty and personal adequacy on consumption

Even within the more affluent world a growing majority of people learn from early childhood that to be without the fashions and consumer goods that their society defines as desirable is to be inadequate. A range of personal-care products, from deodorants to plastic surgery, emphasise the message that beauty is something that is skin deep and can be purchased for a price. This is what Peiss (1999) called 'hope in a jar'. As a number of researchers have detected, women (but increasingly men as well) read fashion and beauty magazines in the hope of finding a way to feel better about themselves; but faced with the impossibly young, slender and shapely models encountered in these publications, they come away feeling only depression (Winship 1987, Wolf 1990, McCracken 1993, Scanlon 1995, Beetham 1996, Currie 1999). Men also stoke their consumer desires by reading magazines and browsing the Internet (Belk forthcoming, Turkle 1995). Important questions remain in terms of consumer well-being within beauty culture. As Charles Revlon, the founder of Revlon, once said, 'In the factory we make cosmetics; in the store we sell hope.' Are we indeed better off without his hope?

Consumption versus the environment

Consumerism also brings in its wake concerns about the physical environment. How we consume, how we get from one place to another, our travel proclivities, how we read and write, our use, reuse, and disposal of our consumer goods and packaging, how we wash and dry our clothes, how we heat and cool ourselves, how we light our homes, how many electric and electronic appliances we use, and, generally, how much we consume, all have a direct impact on the environment. A further consequence of living in a global world is that consumption in one part of the world impacts the entire planetary ecosystem. These are critical consumption issues that have been relatively neglected in our zeal to embrace the new ethos of pro-consumption research. I recently attended a conference hosted by Mihaly Csikmenthalyi in which four groups of scholars who had met independently came together in an attempt to map out positive alternatives to consumer materialism. It was generally agreed that voluntary simplicity, downshifting and other sacrificial reductions in consumption are unlikely to be successful without some cataclysmic imperative (although Etzioni 1998 and Schor 1998 believe otherwise). Unfortunately, little in the way of feasible suggestions emerged from this gathering of some of the best minds studying such issues. The problems of environmental degradation and materialism beg for creative solutions and research.

Positive aspects of consumption

Despite the problematic aspects of consumerism, we are increasingly realising that consumption is very much the way of the world. This means that we increasingly seek, and often find, our hopes, dreams, myths, rituals and enchanted fantasies through consumption. Gift-giving is just one example of the interpersonal aspects of consumption. Our holidays celebrate friends, family and nation through consumption (Santino 1994b), while still stopping short of deifying Ronald McDonald and his kin. Mass media and advertising have largely replaced folklore. Alan Warde in this volume outlines a number of other potentially positive aspects of consumption.

We need to know much more about consumer desires, hopes, wishes and striving, as well as more about the consequences of achieving and failing to achieve these desired ends. It may well be that we have a desire for desire and that it is this desire that we crave more than its fulfilment (Campbell 1987, Belk *et al.* 2000). In an affluent society, our quest for reinitiating our desires through shopping, cinema-going, magazine reading, Internet surfing and observation of others' consumption, may be something like auto-eroticism. Indeed consumer desire shares much in common with sexual desire, religious passion, romantic love and addiction. Each of these may be useful models for understanding more about the nature of the benefits we seek to derive from our consumption.

Conclusion

As this chapter has tried to suggest, these are exciting times for Consumer Research. Consumer Research would exist without the current rise of global consumer culture, but it is much enhanced by these events. It is also a field of rising human consequence. There is much to be studied, theorised and learned about consumption as a field or fields of scholarly inquiry. Moreover, the impacts of consumption on human well-being, interpersonal bonding, intergroup strife and the ecological environment, make consumption a key to understanding contemporary life. It is highly encouraging to me to see the enthusiasm generated by the Plymouth conference on consumption and to see this volume bring together the best of the work that began there.

References

Barker, A. M. (ed.) (1999) *Consuming Russia: Popular Culture, Sex, and Society Since Gorbachev*, Durham, NC: Duke University Press.

Bayley, S. (1991) *Taste: the Secret Meaning of Things*, New York: Pantheon.

Beetham, M. (1996) *A Magazine of Her Own: Domesticity and Desire in the Woman's Magazine, 1800–1914*, London: Routledge.

Belk, R. W. (1988) 'Third World consumer culture', in E. an Kumcu and A. Fuat Firat (eds) *Marketing and Development: Toward Broader Dimension*, Greenwich, CT: JAI Press.

—— (1995) *Collecting in a Consumer Society*, London: Routledge.

—— (1996) 'Hyperreality and globalization: culture in the age of Ronald McDonald', *Journal of International Consumer Marketing* 8(3 and 4), 23–38.

—— (2000) 'Wolf brands in sheep's clothing: global appropriation of the local', in J. Pavitt (ed.) *Brand.New*, London: Victoria & Albert Museum.

—— (forthcoming) 'Specialty magazines and flights of fancy: feeding the desire to desire', in A. Groeppel-Klein and F.-R. Esch (eds) *European Advances in Consumer Research*, Berlin: Association for Consumer Research.

Belk, R. W., Ger, G. and Askegaard, S. (2000) 'The missing streetcar named desire', in S. Ratneshwar, D. G. Mick and C. Huffman (eds) *The Why of Consumption: Contemporary Perspectives on Consumer Motives, Goals, and Desires*, London: Routledge.

Belk, R. W., Wallendorf, M. and Sherry, J. F. Jr (1989) 'The sacred and the profane in Consumer Behavior: theodicy on the odyssey', *Journal of Consumer Research* 15(June): 1–38.

Beng-Huat, C. (ed) (2000) *Consumption in Asia: Lifestyles and Identity*, London: Routledge.

Benjamin, W. (1999) *The Arcades Project*, Cambridge, MA: Belknap Press.

Benson, A. (ed.) (2000) *I Shop Therefore I Am: Compulsive Spending and the Search for Self*, Northvale, NJ: Jason Aronson Press.

Benstock, S. and Ferriss, S. (eds.) (2001) *Footnotes: On Shoes*, New Brunswick, NJ: Rutgers University Press.

Berking, H. (1999) *The Sociology of Giving*, Patrick Camiller (trans.), London: Sage.

Berry, C. J. (1994) *The Idea of Luxury: a Conceptual and Historical Investigation*, Cambridge: Cambridge University Press.

Boorstin, D. (1973) *The Americans: the Democratic Experience*, New York: Random House.

Bosker, G. and Lencek, L. (1999) *The Beach: the History of Paradise on Earth*, New York: Penguin.

Boym, S. (1994) *Common Places: Mythologies of Everyday Life in Russia*, Cambridge: Harvard University Press.

Brewer, J. and Porter, R. (eds) (1993) *Consumption and the World of Goods*, London: Routledge.

Brouwer, S., Gifford, P. and Rose, S. D. (1996) *Exporting the American Gospel: Global Christian Fundamentalism*, New York: Routledge.

Brown, S. and Turley, D. (1997) *Consumer Research: Postcards from the Edge*, London: Routledge.

Buck-Morss, S. (1991) *The Dialectics of Seeing: Walter Benjamin and the Arcades Project*, Boston, MA: MIT Press.

Burke, T. (1996) *Lifebuoy Men, Lux Women: Commodification, Consumption, and Cleanliness in Modern Zimbabwe*, Durham, NC: Duke University Press.

Campbell, C. (1987) *The Romantic Ethic and the Spirit of Modern Consumerism*, Oxford: Blackwell.

Carrier, J. G. (1995) *Gifts and Commodities: Exchange and Western Capitalism since 1700*, London: Routledge.

Cheal, D. (1988) *The Gift Economy*, London: Routledge.

Chin, Elizabeth (2001) *Purchasing Power: Black Kids and American Consumer Culture*, Minneapolis: University of Minnesota Press.

Clammer, J. (1997) *Contemporary Urban Japan: a Sociology of Consumption*, Oxford: Blackwell.

Clark, C. D. (1995) *Flights of Fancy, Leaps of Faith: Children's Myths in Contemporary America*, Chicago: University of Chicago Press.

Classen, C., Howes, D. and Synnott, A. (1994) *Aroma: the Cultural History of Smell*, London: Routledge.

Corbin, A. (1988) *The Foul and the Fragrant: Odor and the French Social Imagination*, Cambridge, MA: Harvard University Press.

Costa, J. A. (ed.) (1994) *Gender Issues and Consumer Behavior*, Thousand Oaks, CA: Sage.

Costa, J. A. and Bamossy, G. J. (eds) (1995) *Marketing in a Multicultural World: Ethnicity, Nationalism and Cultural Identity*, Newbury Park, Thousand Oaks, CA: Sage.

Cross, G. S. (2000) *An All-Consuming Century: Why Commercialism Won in Modern America*, New York: Columbia University Press.

Culver, S. (1988) 'What manikins want: the wonderful world of Oz and the art of decorating dry goods windows', *Representations* 21(Winter): 97–116.

Currie, D. H. (1999) *Girl Talk: Adolescent Magazines and Their Readers*, Toronto: University of Toronto Press.

Davis, D. (ed) (2000) *The Consumer Revolution in Urban China*, Berkeley: University of California Press.

Davis, E. (1998) *Techgnosis: Myth, Magic and Mysticism in the Age of Information*, New York: Three Rivers Press.

de Grazia, V. and Furlough, E. (eds) (1996) *The Sex of Things: Gender and Consumption in Historical Perspective*, Berkeley, CA: University of California Press.

Douglas, M. and Isherwood, B. (1996, revised edition) *The World of Goods: Towards an Anthropology of Consumption*, London: Routledge.

Edgell, S., Hetherington, K. and Warde, A. (eds) (1996) *Consumption Matters*, Oxford: Blackwell.

Etzioni, A. (1998) 'Voluntary simplicity: characterization, select psychological implications, and societal consequences', *Journal of Economic Psychology* 19(October): 619–43.

Eyerman, R. and Löfgren, O. (1995) 'Romancing the road: road movies and images of mobility', *Theory, Culture, and Society* 12: 53–79.

Falk, P. and Campbell, C. (1997) *The Shopping Experience*, London: Sage.

Fine, G. A. (1983) *Shared Fantasy: Role-Playing Games as Social Worlds*, Chicago: University of Chicago Press.

Finkelstein, J. (1989) *Dining Out: A Sociology of Modern Manners*, Cambridge: Polity Press.

Folkes, V. (2001) 'ACR from the 20th to the 21st century: what the numbers tell us', *ACR News*, March/April: 2–4.

Ger, G. and Belk, R. (1996a) 'Cross-cultural differences in materialism', *Journal of Economic Psychology* 17(1) February: 55–78.

—— (1996b) 'I'd like to buy the world a Coke: consumptionscapes of the less affluent world', *Journal of Consumer Policy* 19(3): 271–304.

Gillis, J. R. (1996) *A World of Their Own Making: Myth, Ritual, and the Quest for Family Values*, New York: Basic Books.

Glickman, L. B. (ed.) (1999) *Consumer Society in American History: a Reader*, Ithaca, NY: Cornell University Press.

Godbout, J. and Caille, A. (1998) *The World of the Gift*, Montreal: McGill–Queens University Press.

Godelier, M. (1999) *The Enigma of the Gift*, Cambridge: Polity Press.

Goldman, R. and Papson, S. (1998) *Nike Culture*, London: Sage.

Goodwin, N., Ackerman, F. and Kiron, D. (eds) (1997) *The Consumer Society (Frontiers of Economic Thought)*, Washington, D.C.: Island Press.

Gottdiener, M. (1997) *The Theming of America: Dreams, Visions, and Commercial Spaces*, Boulder, CO: Westview Press.

Hannigan, J. (1998) *Fantasy City: Pleasure and Profit in the Postmodern Metropolis*, London: Routledge.

Hearn, J. and Roseneil, S. (1999) *Consuming Cultures: Power and Resistance*, Basingstoke: Macmillan.

Heim, M. (1993) *The Metaphysics of Virtual Reality*, Oxford: Oxford University Press.

Hendry, J. (1995) *Wrapping Culture: Politeness, Presentation, and Power in Japan and Other Societies*, Oxford: Clarendon Press.

Hogg, M. A. and Abrams, D. (1988) *Social Identifications: a Social Psychology of Intergroup Relations and Group Processes*, London: Routledge.

Holt, D. B. (1998) 'Does cultural capital structure American consumption?', *Journal of Consumer Research*, 25(June) 1–25.

Howes, D. (ed.) (1996) *Cross-Cultural Consumption: Global Markets, Local Realities*, London: Routledge.

Jardine, L. (1996) *Worldly Goods: a New History of the Renaissance*, Basingstoke: Macmillan.

Jing, J. (2000) *Feeding China's Little Emperors: Food, Children and Social Change*, Stanford, CA: Stanford University Press.

Kates, S. M. (1998) *Twenty Million New Consumers: Understanding Gay Men's Consumer Behavior*, New York: Haworth Press.

Komter, A. E. (ed.) (1996) *The Gift: an Interdisciplinary Perspective*, Amsterdam: Amsterdam University Press.

Kowinski, W. S. (1985) *The Malling of America: an Inside Look at the Great Consumer Paradise*, New York: William Morrow.

Leach, W. (1993) *Land of Desire: Merchants, Power, and the Rise of a New American Culture*, New York: Vintage.

Lears, J. (1994) *Fables of Abundance: a Cultural History of Advertising in America*, New York: Basic Books.

Li, C. (1998) *China: the Consumer Revolution*, Singapore: John Wiley.

Liebes, T. and Katz, E. (1990) *The Export of Meaning: Cross-Cultural Readings of Dallas*, New York: Oxford University Press.

Lukenbill, G. (1999) *Untold Millions: Secret Truths About Marketing to Gay and Lesbian Consumers*, New York: Harrington Park Press.

MacCannell, D. (1999) *The Tourist: a New Theory of the Leisure Class*, Berkeley, CA: University of California Press.

McCracken, E. (1993) *Decoding Women's Magazines, From* Mademoiselle *to* Ms., New York: St Martin's Press.

McCracken, G. (1991) *Culture and Consumption: New Approaches to the Symbolic Character of Consumer Goods and Activities*, Bloomington, IN: Indiana University Press.

McDannell, C. (1998) *Material Christianity, Religion and Popular Culture in America*, New Haven, CT: Yale University Press.

McDowell, C. (1989) *Shoes: Fashion and Fantasy*, New York: Rizzoli.

Marling, K. A. (2000) *Merry Christmas! Celebrating America's Greatest Holiday*, Cambridge, MA: Harvard University Press.

Martinez, K. and Shapiro, K. (eds) (1997) *The Material Culture of Gender/the Gender of Material Culture*, Winterthur, DL: Henry Francis du Point Winterthur Museum.

Miles, S. (1998) *Consumerism as a Way of Life*, London: Sage.

Miller, D. (ed.) (1993) *Unwrapping Christmas*, Oxford: Clarendon Press.

—— (1998) *A Theory of Shopping*, Ithaca, NY: Cornell University Press.

Miller, D. and Slater, D. (2000) *The Internet: an Ethnographic Approach*, Oxford: Berg.

Miller, D., Holbrook, B., Jackson, P. and Thrift, N. (eds) (1998) *Shopping, Place, and Identity*, London: Routledge.

Miller, M. B. (1981) *The Bon Marché Bourgeois Culture and the Department Store, 1869–1920*, Princeton, NJ: Princeton University Press.

Muensterberger, W. (1994) *Collecting: an Unruly Passion*, Princeton, NJ: Princeton University Press.

Muniz, A. M., Jr and O'Guinn, T. C. (2001) 'Brand community', *Journal of Consumer Research* 27(March): 412–32.

Nissenbaum, S. (1996) *The Battle For Christmas: a Social and Cultural History of Christmas that Shows How it Was Transformed from an Unruly Carnival Season into the Quintessential American Family Holiday*, New York: Alfred A. Knopf.

Noble, D. F. (1999) *The Religion of Technology: the Divinity of Man and the Spirit of Invention*, New York: Penguin.

Otnes, C. and Beltramini, R. F. (eds) (1996) *Gift Giving: a Research Anthology*, Bowling Green, OH: Bowling Green University Popular Press.

Park-Curry, P. and Jiobu, R. M. (1982) 'The computer as fetish: electronic pop god', in R. B. Browne (ed.) *Objects of Special Devotion: Fetishism in Popular Culture*, Bowling Green, OH: Bowling Green University Popular Press.

Pavitt, J. (ed.) (2000) *Brand.New*, London: V&A Publications.

Peiss, K. (1999) *Hope in a Jar: the Making of America's Beauty Culture*, San Francisco: Owl Books.

Pesce, M. (2000) *How Technology is Transforming Our Imagination: the Playful World*, New York: Ballantine Books.

Pinches, M. (ed.) (1999) *Culture and Privilege in Capitalist Asia*, London: Routledge.

Pine, B. J., Gilmore, J. H. and Pine, B. J. II. (1999) *The Experience Economy*, Cambridge, MA: Harvard Business School Press.

Ratneshwar, S., Mick, D. J. and Huffman, C. (eds) (2000) *The Why of Consumption: Contemporary Perspectives on Consumer Motives, Goals, and Desires*, London: Routledge.

Reekie, G. (1990) *Temptations: Sex, Selling and the Department Store*, St Leonards, NSW: Allen & Unwin.

Restad, P. L. (1995) *Christmas in America: a History*, Oxford: Oxford University Press.

Richards, B. (1994) *Disciplines of Delight: the Psychoanalysis of Popular Culture*, London: Free Association Books.

Ritson, M. and Elliott, R. (1999) 'The social uses of advertising: an ethnographic study of adolescent advertising', *Journal of Consumer Research* December: 260–77.

Ritzer, G. (1999) *Enchanting a Disenchanted World: Revolutionizing the Means of Consumption*, Thousand Oaks, CA: Pine Forge Press.

Roach, M. E. and Bubolz Eicher, J. (1985) *Dress, Adornment, and the Social Order*, New York: Wiley.

Robison, R. and Goodman, D. S. G. (eds) (1996) *The New Rich in Asia: Mobile Phones, McDonald's and Middle-Class Revolution*, London: Routledge.

Rossi, W. A. (1993) *The Sex Life of the Foot and Shoe*, Malabar, FL: Krieger.

Sachs, W. (1992) *For Love of the Automobile: Looking Back into the History of Our Desires*, Berkeley, CA: University of California Press.

—— (1994b) *All Around the Year: Holidays and Celebrations in America*, Urbana, IL: University of Illinois Press.

—— (1996) *New Old Fashioned Ways: Holidays and Popular Culture*, Knoxville, TN: University of Tennessee Press.

Scanlon, J. (1995) *Inarticulate Longings: the Ladies' Home Journal, Gender, and the Promises of Consumer Culture*, London: Routledge.

—— (ed.) (2000) *The Gender and Consumer Culture Reader*, New York: New York University Press.

Schama, S. (1987) *The Embarrassment of Riches: an Interpretation of Dutch Culture in the Golden Age*, New York: Alfred A. Knopf.

Schmidt, L. E. (1995) *Consumer Rites: the Buying & Selling of American Holidays*, Princeton, NJ: Princeton University Press.

Schor, J. B. (1998) *The Overspent American: Upscaling, Downshifting, and the New Consumer*, New York: Basic Books.

Schor, J. B. and Holt, D. (eds) (2000) *The Consumer Society Reader*, Boston: New Press.

Sherman, A. L. (1997) *The Soul of Development: Biblical Christianity and Economic Transformation in Guatemala*, New York: Oxford.

Sherry, H. F. Jr. (ed) (1995) *Contemporary Marketing and Consumer Behavior: an Anthropological Sourcebook*, Newbury Park, CA: Sage.

Shultz, C. III, Belk, R. and Ger, G. (eds) (1994) *Consumption in Marketizing Economies*, Greenwich, CT: JAI Press.

Silverstone, R. and Hirsch, E. (eds) (1992) *Consuming Technologies: Media and Information in Domestic Spaces*, London: Routledge.

Slater, D. (1997) *Consumer Culture and Modernity*, Cambridge: Polity Press.

Solomon, M. R. (1988) 'Mapping product constellations: a social categorization approach to symbolic consumption', *Psychology and Marketing* 5(3): 233–58.

Sparke, P. (1995) *As Long as It's Pink: the Sexual Politics of Taste*, London: Pandora.

Stan, L. (ed.) (1997) *Romania in Transition*, Aldershot, UK: Dartmouth Press.

Steerns, P. N. (2001) *Consumerism in World History: The Global Transformation of Human Desire*, London: Routledge.

Strasser, S., McGovern, C. and Judt, M. (eds) (1998) *Getting and Spending: European and American Consumer Societies in the Twentieth Century*, Cambridge: Cambridge University Press.

Sulkunen, P., Holmwood, J., Radner, H. and Schulze, G. (eds) (1997) *Constructing the New Consumer*, London: Macmillan.

Susman, W. (1984) *Culture as History: the Transformation of American Society in the Twentieth Century*, New York: Pantheon.

Sutton-Smith, B. (1986) *Toys as Culture*, New York: Gardner Press.

Tester, K. (ed) (1994) *The Flaneur*, London: Routledge.

Tobin, J. (ed.) (1992) *Remade in Japan: Everyday Life and Consumer Taste in a Changing Society*, New Haven, CT: Yale University Press.

Turkle, S. (1995) *Life on the Screen: Identity in the Age of the Internet*, New York: Simon and Schuster.

Twitchell, J. B. (1999) *Lead Us Into Temptation: the Triumph of American Materialism*, New York: Columbia University Press.

Urry, J. (1990) *The Tourist Gaze: Leisure and Travel in Contemporary Societies*, London: Sage.

Varnedoe, K. and Gopnik, A. (eds) (1990) *Modern Art and Popular Culture: Readings in High and Low*, New York: Museum of Modern Art.

Waits, W. B. (1993) *The Modern Christmas in America: a Cultural History of Gift Giving*, New York: New York University Press.

Walton, J. K. (1998) *Blackpool*, Edinburgh: Edinburgh University Press.

Warde, A. (1997) *Consumption, Food, and Taste: Culinary Antimonies and Commodity Culture*, London: Sage.

Warde, A. and Martens, L. (2000) *Eating Out: Social Differentiation, Consumption, and Pleasure*, Cambridge: Cambridge University Press.

Wardlow, D. L. (ed.) (1996) *Gays, Lesbians, and Consumer Behavior: Theory, Practice, and Research Issues in Marketing*, New York: Haworth Press.

Watson, J. L. (ed.) (1997) *Golden Arches East: McDonald's in East Asia*, Stanford, CA: Stanford University Press.

Weiss, B. (1996) *The Making and Unmaking of the Haya Lived World: Consumption, Commoditization, and Everyday Practice*, Durham, NC: Duke University Press.

Wertheim, M. (1999) *The Pearly Gates of Cyberspace: a History of Space from Dante to the Internet*, New York: W. W. Norton.

Wilk, R. (1993) '"It's destroying a whole generation": television and moral discourse in Belize', *Visual Anthropology* 5: 229–44.

Williams, R. (1982) *Dream Worlds: Mass Consumption in Late Nineteenth-Century France*, Berkeley, CA: University of California Press.

Index